# The Practical Evaluation of PHYTO PHARMACEUTICAL

# The Practical Evaluation of PHYTO PHARMACEUTICAL

**Arun Rastogi**

**ANMOL PUBLICATIONS PVT. LTD.**
**NEW DELHI-110 002 (INDIA)**

**ANMOL PUBLICATIONS PVT. LTD.**
**Regd. Office:** 4360/4, Ansari Road, Daryaganj,
New Delhi-110002 (India)
Tel.: 23278000, 23261597, 23286875, 23255577
Fax: 91-11-23280289
*Email:* anmolpub@gmail.com
*Visit us at:* www.anmolpublications.com

**Branch Office:** No. 1015, Ist Main Road, BSK IIIrd Stage
IIIrd Phase, IIIrd Block, Bangalore-560 085 (India)
Tel.: 080-41723429 • Fax: 080-26723604
*Email:* anmolpublicationsbangalore@gmail.com

*The Practical Evaluation of Phyto Pharmaceutical*



First Edition, 2010

ISBN 978-81-261-4464-8

PRINTED IN INDIA

---

Printed at Mehra Offset Press, Delhi.

# Contents

# Preface

Phyto Pharmaceuticals are pharmaceuticals using traditional compounds derived from botanicals instead of chemicals. Natural ingredients are more easily and more readily metabolized by the body. Therefore they produce fewer, if any, side effects and provide increased absorption in the bloodstream resulting in more thorough and effective treatments.

Pharmaceuticals made from chemical compounds are prone to adverse side effects. The human body will have a tendency to reject certain chemical compounds which do not occur naturally. These rejections occur in the form of side effects; some as mild as minor headaches, and others as severe as to be potentially lethal. It is important to note while phytopharmaceuticals produce fewer to no side effects, chemical interactions with other prescription drugs can occur.

While therapies such as herbal remedies and phytopharmaceuticals have been used for centuries, if not millennia, modern science has been reluctant to accept this discipline. As this industry continues to grow, the public must be aware and research the different therapies they are considering.

*Author*

## Chapter 1

# Alkaloid

Alkaloids are naturally occurring chemical compounds containing basic nitrogen atoms. The name derives from the word alkaline and is used to describe any nitrogen-containing base and organic compounds with one or more of the following features: a heterocyclic compound containing nitrogen, with an alkaline pH and a marked physiological action on animal physiology. However, there are exceptions to each of these criteria. Alkaloids are produced by a large variety of organisms, including bacteria, fungi, plants, and animals and are part of the group of natural products . Many alkaloids can be purified from crude extracts by acid-base extraction. Many alkaloids are toxic to other organisms.

They often have pharmacological effects and are used as medications, as recreational drugs, or in entheogenic rituals. Examples are the local anesthetic and stimulant cocaine, the stimulant caffeine, nicotine, the analgesic morphine, or the antimalarial drug quinine. Most alkaloids have a bitter taste.

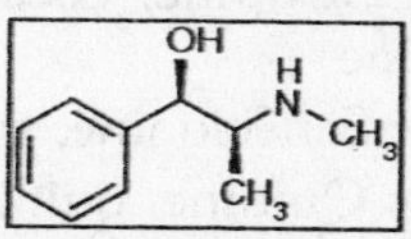


**Fig.** Chemical Structure of Ephedrine, a Phenethylamine Alkaloid

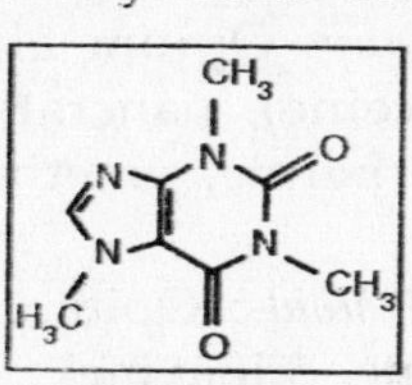


**Fig**. Caffeine, a Purine Alkaloid

## ALKALOID CLASSIFICATIONS

The classification of the alkaloids is complex and may be guided by a set of rules that take into account the structure and other chemical features of the alkaloid molecule, its biological origin, as well as the biogenetic origin where known.

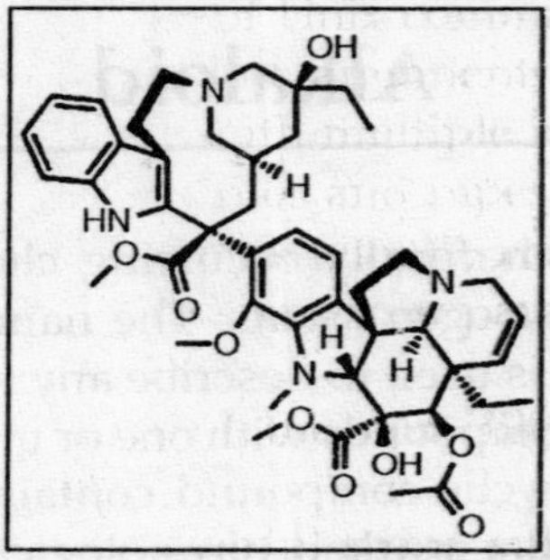

Fig. Chemical Structure of Vinblastine

For example, where the biosynthesis pathway of an alkaloid is unknown, it may be grouped based on structural similarities with known compounds, including non-nitrogenous compounds, or by the organism(s) from which the alkaloid was isolated.

- *Pyridine group*: Piperine, coniine, trigonelline, arecoline, arecaidine, guvacine, cytisine, lobeline, nicotine, anabasine, sparteine, pelletierine.
- *Pyrrolidine group*: Hygrine, cuscohygrine, nicotine
- *Tropane group*: Atropine, cocaine, ecgonine, scopolamine, catuabine
- *Indolizine group*: Senecionine, swainsonine
- *Quinoline group*: Quinine, quinidine, dihydroquinine, dihydroquinidine, strychnine, brucine, veratrine, cevadine
- *Isoquinoline group*: Opium alkaloids (papaverine, narcotine, narceine), pancratistatin, sanguinarine, hydrastine, berberine, emetine, berbamine, oxyacanthine
- *Phenanthrene alkaloids*: Opium alkaloids (morphine, codeine, thebaine, oripavine)

- *Phenethylamine group*: Mescaline, ephedrine, dopamine
- Indole group:
  - *Tryptamines*: Serotonin, DMT, 5-MeO-DMT, bufotenine, psilocybin
  - *Ergolines (the ergot alkaloids)*: Ergine, ergotamine, lysergic acid
  - *Beta-carbolines*: Harmine, harmaline, tetrahydr-oharmine
  - *Yohimbans*: Reserpine, yohimbine
  - *Vinca alkaloids*: Vinblastine, vincristine
  - *Kratom (Mitragyna speciosa) alkaloids*: Mitragynine, 7-hydroxymitragynine
  - *Tabernanthe iboga* alkaloids: Ibogaine, voacangine, coronaridine
  - *Strychnos nux-vomica alkaloids*: Strychnine, brucine
- *Purine group*:
  - *Xanthines*: Caffeine, theobromine, theophylline
- *Terpenoid group*:
  - *Aconitum alkaloids*: Aconitine
  - Steroid alkaloids (containing a steroid skeleton in a nitrogen containing structure):
    - (a) *Solanum* (e.g. potato and tomato) alkaloids (solanidine, solanine, chaconine)
    - (b) *Veratrum* alkaloids (veratramine, cyclopamine, cycloposine, jervine, muldamine)
    - (c) Fire Salamander alkaloids (samandarin)
    - (d) *Others*: conessine
- *Quaternary ammonium compounds*: Muscarine, choline, neurine
- *Miscellaneous*: Capsaicin, cynarin, phytolaccine, phytolaccotoxin

## PHYSICOCHEMICAL PROPERTIES

Low-molecular weight alkaloids without hydrogen bond donors such as hydroxy groups are often liquid at room temperature, examples are nicotine, sparteine, coniine, and phenethylamine. The basicity of alkaloids depends on the lone pairs of electrons on their nitrogen atoms. As organic bases, alkaloids form salts with mineral acids such as hydrochloric acid and sulfuric acid and organic acids such as tartaric acid or maleic acid. These salts are usually more water-soluble than their free base form.

With the exception of caffeine, alkaloids are one of several classes of compound which are generally precipitated from aqueous solutions by tannins, a fact which is important in herbalism.

## EPHEDRINE

Ephedrine is a sympathomimetic amine commonly used as a stimulant, appetite suppressant, concentration aid, decongestant, and to treat hypotension associated with anaesthesia. Ephedrine is similar in structure to the (semi-synthetic) derivatives amphetamine and methamphetamine. Chemically, it is an alkaloid derived from various plants in the genus *Ephedra* (family Ephedraceae). It is most usually marketed in the *hydrochloride* and *sulfate* forms.

In traditional Chinese medicines, the herb *ma huang* (*Ephedra sinica*) contains ephedrine and pseudoephedrine as its principal active constituents. The same is true of other herbal products containing extracts from *Ephedra* species.

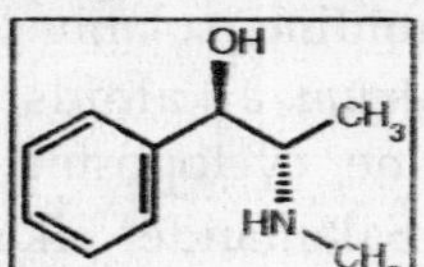


Fig. Ephedrine

### Chemistry of Ephedrine

Ephedrine exhibits optical isomerism and has two chiral centres, giving rise to four diastereomers. By convention the enantiomers with opposite stereochemistry around the chiral centres (1R,2S and 1S,2R) are designated ephedrine, while pseudoephedrine has same stereochemistry around the chiral carbons (1R,2R and 1S,2S).

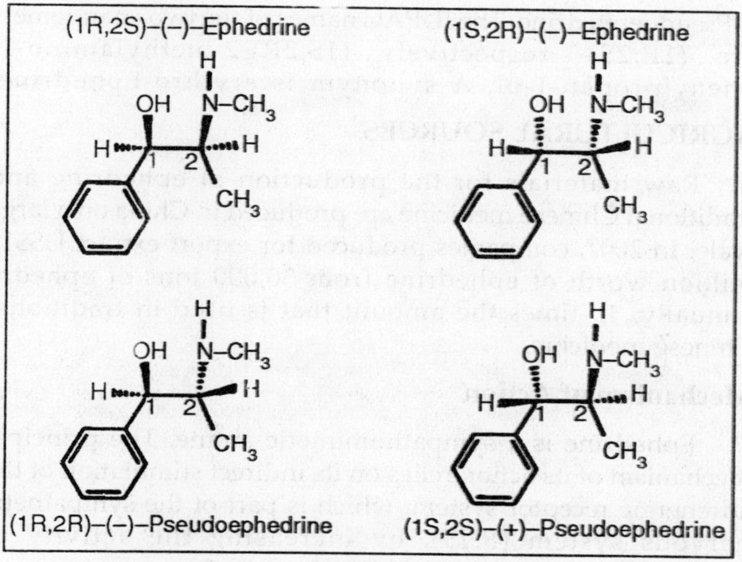


**Fig. The Four Diastereoisomers of Ephedrine.**

Ephedrine is a substituted amphetamine and a structural methamphetamine analogue. It differs from methamphetamine only by the presence of a hydroxyl (OH). Amphetamines, however, are more potent and have additional biological effects. The isomer which is marketed is (–)-(1R,2S)-ephedrine. Ephedrine hydrochloride has a melting point of 187-188°C.

## NOMENCLATURE

The dextrorotary (+)– or d– enantiomer is (1S,2R)-Ephedrine, whereas the levorotating (–)- or l- form is (1R,2S)-Ephedrine. In the outdated D/L system (+)-Ephedrine is also referred to as L-Ephedrine and (—)-Ephedrine as D-Ephedrine (in the Fisher projection then the phenylring is drawn at bottom).

Often the D/L system (with small caps) and the d/l system (with lower-case) are confused. The result is that the levorotary l-Ephedrine is wrongly named L-Ephedrine and the dextrorotary d-Pseudoephedrine (the diastereomer) wrongly

D-Pseudoephedrine. The IUPAC names of the two enantiomers are (1R,2S)- respectively (1S,2R)-2-methylamino-1-phenylpropan-1-ol. A synonym is erythro-Ephedrine.

## AGRICULTURAL SOURCES

Raw materials for the production of ephedrine and traditional Chinese medicine are produced in China on a large scale. In 2007, companies produced for export extract US$13 million worth of ephedrine from 30,000 tons of ephedra annually, 10 times the amount that is used in traditional Chinese medicine.

### Mechanism of Action

Ephedrine is a sympathomimetic amine. The principal mechanism of its action relies on its indirect stimulation of the adrenergic receptor system, which is part of the sympathetic nervous system (*SNS*), by increasing the activity of noradrenaline at the post-synaptic α- and β-receptors.

The presence of direct interactions with α-receptors is unlikely, but still controversial.

Acting upon the central nervcus system (*CNS*) is limited because ephedrine only crosses the blood-brain barrier weakly and not very efficiently.

The presence of an *N*-methyl group decreases binding affinities at α-receptors, compared with norephedrine. On the other hand ephedrine binds better than *N*-methylephedrine, which has an additional methyl group at the N-atom. Also the steric orientation of the hydroxyl group is important for receptor binding and functional activity

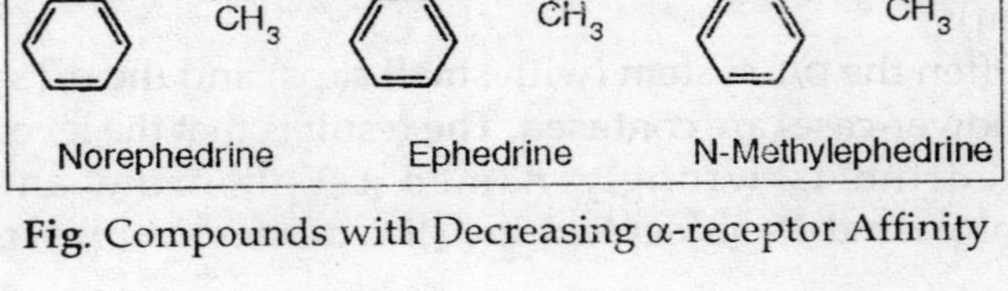


**Fig.** Compounds with Decreasing α-receptor Affinity

## MEDICAL USE

### Indications

In traditional Chinese medicine, ephedrine has been used in the treatment of asthma and bronchitis for centuries.

Both ephedrine and pseudoephedrine act as a bronchodilator, but pseudoephedrine has considerably less effect. Both also increase blood pressure, with again pseudoephedrine being considerably less effective.

An ECA stack is a component found in thermogenic weight loss pills, composed of ephedrine, caffeine and aspirin (many supplement manufacturers include salicin instead of aspirin) working to speed up the metabolism and thus cause food energy to burn faster. The ECA stack is a popular supplement taken by body builders before workouts due to the increased amount of energy and alertness.

For many years, the US Coast Guard recommended ephedrine together with an equal 25 mg dose of promethazine to its sailors to combat seasickness. Promethazine manages nausea and ephedrine fights the ensuing drowsiness. Commonly referred to as the Coast Guard cocktail, ephedrine may still be available for prescription for this purpose.

### Adverse Effects

Adverse drug reactions (ADRs) are more common with systemic administration (e.g. injection or oral administration) compared to topical administration (e.g. nasal instillations).

*ADRs associated with ephedrine therapy include*:

- *Cardiovascular*: Tachycardia, cardiac arrhythmias, angina pectoris, vasoconstriction with hypertension
- *Dermatological*: Flushing, sweating, acne vulgaris
- *Gastrointestinal*: Anorexia, nausea
- *Genitourinary*: Diuresis (increased urination) due to increased blood flow (difficulty urinating is not uncommon, as alpha-agonists such as ephedrine constrict the internal urethral sphincter, mimicking the effects of sympathetic nervous system stimulation)

- *Nervous system*: Restlessness, confusion, insomnia, mild euphoria, mania/hallucinations (rare except in previously existing psychiatric conditions), delusions, formication (may be possible, but lacks documented evidence) paranoia, hostility, panic, agitation
- *Respiratory*: Dyspnea, pulmonary edema
- *Miscellaneous*: Dizziness, headache, tremor, hyperglycemic reactions, dry mouth

The neurotoxicity of l-Ephedrine is disputed.

## Contraindications

Ephedrine should not be used in conjunction with certain antidepressants, namely SNRIs (serotonin-norepinephrine re-uptake inhibitors), as this increases the risk of the above symptoms due to excessive serum levels of norepinephrine.

Bupropion is an example of an antidepressant with an amphetamine-like structure similar to ephedrine, and it is known as an NDRI (norepinephrine-dopamine re-uptake inhibitor). It has an action which bears more resemblance to amphetamine than to fluoxetine in that its primary mode of therapeutic action involves norepinephrine and to a lesser degree dopamine, but it also releases some serotonin from presynaptic clefts. It should not be used with ephedrine as it may increase the likelihood of the above side effects.

Ephedrine should be used with caution in patients with inadequate fluid replacement, impaired adrenal function, hypoxia, hypercapnia, acidosis, hypertension, hyperthyroidism, prostatic hypertrophy, diabetes mellitus, cardiovascular disease, during delivery if maternal BP > 130/80 mmHg, and lactation.

Contraindications for the use of ephedrine include: closed angle glaucoma, phaeochromocytoma, asymmetric septal hypertrophy (idiopathic hypertrophic subaortic stenosis), concomitant or recent (previous 14 days) monoamine oxidase inhibitor (MAOI) therapy, general anaesthesia with halogenated hydrocarbons (particularly halothane), tachyarrhythmias or ventricular fibrillation, hypersensitivity to ephedrine or other stimulants.

Ephedrine should not be used at any time during pregnancy unless specifically indicated by a qualified physician and only when other options are unavailable.

**Recreational and Illicit use**

Anecdotal reports have suggested that ephedrine helps studying, thinking, or concentrating to a greater extent than caffeine. Some students and some white-collar workers have used ephedrine (or Ephedra-containing herbal supplements) for this purpose, as well as some professional athletes and weightlifters.

It is common for many athletes to use stimulants while exercising. Such use of ephedrine has been associated with stimulant dependence, as well as deaths from heatstroke in athletes and circulatory problems such as aortic aneurysm in weightlifters, though these side effects are rare.

As a phenylethylamine, ephedrine has a similar chemical structure to amphetamines and is a methamphetamine analogue having the methamphetamine structure with a hydroxyl group at the β position. Because of ephedrine's structural similarity to methamphetamine it can be used to create methamphetamine using chemical reduction in which ephedrine's hydroxy group is removed; this has made ephedrine a highly sought-after chemical precursor in the illicit manufacture of methamphetamine.

The most popular method for reducing ephedrine to methamphetamine is similar to the Birch reduction, in that it uses anhydrous ammonia and lithium metal in the reaction. The second most popular method uses red phosphorus, iodine, and ephedrine in the reaction.

In *E for Ecstasy* (a book examining the uses of the drug MDMA in the UK) the writer, activist and Ecstasy advocate Nicholas Saunders highlighted test results showing that certain consignments of the drug also contained ephedrine. Consignments of Ecstasy known as "Strawberry" contained what Saunders described as a "potentially dangerous combination of ketamine, ephedrine and selegiline," as did a consignment of "Sitting Duck" Ecstasy tablets.

## USES OF EPHEDRINE

Ephedrine is used to relieve congestion due to colds, flu, hay fever, and allergies, and for temporary relief of shortness of breath, chest tightness, and wheezing due to bronchial asthma. Ephedrine may also be used for other conditions as determined by your doctor. Ephedrine is a decongestant and bronchodilator. It works by reducing swelling and constricting blood vessels in the nasal passages and widening the airway, allowing you to breathe more easily.

*Do not use ephedrine if*:

- you are allergic to this medication.
- you are taking furazolidone or have taken a monoamine oxidase (MAO) inhibitor (eg, phenelzine) in the last 14 days.
- you have severe high blood pressure, severe heart blood vessel disease, a rapid heartbeat, or severe heart problems.

Contact your doctor or health care provider right away if any of these apply to you.

### Before Using Ephedrine

Some medical conditions may interact with ephedrine. Tell your doctor or pharmacist if you have any medical conditions, especially if any of the following apply to you:

- if you are pregnant, planning to become pregnant, or are breast-feeding.
- if you are taking any prescription or nonprescription medicine, herbal preparation, or dietary supplement.
- if you have allergies to medicines, foods, or other substances.
- if you have a history of heart problems, diabetes, glaucoma, an enlarged prostate or other prostate problems, adrenal gland problems, high blood pressure, seizures, stroke, blood vessel problems, an overactive thyroid, or severe asthma.

Some medicines may interact with ephedrine. Tell your health care provider if you are taking any other medicines, especially any of the following:

- Rauwolfia derivatives (eg, reserpine) because the effectiveness of may be decreased.
- Beta-blockers (eg, propranolol), cocaine, furazolidone, indomethacin, methyldopa, MAO inhibitors (eg, phenelzine), oxytocic medicines (eg, oxytocin), rauwolfia derivatives (eg, reserpine), or tricyclic antidepressants (eg, amitriptyline) because the actions and side effects of ephedrine may be increased.
- Bromocriptine, catechol-O-methyltransferase (COMT) inhibitors (eg, entacapone), digoxin, or droxidopa because the actions and side effects of these medicines may be increased.
- Guanadrel, guanethidine, mecamylamine, methyldopa, or reserpine because its effectiveness may be decreased by ephedrine.

This may not be a complete list of all interactions that may occur. Ask your health care provider if ephedrine may interact with other medicines that you take. Check with your health care provider before you start, stop, or change the dose of any medicine.

## How to Use Ephedrine

Use this medication as directed by your doctor. Check the label on the medicine for exact dosing instructions. Check the label on the medicine for exact dosing instructions.

- *Ephedrine may be taken with or without food*: If stomach upset occurs, take with food to reduce stomach irritation.
- If you miss a dose of ephedrine and are taking it regularly, take it as soon as possible. If it is almost time for your next dose, skip the missed dose and go back to your regular dosing schedule. Do not take 2 doses at once.

Ask your health care provider any questions you may have about how to use ephedrine.

## Important Safety Information

- *Ephedrine may cause dizziness*: Do not drive, operate

machinery, or do anything else that could be dangerous until you know how you react to ephedrine. Using ephedrine alone, with certain other medicines, or with alcohol may lessen your ability to drive or perform other potentially dangerous tasks.

- If your symptoms do not improve within 7 days or if you develop a high fever, check with your doctor.
- If you have trouble sleeping, ask your pharmacist or doctor about the best time to take this medication.
- Do not take diet or appetite control medicines while you are taking ephedrine.
- Before you begin taking any new prescription or nonprescription medicine, read the ingredients to see if it also contains ephedrine. If it does or if you are uncertain, contact your doctor or pharmacist.
- *Diabetes patients*: Ephedrine may affect your blood sugar. Check blood sugar levels closely and ask your doctor before adjusting the dose of your diabetes medicine.
- Use this medication with caution in the elderly because they may be more sensitive to its effects.
- *Use ephedrine with extreme caution in children*: Safety and effectiveness have not been confirmed.
- *Pregnancy and breast-feeding*: It is unknown if this medication can cause harm to the fetus. If you become pregnant while taking ephedrine, discuss with your doctor the benefits and risks of using ephedrine during pregnancy. It is unknown if ephedrine is excreted in breast milk. If you are or will be breast-feeding while you are using ephedrine, check with your doctor or pharmacist to discuss the risks to your baby.

## GENERIC NAME: EPHEDRINE

- *Warning*: This drug should not be used in combination with other stimulant products (e.g., caffeine), other cough-and-cold products, or as a dietary supplement for the purpose of weight loss or body building. Doing so may increase your risk of unlikely but potentially fatal side effects including: stroke, heart attack, seizures, or severe mental disorders. In addition, dietary supplements containing ephedrine should not exceed 8 mg as a single ephedrine dose, 24 mg of ephedrine per day (24 hours), or be given for longer than 7 days, as recommended by the FDA. Exceeding the recommended ephedrine dose increases your risk of the side effects noted above. For detailed information, consult your pharmacist. Check all product labels carefully to see if they contain ephedrine or ephedra/ma huang.

- *Uses*: Ephedrine is a central nervous system stimulant used to treat breathing problems (as a bronchodilator), nasal congestion (as a decongestant), low blood pressure problems (orthostatic hypotension), or myasthenia gravis.
- *Other Uses*: This drug has also been used to treat certain sleep disorders (narcolepsy), menstrual problems (dysmenorrhea), or urine-control problems (incontinence or enuresis).
- *How To Use*: Take this medication by mouth usually every 4 hours as needed; or as directed by your doctor. The dosage is based on your medical condition and response to therapy. For prescription ephedrine, do not exceed 150 mg per day in adults or 75 mg per day in children. Do not combine prescription ephedrine with ephedrine/ephedra/ma huang from dietary supplement products, since they are the same medicine. Use this medication exactly as prescribed. Do not increase your dose, take it more frequently, or use it for a longer period of time than prescribed because this drug can be habit-forming and you may increase for your risk for serious side effects. When used for an extended period, this medication may not work as well and may require different dosing. Talk with your doctor if this

medication stops working well. Your doctor may recommend "drug holidays" where your medication is stopped temporarily. Doing so may help this medication work more effectively.

- *Side Effects*: Nervousness, anxiety, dizziness, headache, nausea, loss of appetite, or trouble sleeping may occur. If any of these effects persist or worsen, notify your doctor promptly. Tell your doctor immediately if any of these serious side effects occur: chest pain, unusually fast or irregular heartbeat, vomiting, tremor/shakiness, sweating, severe weight loss, difficult or painful urination, stomach pain.

  Tell your doctor immediately if any of these unlikely but serious side effects occur: severe mental/mood changes, fever, trouble breathing, one-sided weakness, confusion, vision problems, slurred speech. If you notice other effects not listed above, contact your doctor or pharmacist.

- Precautions: This medication is not recommended for use if you have the following medical conditions: glaucoma (closed-angle type), certain psychiatric conditions (e.g., psychoneurosis). Tell your doctor your medical history, especially of: heart problems (e.g., arrhythmias, chest pain), blood vessel problems (e.g., stroke or TIA), diabetes, over-active thyroid (hyperthyroidism), prostate problems, high blood pressure (hypertension), kidney problems, any allergies. This medication should be used only when clearly needed during pregnancy. Discuss the risks and benefits with your doctor. It is not known whether this drug passes into breast milk. Due to the potential risk to the infant, breast-feeding while using this drug is not recommended.

- *Drug Interactions*: This drug is not recommended for use with other adrenalin-like drugs (e.g., caffeine, epinephrine, methylphenidate, pseudoephedrine). Also, avoid taking any MAO inhibitors (e.g., furazolidone, isocarboxazid, linezolid, moclobemide, phenelzine, procarbazine, selegiline, tranylcypromine) for at least 2 weeks before or after using this drug. Tell your doctor of all prescription and nonprescription medication you may use, especially: beta-blockers (e.g., metoprolol, propranolol), other blood pressure medicine (e.g., guanethidine, methyldopa, reserpine, or alpha-blockers such as prazosin and terazosin), tricyclic antidepressants (e.g., amitriptyline, desipramine), "water pills" (e.g., furosemide, hydrochlorothiazide), digoxin, atropine, theophylline, oxytocin, certain anesthetics used in surgery (e.g., cyclopropane, halothane), certain herbal/natural medications (e.g., ma huang, St John's wort). Check the labels on all your medicines (e.g., cough-and-cold products, diet aids, natural products) because they may contain ingredients that could increase your heart rate or blood pressure.

The use of ephedrine with these products is not recommended. Do not start or stop any medicine without doctor or pharmacist approval.

- *Overdose*: If overdose is suspected, contact your local poison control centre or emergency room immediately. Symptoms of overdose may include: seizures, cold sweats, vision problems (dilated pupils).
- *Notes*: Do not share this medication with others, it is against the law. Laboratory and/or medical tests (e.g., blood pressure) will be performed to monitor your progress.
- *Missed Dose*: If you miss a dose, use it as soon as you remember. If it is near the time of the next dose, skip the missed dose and resume your usual dosing schedule. Do not double the dose to catch up.
- *Storage*: Store at room temperature between 59 and 86 degrees F (15 and 30 degrees C) away from light.

## EPHEDRINE FOR WEIGHT LOSS

### Ephedrine and Dieting

Lately, the diet product market has been flooded with pills that make all sorts of wild claims about ephedrine. Some go so far as to call the chemical stimulant an herbal alternative to "Phen-Fen." It has also been touted for use as an energy booster or muscle mass builder.

However, as recently as a year ago, the Food and Drug Administration has issued a proposal calling for these diet product manufacturers to include a warning to their customers about the dangers of high doses of ephedrine.

### The Dangers of Using Ephedrine

Powerful enough to be sought out by recreational drug users, ephedrine is a stimulant whose effects are comparable to amphetamines (better known as speed). The drug is often derived from plants and works on both the nervous system and the heart. Its effects are strong enough to even induce seizures in certain people.

As for those diet supplements, the FDA is concerned that consumers will buy the products hoping to achieve quick results. This becomes a problem in terms of overdoing it, since both higher levels of dosing, as well as long-term use of ephedrine have been associated with increased risk of adverse effects.

After all, a person's natural impulse is to take higher doses of the drug in order to achieve larger, more powerful effects. The FDA wants warnings on all ephedrine-containing products, advising consumers not to exceed the recommended dose, and to use the product for no more than seven consecutive days.

Additionally, combining ephedrine's effects on the body with those of caffeine can really be dangerous, since the two drugs together are an extremely potent combination - this is definitely worrisome for the college crowd, where caffeine is often a way of life. In short, the diet pills are essentially a stimulant, much like the caffeine weight loss pills of old.

## Ephedrine's Medical Uses

Ephedrine and its chemically related cousin, pseudoephedrine, however, are used for legitimate medical purposes, especially for treating colds and other breathing disorders. Ever felt like you were breathing rapidly or that you had just consumed too much caffeine after taking some over the counter cold preparation? Chances are, that was the ephedrine-like compound kicking in. At these low doses, that stimulated feeling is about the worst of it for most people. However, these drugs all come with warnings advising anyone with high blood pressure, glaucoma, or heart or who is taking certain types of antidepressants (MAO inhibitors), against using the medications. Ephedrine is also not recommended for use in children under 12, pregnant women, or the elderly.

## The Bottom Line

Whatever weight loss may be attributed to this kind of diet pill - if any at all - is only going to be short term. As it has been said time and time again, the only safe and effective way to achieve permanent weight loss is through healthy eating and regular exercise.

## DANGERS OF EPHEDRINE

Ephedrine, the main ingredient in many popular decongestant cold remedies, is banned from the competitive arena by the IOC, the IAAF, the USOC, the NCAA, and the Boy and Girl Scouts of America, and several well-known athletes have been suspended from competition because ephedrine occupied a too-prominent position in their urine. Despite these banishments, athletes continue to use the stuff. Ice-hockey players pop ephedrine tabs before games, weight lifters swallow the stuff to give their workouts a boost, runners devour it before interval sessions, and a variety of different athletes (and non-athletes) ingest ephedrine in hopes of losing weight. Ephedrine has become one of the most popular 'supplements' used by athletes; the 'word on the street' is that it is a rather powerful stimulant which can speed up interval workouts, increase strength, and also assist with weight loss...

For more high quality information on Sports Supplements, subscribe to Peak Performance here and receive a bundle of free reports.

Strangely enough, however, until now not a single scientific study has linked ephedrine with improved athletic performance. In fact, classic research carried out in the 1970s showed that ephedrine had no effect at all on physical work capacity. More recently, studies demonstrated that ephedrine did not improve 40-K bicycle race times, nor did it increase maximal power and muscular endurance in experienced, competitive cyclists...

But you may have noticed that we began the last paragraph with the phrase 'until now'. Indeed, there is new research which indicates that ephedrine can boost performance during intense efforts which last for about 15 minutes or so (for example, a 5-K running race). However, this new study indicates that ephedrine works its magic only when it is ingested along with caffeine...

**Putting it to the Test**

Scientists at the Defence and Civil Institute of Environmental Medicine in North York, Ontario, Canada, asked twelve male cyclists to take part in a rugged, exercise-cycle workout which was designed to produce complete exhaustion in about 12 to 13 minutes (in this session, the individuals simply warmed up with five minutes of easy riding and then pedalled for as long as possible at a fixed, high percentage of *VO2max*). On one occasion, the subjects attempted this workout 90 minutes after ingesting 1 mg of ephedrine per kilogram of body weight. On another day, the athletes hit the session 90 minutes after swallowing 5 mg of caffeine per kilo of body weight (research has shown that it takes about 90 minutes for ephedrine and caffeine to attain peak concentrations in the blood after they are ingested). In yet another situation, the athletes took both the epehedrine and caffeine before stepping on to their bikes. And of course, they also tried the red-hot session after taking in only a *placebo*.

Ephedrine, when taken alone, failed to increase

performance time (which was defined as the amount of time a cyclist could sustain the required, high-percentage-of-VO2max intensity without becoming too exhausted to continue).

However, ephedrine combined with caffeine proved to be a powerful ergogenic concoction. Average performance time increased by about 39 per cent with ephedrine plus caffeine, compared to placebo, and all eight subjects improved their performances with ephedrine and caffeine together. In addition, the subjects' heart rates were higher with the ephedrine-caffeine combo, yet the workout actually felt easier with the ephedrine and caffeine on board...

**Why it Works**

Why did the ephedrine-plus-caffeine mix work so well? Blood-glucose levels were highest after the ephedrine-caffeine intake, suggesting that perhaps there was greater fuel available for leg muscles after ephedrine-caffeine ingestion, or that more glucose was getting to the brain, allaying mental fatigue. However, neither of these possibilities represents a likely explanation for the superiority of the ephedrine-plus-caffeine mix: The workouts were so short that fuel should not have become limiting, and indeed blood-glucose levels were normal in the placebo, isolated caffeine, and isolated ephedrine trials. In other words, there was plenty of carbohydrate fuel available in all situations...

Since the exercise felt about 25 per cent easier after ephedrine and caffeine were taken together (ie, ratings of perceived exertion were 25 per cent lower), it's likely that the ephedrine and caffeine worked together - by some as yet unknown mechanism - on the central nervous system, masking feelings of fatigue and thus allowing the athletes to work for a longer period of time. We do know (from previous research) that ephedrine and caffeine, when taken together, can fairly dramatically speed up *metabolism*. Thus, the ephedrine-caffeine combination may be a fairly potent stimulant of nervous-system function and may also spur other physiological processes, including muscle contractility...

However, all was not a bed of roses for the caffeine-ephedrine ingesters. About 33 per cent of them suffered from nausea during the workout after they had ingested the high-octane, ephedrine-caffeine cocktail and were unable to complete the session (thus, the number of subjects actually analysed dropped from 12 to eight). In addition, of course, ephedrine is a banned drug, so you run the risk of being both disqualified from your race and suspended from competition indefinitely if you use it. And finally, some individuals have severe reactions to ephedrine, ranging from nervousness and irritability to irregular heart rhythms, convulsions, and even death. It's not something you want to fool around with!

## Caffeine

Why didn't caffeine boost exercise performance, since a number of other studies have shown it to be an ergogenic substance? For one thing, the participants in the Ontario study were regular caffeine users (they drank at least seven cups of caffeinated coffee per week), so perhaps they were less sensitive to caffeine than irregular users would be (research suggests that caffeine's effects are blunted if it is ingested frequently). The subjects were also not in a high state of fitness, and there is some evidence that caffeine works better in highly trained athletes, compared to average people...

As we have mentioned before in Peak Performance, caffeine - taken in moderate amounts - is a 'legal' performance booster. Taking too much of the stuff will get you banned, but as it turns out, the amount needed for banishment actually hurts performances, while lesser quantities increase athletic capacity...

*The true scoop on caffeine is as follows*:

- Although most endurance runners believe that caffeine can help marathon performances, the truth is that it helps individuals engaged in shorter races, but not marathoners. Not a single published study has linked caffeine intake with improved marathon performance, but strong evidence indicates that caffeine (specifically, the amount in about two cups of strong coffee, which is a legal intake) can improve one-mile race time by about four seconds and also heighten kicking speed at the end of a 1500-metre or one-mile race by around 3 per cent.

- The caffeine in a caffeine tablet is much more effective (ie, performance-enhancing) than the caffeine in coffee, because coffee itself contains chemical constituents which dull caffeine's physiological activity.
- It's likely that caffeine can add some real sizzle to 10-K performances. In a recent study carried out at the University of Guelph in Canada, subjects were asked to run for as long as possible at an intensity of about 91 per cent of maximal heart rate (similar to the heart rate which prevails during the greater portion of a 10K). Individuals who ingested placebo (sugar) tablets lasted only 22 minutes at this intensity, while runners who took in decaf coffee, regular coffee, or decaf coffee plus added caffeine kept going for 26 minutes. The best strategy by far, however, was using caffeine tablets, which allowed athletes to buzz along for 41 minutes at 91 per cent of max heart rate. All of the runners improved their performances after taking in caffeine pills, compared to swilling real coffee. The dosage used in all cases was 4.5 mg of caffeine per kilogram of body weight (which usually leads to perfectly legal caffeine concentrations in the urine).
- Caffeine can also improve the quality of interval workouts. One piece of research determined that ingesting six mg of caffeine per kilogram of body weight (approximately the amount in three to four cups of strong coffee, which will still be a legal dose for most athletes) boosts performance by about 20 per cent during an interval workout which consists of two-minute intervals at an intensity of 100% VO2max.
- Other studies have linked caffeine with improve-

ments in both sprinting ability on a bicycle and 100-metre swim times.

- Although caffeine can act as a diuretic, it does not appear to increase the risk of dehydration when taken shortly (about an hour) before exercise, probably because the exercise itself tends to tone down urine production. For example, in one study, a jolt of caffeine exaggerated urine production by 31 per cent when no exercise was undertaken but had basically no effect on urine output when the caffeine was combined with exercise.
- If you are interested in using caffeine to put a charge in your interval sessions or race performances, the 'right' dose appears to be about 300 mg, taken 60 to 90 minutes before you start exercising. This practice is legal, but is it ethical? If you always drank three cups of coffee one hour before your races or intense workouts, even before you knew that caffeine was ergogenic, you could argue that your caffeine intake was a normal and natural part of your life, ie, that you were just following your routine dietary practices (however, bear in mind that coffee is less ergogenic than straight caffeine). However, in other situations, the truth is that caffeine intake is not ethical. You are basically using a drug to enhance your performance, and the only reason such a practice won't lead to penalties is that the governing bodies are too stupid to recognize the ergogenic potential of small quantities of caffeine.
- Caffeine is not included in most sports drinks, but it would probably have great performance-promoting value there. For example, in research carried out at McMaster University in Ontario, Canada, cyclists who ingested caffeine exhibited greater strength and endurance at the end of prolonged rides. This may be one reason why so many athletes sip Coke during extended race efforts.
- Should you try ephedrine - or mix ephedrine with

caffeine - prior to your rugged workouts or race efforts? Not a chance! Ephedrine plus caffeine would probably be an ergogenic combination for many athletes, but ephedrine produces too many side effects to be used safely, and the amount required to produce an effect is definitely illegal.

## HYOSCYAMINE

Hyoscyamine, is a tropane alkaloid and the levorotary isomer to atropine. It is a secondary metabolite found in certain plants of the Solanaceae family, including henbane (*Hyoscyamus niger*), mandrake (*Mandragora officinarum*), jimsonweed (*Datura stramonium*), and deadly nightshade (*Atropa belladonna*).

### USES

Hyoscyamine is used to provide symptomatic relief to various gastrointestinal disorders including spasms, peptic ulcers, irritable bowel syndrome, pancreatitis, colic and cystitis. It has also been used to relieve some heart problems, control some of the symptoms of Parkinson's disease, as well as for control of respiratory secretions in palliative care. It may be useful in pain control for neuropathic pain treated with opioids as it increases the level of analgesia obtained. Several mechanisms are thought to contribute to this effect. The closely related drugs atropine and scopolamine and other members of the anticholinergic drug group like cyclobenzaprine, trihexyphenidyl, and orphenadrine are also used for this purpose. When hyoscyamine is used along with opioids or other anti-peristaltic agents, measures to prevent constipation are especially important given the risk of paralytic ileus.

### SIDE EFFECTS

Side effects include dry mouth and throat, eye pain, blurred vision, restlessness, dizziness, arrythmia, flushing, and faintness. An overdose will cause headache, nausea, vomiting, and central nervous system symptoms including disorientation, hallucinations, euphoria, sexual arousal, short-term memory loss, and possible coma in extreme cases. Some people can experience transient combativeness. The euphoric and sexual effects are stronger than those of atropine but weaker than those of scopolamine, as well as dicycloverine, orphenadrine, cyclobenzaprine, trihexyphenidyl, ethanolamine antihistamines like phentyltoloxamine and the like.

## PHARMACOLOGY

Hyoscyamine is an anticholinergic, specifically an antimuscarinic, working by blocking the action of acetylcholine at parasympathetic sites in smooth muscle, secretory glands and the CNS; increases cardiac output, dries secretions, and antagonizes serotonin. At comparable doses, hyoscyamine has 98 per cent of the anticholinergic power of atropine and the other major belladonna-derived drug scopolamine having 92 per cent of the antimuscarinic potency of atropine.

### Isolation

Hyoscyamine can be extracted from plants of the *Solanaceae* family, notably *Datura stramonium*. Empirically it is $C_{17}H_{23}NO_3$. Its structural name is α-(hydroxymethyl)-, 8-methyl-8-azabicyclo[3.2.1]oct-3-yl ester, [3(S)-endo]-1αH,5αH-Tropan-3α-ol.

### medication prescribed

Hyoscyamine is used to control symptoms associated with disorders of the gastrointestinal (GI) tract. It works by decreasing the motion of the stomach and intestines and the secretion of stomach fluids, including acid. Hyoscyamine is also used in the treatment of bladder spasms, peptic ulcer disease, diverticulitis, colic, irritable bowel syndrome, cystitis, and pancreatitis. Hyoscyamine may also be used to treat certain heart conditions, to control the symptoms of Parkinson's disease and rhinitis (runny nose), and to reduce excess saliva production.

### Use OF Hyoscyamine

Hyoscyamine comes as a tablet, an extended-release (long-acting) capsule, a liquid to take by mouth, and in an injectable form. The tablets and liquid are usually taken three or four times a day. The extended-release capsules are usually taken twice a day. Do not crush, chew, or divide the extended-release capsules. Hyoscyamine injections are given by qualified healthcare professionals. Follow the directions on your prescription label carefully, and ask your doctor or pharmacist to explain any part you do not understand. Take hyoscyamine exactly as directed. Do not take more or less of it or take it more often than prescribed by your doctor.

Hyoscyamine controls symptoms associated with disorders of the GI tract, but it does not cure the disorders. Continue to take hyoscyamine even if you feel well. Do not stop taking hyoscyamine without talking to your doctor.

## Special Precautions for Hyoscyamine

Before taking hyoscyamine,

- Tell your doctor and pharmacist if you are allergic to hyoscyamine or any other drugs.
- Tell your doctor and pharmacist what prescription and nonprescription medications you are taking, especially amantadine (Symadine, Symmetrel), amitriptyline (Elavil), chlorpromazine (Thorazine), clomipramine (Anafranil), desipramine (Norpramin), doxepin (Sinequan), fluphenazine (Prolixin), haloperidol (Haldol), imipramine (Tofranil), medications containing belladonna (Donnatal), mesoridazine (Serentil), nortriptyline (Pamelor), perphenazine (Trilafon), phenelzine (Nardil), prochlorperazine (Compazine), promazine (Sparine), promethazine (Phenergan), protriptyline (Vivactil), thioridazine (Mellaril), tranylcypromine (Parnate), trifluoperazine (Stelazine), triflupromazine (Vesprin), trimeprazine (Temaril), trimipramine (Surmontil), and vitamins.
- Be aware that antacids may interfere with hyoscyamine, making it less effective. Take hyoscyamine 1 hour before or 2 hours after antacids.

- Tell your doctor if you have or have ever had glaucoma; heart, lung, liver, or kidney disease; a urinary tract or intestinal obstruction; an enlarged prostate; ulcerative colitis; or myasthenia gravis.
- Tell your doctor if you are pregnant, plan to become pregnant, or are breast-feeding. If you become pregnant while taking hyoscyamine, call your doctor.
- If you are having surgery, including dental surgery, tell your doctor or dentist that you take hyoscyamine.
- You should know that this drug may make you drowsy. Do not drive a car or operate machinery until you know how hyoscyamine will affect you.
- Remember that alcohol can add to the drowsiness caused by this drug.

## Side Effects of Hyoscyamine

Hyoscyamine may cause side effects. Tell your doctor if any of these symptoms are severe or do not go away:

- Drowsiness
- Dizziness or lightheadedness
- Headache
- Blurred vision
- Flushing (feeling of warmth)
- Dry mouth
- Constipation
- Difficulty urinating
- Increased sensitivity to light

*If you experience any of the following symptoms, call your doctor immediately*:

- Diarrhea
- Skin rash
- Eye pain
- Fast or irregular heartbeat

## Storage Conditions for Hyoscyamine

Keep this medication in the container it came in, tightly closed, and out of reach of children. Store it at room temperature and away from excess heat and moisture (not in the bathroom). Throw away any medication that is outdated or no longer needed. Talk to your pharmacist about the proper disposal of your medication.

## HYOSCYAMINE AND HYOSCINE THERAPY

The possession of decided hypnotic qualities has led to the use of hyoscyamine and hyoscine in the treatment of various mental disorders (Prideaux, Lawson, and others). Prideaux makes the important practical distinction, that it acts with different degrees of rapidity and potency under varying conditions of insanity. In acute mania with depression, one sixteenth of a grain will have a marked effect, while in the excitement of chronic mania large doses will be necessary. In chronic mania with exacerbations, he gives one quarter, one half, and even one grain by the stomach, or one tenth of a grain subcutaneously.

The latter mode of administration he regards preferable in these cases. In cases of mania with great motor excitement, and of a destructive character, Prideaux regards hyoscyamine as "the most rapid and reliable narcotic we possess." In the epileptic mania of the epileptic status, he says, it diminishes the number and violence of the attacks. In delusional insanity he finds it brings about, under favorable circumstances, mental restoration.

In chronic dementia, with destructive tendencies and sleeplessness, improvement is sometimes noted from the persistent use of small doses. Reinhard also has administered this agent in the dose of a milligramme (about one sixty-fifth of a grain) subcutaneously in cases of mania and epilepsy, with distinctly good results.

In eight of fifteen cases of mania, calmative effects were produced and permanent good was accomplished; and in five of twelve epileptics with maniacal attacks, the number and severity of the seizures were lessened. Drs. Sapilli and Riva, eminent Italian alienists, have found hyoscyamine very useful in recurrent mania. Gill, Ringer, and Lawson have also had good effects from hyoscyamine, in suitable cases, as an hypnotic.

Stramonium and hyoscyamus may be used like belladonna for the relief of painful affections, the neuralgiae; but they possess no special advantages over their more powerful congener. Oulmont has used the hypodermatic injection of hyoscyamine with remarkable success in several cases of neuralgia, but he does not regard it as more conspicuous and rapid in this disease than are opium and belladonna.

In affections characterized by spasm, as asthma, laryngeal cough, hepatic, intestinal, renal, and uterine colic, stramonium and hyoscyamus may be given with advantage, in place of or in combination with belladonna. The hypodermatic injection of hyoscyamine or daturine is an excellent expedient for procuring relief in these cases, but these alkaloids are not more effective than atropine.

Hyoscyamus, especially in the form of tincture, is frequently prescribed in irritable states of the bladder due to the presence of stone, enlargement of the prostate, and in catarrh of the bladder arising by transference of irritation from the urethra. It should not be forgotten that liquor potassae, so much prescribed in a mixture with hyoscyamus, is incompatible.

M. Oulmont refers, in terms which may seem to be exaggerated, to the great efficiency of hyoscyamine in the treatment of mercurial tremor, senile tremor, paralysis agitans, locomotor ataxia, and tetanus. In mercurial and senile tremor cures were obtained, but, as might be expected, only amelioration in paralysis agitans, locomotor ataxia, and tetanus.

The remarkable benefit obtained from this remedy in paralysis agitans is testified to by Empis, Joffroy, Charcot, and many other observers. The dose which Oulmont found effective was the one thirty-second of a grain of hyoscyamine, gradually increased to the one fifteenth of a grain.

The hypnotic quality is much more conspicuous in hyoscyamus than in belladonna or stramonium. In children it has long been known that, when opium is not well borne, hyoscyamus is an efficient substitute. Recent experience in asylum practice has shown that hyoscyamus in large doses is a very valuable hypnotic.

According to Dr. Campbell, two and a half drachms of the tincture are equivalent in hypnotic power to thirty grains of chloral hydrate. In order to procure efficient hypnotic effects, from two drachms to an ounce of the tincture is necessary, and this large quantity appears to be free from danger.

Extract of hyoscyamus is used in combination with purgatives, with the object—which abundant clinical observation confirms—of rendering their operation more efficient, no doubt, because of its action on the muscular layer of the intestine.

The ointment of stramonium is a favourite application to irritable ulcers, superficial inflammations, etc.

### Use of Hyoscyamine

Hyoscyamine is used to treat a wide variety of bladder, stomach and intestinal problems by acting on the wall of the stomach and also the bladder. Some of the conditions wherein this drug can be used to treat would include diverticulitis, peptic ulcers, pancreatitis, irritable bowel syndrome, colitis and diarrhea.

Other than that, hyoscyamine has also been popularly used to prevent motion sickness or to control bed-wetting. This can also be used for the treatment of rhinitis and to relieve some symptoms of Parkinson's disease.

Hyoscyamine can also be used for a lot of other conditions aside from the ones stated above.

For a doctor to give a patient a prescription for hyoscyamine, the doctor has to know if the patient has glaucoma, heart disease, a history of a heart attack, ulcerative colitis, any allergies particularly to hyoscyamine, stomach obstruction, pregnant, lactating or having prostate problems.

If this medicine should be used on children, make sure to ask a pediatrician as special caution may be needed. While hyoscyamine may be prescribed for children less than 12 years of age, there may be additional precautions that will be specified by the doctor.

The right dosage for any specific condition will be specified by the doctor. After taking the dose, make sure to follow it with one glass of water and follow further instructions from the prescription label.

Doses should be taken at regular intervals and not more than what the doctor has indicated. If overdose for this medicine is suspected, seek medical help immediately.

If a dose should be missed, it should be taken as soon as remembered. If it is close to the schedule for the next dose, forfeit the missed dose and take the next dose instead. Never take double doses or more than what the doctor has instructed.

Some mild side effects that hyoscyamine can bring about would be nausea, altered taste and constipation. Though these side effects basically do not need any medical attention, if they do not disappear in time, make sure to seek medical help.

Other side effects of this drug that would require medical attention immediately would be palpitations, difficulty in urinating, vomiting, anxiety, nervousness, dizziness, fever and fatigue.

This may not be a complete list of all the side effects that hyoscyamine would bring about. Considering that, make sure to report to a doctor whenever any discomfort or any suspected side effects would come out while taking this drug.

Hyoscyamine may interact with medicines such as antacids, donepezil, amantadine, benztropine, galantamine, medicines for allergies, medicines for hay fever, medicines for mental conditions, medicines for depression, tacrine, and rivastigmine.

There are many other drugs and food that may interact with hyoscyamine. With this, the doctor should know what the patient is ingesting. Thus, the doctor should have a list of whatever the patient takes whether it would be vitamins, minerals, supplements or any herbal products. The doctor should also be aware of a patient's smoking and drinking habits.

As this drug may cause dizziness, anyone taking it should avoid driving or operating heavy machinery after taking it. To avoid dizziness, do not stand up or sit immediately.

This side effect may affect older adults more. As the dizziness can also be caused by exposure to light, wearing of sunglasses is also advised.

*Hyoscyamine has the following structural formula:*

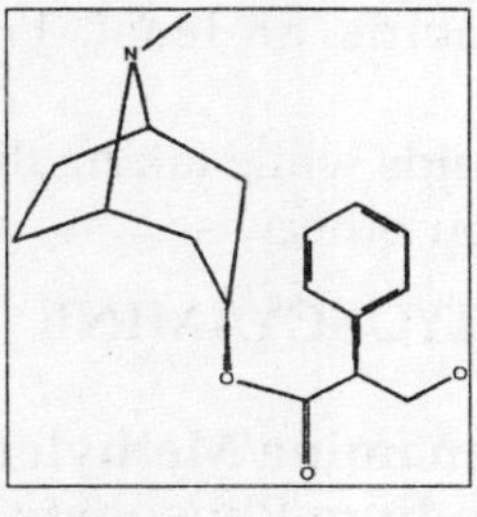

## Hyoscyamine Oral Uses

Hyoscyamine is used to treat a variety of stomach/ intestinal problems such as cramps and irritable bowel syndrome.

It is also used to treat other conditions such as bladder and bowel control problems, cramping pain caused by kidney stones and gallstones, and Parkinson's disease. In addition, it is used to decrease side effects of certain medications (drugs used to treat myasthenia gravis) and insecticides.

This medication works by decreasing acid production in the stomach, slowing down the natural movements of the gut, and relaxing muscles in many organs (e.g., stomach, intestines, bladder, kidney, gallbladder).

Hyoscyamine also lessens the amount of certain body fluids (e.g., saliva, sweat). This medication belongs to a class of drugs known as anticholinergics/antispasmodics.

## How to Use Hyoscyamine Oral

Take this medication by mouth as prescribed, usually 30-60 minutes before meals, or as directed by your doctor.

Dosage is based on your medical condition and response to therapy. Do not increase your dose or take it more often than prescribed without consulting your doctor.

Adults and children 12 years and older should not take more than 1.5 milligrams in 24 hours. Children aged 2 to 12 years should not take more than 0.75 milligrams in 24 hours. Ask your doctor or pharmacist for more information.

Antacids lower the absorption of hyoscyamine. If you use antacids, take them after meals and take hyoscyamine before meals; or take antacids at least 1 hour after taking hyoscyamine.

Drink plenty of fluids while taking this medication unless your doctor directs you otherwise.

## SIDE EFFECTS OF HYOSCYAMINE

### Hyoscyamine/Methenamine/Methylene Blue /Phenyl Salicylate/Sodium Phosphate

All medicines may cause side effects, but many people have no, or minor, side effects. Check with your doctor if any of these most COMMON side effects persist or become bothersome when using Hyoscyamine/Methenamine/ Methylene Blue/Phenyl Salicylate/Sodium Phosphate.

### Dry Mouth; Flushing; Nausea; Vomiting

Seek medical attention right away if any of these SEVERE side effects occur when using Hyoscyamine/Methenamine/ Methylene Blue/Phenyl Salicylate/Sodium Phosphate.

Severe allergic reactions (rash; hives; itching; difficulty breathing; tightness in the chest; swelling of the mouth, face, lips, or tongue); blurred vision; difficulty urinating; dizziness; fast or irregular heartbeat.

### Hyoscyamine

All medicines may cause side effects, but many people have no, or minor side effects. Check with your doctor if any of these most COMMON side effects persist or become bothersome when using Hyoscyamine.

Bloated feeling; blurred vision; constipation; decreased sweating; dizziness; drowsiness; dry mouth; enlarged pupils; excitability; headache; nausea; nervousness; trouble sleeping; weakness. Seek medical attention right away if any of these SEVERE side effects occur when using Hyoscyamine.

Severe allergic reactions (rash; hives; itching; difficulty breathing; tightness in the chest; swelling of the mouth, face, lips, or tongue); agitation; behaviour changes; confusion; decreased sexual ability; diarrhea; difficulty focusing eyes; disorientation; exaggerated sense of well-being; fast or irregular heartbeat; hallucinations; loss of consciousness; loss of coordination; memory loss; mental or mood changes; severe or persistent trouble sleeping; speech changes; taste changes or loss; trouble urinating; unusual tiredness or weakness; vision changes; vomiting.

## Hyoscyamine/Phenyltoloxamine

All medicines may cause side effects, but many people have no, or minor, side effects. Check with your doctor if any of these most COMMON side effects persist or become bothersome when using Hyoscyamine/Phenyltoloxamine.

Bloated feeling; blurred vision; constipation; decreased sweating; dizziness; drowsiness; dry mouth; enlarged pupils; excitability; headache; nausea; nervousness; trouble sleeping; weakness. Seek medical attention right away if any of these Severe side effects occur when using Hyoscyamine Phenyltoloxamine.

Severe allergic reactions (rash; hives; itching; difficulty breathing; tightness in the chest; swelling of the mouth, face, lips, or tongue); agitation; behaviour changes; confusion; decreased sexual ability; diarrhea; difficulty focusing eyes; disorientation; exaggerated sense of well-being; fast or irregular heartbeat; fever; hallucinations; loss of consciousness; loss of coordination; memory loss; mental or mood changes; severe or persistent trouble sleeping; speech changes; taste changes or loss; trouble urinating; unusual tiredness or weakness; vision changes; vomiting.

## Hyoscyamine Controlled-Release Tablets

All medicines may cause side effects, but many people have no, or minor side effects. Check with your doctor if any of these most COMMON side effects persist or become bothersome when using Hyoscyamine Controlled-Release

Tablets: Bloated feeling; blurred vision; constipation; decreased sweating; dizziness; drowsiness; dry mouth; enlarged pupils; excitability; headache; nausea; nervousness; trouble sleeping; weakness. Seek medical attention right away if any of these SEVERE side effects occur when using Hyoscyamine Controlled-Release Tablets:

Severe allergic reactions (rash; hives; itching; difficulty breathing; tightness in the chest; swelling of the mouth, face, lips, or tongue); agitation; behaviour changes; confusion; decreased sexual ability; diarrhea; difficulty focusing eyes; disorientation; exaggerated sense of well-being; fast or irregular heartbeat; hallucinations; loss of consciousness; loss of coordination; memory loss; mental or mood changes; severe or persistent trouble sleeping; speech changes; taste changes or loss; trouble urinating; unusual tiredness or weakness; vision changes; vomiting.

### Hyoscyamine Elixir

All medicines may cause side effects, but many people have no, or minor side effects. Check with your doctor if any of these most COMMON side effects persist or become bothersome when using Hyoscyamine Elixir.

Bloated feeling; blurred vision; constipation; decreased sweating; dizziness; drowsiness; dry mouth; enlarged pupils; excitability; headache; nausea; nervousness; trouble sleeping; weakness.

Seek medical attention right away if any of these SEVERE side effects occur when using Hyoscyamine Elixir:

Severe allergic reactions (rash; hives; itching; difficulty breathing; tightness in the chest; swelling of the mouth, face, lips, or tongue); agitation; behaviour changes; confusion; decreased sexual ability; diarrhea; difficulty focusing eyes; disorientation; exaggerated sense of well-being; fast or irregular heartbeat; hallucinations; loss of consciousness; loss of coordination; memory loss; mental or mood changes; severe or persistent trouble sleeping; speech changes; taste changes or loss; trouble urinating; unusual tiredness or weakness; vision changes; vomiting.

**Hyoscyamine/Phenyltoloxamine**

All medicines may cause side effects, but many people have no, or minor, side effects. Check with your doctor if any of these most COMMON side effects persist or become bothersome when using Hyoscyamine/Phenyltoloxamine:

Bloated feeling; blurred vision; constipation; decreased sweating; dizziness; drowsiness; dry mouth; enlarged pupils; excitability; headache; nausea; nervousness; trouble sleeping; weakness. Seek medical attention right away if any of these SEVERE side effects occur when using Hyoscyamine/ Phenyltoloxamine:

Severe allergic reactions (rash; hives; itching; difficulty breathing; tightness in the chest; swelling of the mouth, face, lips, or tongue); agitation; behaviour changes; confusion; decreased sexual ability; diarrhea; difficulty focusing eyes; disorientation; exaggerated sense of well-being; fast or irregular heartbeat; fever; hallucinations; loss of consciousness; loss of coordination; memory loss; mental or mood changes; severe or persistent trouble sleeping; speech changes; taste changes or loss; trouble urinating; unusual tiredness or weakness; vision changes; vomiting.

**Hyoscyamine Controlled-Release Tablets**

All medicines may cause side effects, but many people have no, or minor side effects. Check with your doctor if any of these most COMMON side effects persist or become bothersome when using Hyoscyamine Controlled-Release Tablets:

Bloated feeling; blurred vision; constipation; decreased sweating; dizziness; drowsiness; dry mouth; enlarged pupils; excitability; headache; nausea; nervousness; trouble sleeping; weakness. Seek medical attention right away if any of these SEVERE side effects occur when using Hyoscyamine Controlled-Release Tablets:

Severe allergic reactions (rash; hives; itching; difficulty breathing; tightness in the chest; swelling of the mouth, face, lips, or tongue); agitation; behaviour changes; confusion; decreased sexual ability; diarrhea; difficulty focusing eyes;

disorientation; exaggerated sense of well-being; fast or irregular heartbeat; hallucinations; loss of consciousness; loss of coordination; memory loss; mental or mood changes; severe or persistent trouble sleeping; speech changes; taste changes or loss; trouble urinating; unusual tiredness or weakness; vision changes; vomiting.

### Hyoscyamine/Methenamine/Methylene Blue/Phenyl Salicylate/Sodium Biphosphate Delayed-Release Tablets

All medicines may cause side effects, but many people have no, or minor, side effects. Check with your doctor if any of these most COMMON side effects persist or become bothersome when using Hyoscyamine/Methenamine/Methylene Blue/Phenyl Salicylate/Sodium Biphosphate Delayed-Release Tablets:

Dry mouth; flushing; nausea; vomiting.

Seek medical attention right away if any of these SEVERE side effects occur when using Hyoscyamine/Methenamine/Methylene Blue/Phenyl Salicylate/Sodium Biphosphate Delayed-Release Tablets:

Severe allergic reactions (rash; hives; itching; difficulty breathing; tightness in the chest; swelling of the mouth, face, lips, or tongue); blurred vision; difficulty urinating; dizziness; fast or irregular heartbeat.

### Hyoscyamine Drops

All medicines may cause side effects, but many people have no, or minor side effects. Check with your doctor if any of these most COMMON side effects persist or become bothersome when using Hyoscyamine Drops:

Bloated feeling; blurred vision; constipation; decreased sweating; dizziness; drowsiness; dry mouth; enlarged pupils; excitability; headache; nausea; nervousness; trouble sleeping; weakness.

Seek medical attention right away if any of these SEVERE side effects occur when using Hyoscyamine Drops: Severe allergic reactions (rash; hives; itching; difficulty breathing;

tightness in the chest; swelling of the mouth, face, lips, or tongue); agitation; behaviour changes; confusion; decreased sexual ability; diarrhea; difficulty focusing eyes; disorientation; exaggerated sense of well-being; fast or irregular heartbeat; hallucinations; loss of consciousness; loss of coordination; memory loss; mental or mood changes; severe or persistent trouble sleeping; speech changes; taste changes or loss; trouble urinating; unusual tiredness or weakness; vision changes; vomiting.

**Hyoscyamine Elixir**

All medicines may cause side effects, but many people have no, or minor side effects. Check with your doctor if any of these most COMMON side effects persist or become bothersome when using Hyoscyamine Elixir:

Bloated feeling; blurred vision; constipation; decreased sweating; dizziness; drowsiness; dry mouth; enlarged pupils; excitability; headache; nausea; nervousness; trouble sleeping; weakness. Seek medical attention right away if any of these SEVERE side effects occur when using Hyoscyamine Elixir:

Severe allergic reactions (rash; hives; itching; difficulty breathing; tightness in the chest; swelling of the mouth, face, lips, or tongue); agitation; behaviour changes; confusion; decreased sexual ability; diarrhea; difficulty focusing eyes; disorientation; exaggerated sense of well-being; fast or irregular heartbeat; hallucinations; loss of consciousness; loss of coordination; memory loss; mental or mood changes; severe or persistent trouble sleeping; speech changes; taste changes or loss; trouble urinating; unusual tiredness or weakness; vision changes; vomiting.

**Hyoscyamine Extended-Release Capsules**

All medicines may cause side effects, but many people have no, or minor side effects. Check with your doctor if any of these most COMMON side effects persist or become bothersome when using Hyoscyamine Extended-Release Capsules:

Bloated feeling; blurred vision; constipation; decreased

sweating; dizziness; drowsiness; dry mouth; enlarged pupils; excitability; headache; nausea; nervousness; trouble sleeping; weakness.

Seek medical attention right away if any of these SEVERE side effects occur when using Hyoscyamine Extended-Release Capsules: Severe allergic reactions (rash; hives; itching; difficulty breathing; tightness in the chest; swelling of the mouth, face, lips, or tongue); agitation; behaviour changes; confusion; decreased sexual ability; diarrhea; difficulty focusing eyes; disorientation; exaggerated sense of well-being; fast or irregular heartbeat; hallucinations; loss of consciousness; loss of coordination; memory loss; mental or mood changes; severe or persistent trouble sleeping; speech changes; taste changes or loss; trouble urinating; unusual tiredness or weakness; vision changes; vomiting.

**Hyoscyamine Extended-Release Tablets**

All medicines may cause side effects, but many people have no, or minor side effects. Check with your doctor if any of these most COMMON side effects persist or become bothersome when using Hyoscyamine Extended-Release Tablets:

Bloated feeling; blurred vision; constipation; decreased sweating; dizziness; drowsiness; dry mouth; enlarged pupils; excitability; headache; nausea; nervousness; trouble sleeping; weakness. Seek medical attention right away if any of these SEVERE side effects occur when using Hyoscyamine Extended-Release Tablets:

Severe allergic reactions (rash; hives; itching; difficulty breathing; tightness in the chest; swelling of the mouth, face, lips, or tongue); agitation; behaviour changes; confusion; decreased sexual ability; diarrhea; difficulty focusing eyes; disorientation; exaggerated sense of well-being; fast or irregular heartbeat; hallucinations; loss of consciousness; loss of coordination; memory loss; mental or mood changes; severe or persistent trouble sleeping; speech changes; taste changes or loss; trouble urinating; unusual tiredness or weakness; vision changes; vomiting.

**Hyoscyamine Orally Disintegrating Tablets**

All medicines may cause side effects, but many people have no, or minor, side effects. Check with your doctor if any of these most COMMON side effects persist or become bothersome when using Hyoscyamine Orally Disintegrating Tablets: Bloated feeling; blurred vision; constipation; decreased sweating; dizziness; drowsiness; dry mouth; enlarged pupils; excitability; headache; nausea; nervousness; trouble sleeping; weakness.

Seek medical attention right away if any of these SEVERE side effects occur when using Hyoscyamine Orally Disintegrating Tablets: Severe allergic reactions (rash; hives; itching; difficulty breathing; tightness in the chest; swelling of the mouth, face, lips, or tongue); agitation; behaviour changes; confusion; decreased sexual ability; diarrhea; difficulty focusing eyes; disorientation; exaggerated sense of well-being; fast or irregular heartbeat; hallucinations; loss of consciousness; loss of coordination; memory loss; mental or mood changes; severe or persistent trouble sleeping; speech changes; taste changes or loss; trouble urinating; unusual tiredness or weakness; vision changes; vomiting.

**Hyoscyamine Spray**

All medicines may cause side effects, but many people have no, or minor side effects. Check with your doctor if any of these most COMMON side effects persist or become bothersome when using Hyoscyamine Spray:

Bloated feeling; blurred vision; constipation; decreased sweating; dizziness; drowsiness; dry mouth; enlarged pupils; excitability; headache; nausea; nervousness; trouble sleeping; weakness.

Seek medical attention right away if any of these SEVERE side effects occur when using Hyoscyamine Spray: Severe allergic reactions (rash; hives; itching; difficulty breathing; tightness in the chest; swelling of the mouth, face, lips, or tongue); agitation; behaviour changes; confusion; decreased sexual ability; diarrhea; difficulty focusing eyes; disorientation; exaggerated sense of well-being; fast or irregular heartbeat;

hallucinations; loss of consciousness; loss of coordination; memory loss; mental or mood changes; severe or persistent trouble sleeping; speech changes; taste changes or loss; trouble urinating; unusual tiredness or weakness; vision changes; vomiting.

### Hyoscyamine Tablets

All medicines may cause side effects, but many people have no, or minor side effects. Check with your doctor if any of these most COMMON side effects persist or become bothersome when using Hyoscyamine Tablets:

Bloated feeling; blurred vision; constipation; decreased sweating; dizziness; drowsiness; dry mouth; enlarged pupils; excitability; headache; nausea; nervousness; trouble sleeping; weakness.

Seek medical attention right away if any of these SEVERE side effects occur when using Hyoscyamine Tablets:

Severe allergic reactions (rash; hives; itching; difficulty breathing; tightness in the chest; swelling of the mouth, face, lips, or tongue); agitation; behaviour changes; confusion; decreased sexual ability; diarrhea; difficulty focusing eyes; disorientation; exaggerated sense of well-being; fast or irregular heartbeat; hallucinations; loss of consciousness; loss of coordination; memory loss; mental or mood changes; severe or persistent trouble sleeping; speech changes; taste changes or loss; trouble urinating; unusual tiredness or weakness; vision changes; vomiting.

### Side Effects by Body System

- *Cardiovascular*: Cardiovascular side effects have included tachycardia, premature ventricular depolarizations, and ventricular tachycardia.
- *Gastrointestinal*: Gastrointestinal side effects due to the anticholinergic effects of hyoscyamine have commonly included dry mouth and mucous membranes. Other reported side effects include delayed gastric emptying time, reduced gastric acid secretion, constipation, and gastroesophageal reflux.

- *General*: Hyoscyamine toxicity (anticholinergic side effects) often presents as fever, tachycardia, agitation, and dry skin/mucous membranes.
- *Genitourinary*: Genitourinary complications include urinary retention (due to anticholinergic effects on the urinary sphincter), which is common and dose-related, and impotence in male patients.
- *Hypersensitivity*: Hypersensitivity reactions to hyoscyamine are rare. Reactions can include urticaria, eczema, papillary hyperplasia, mucopurulent discharge, eosinophilia, pruritus, edema, hypotension, abdominal pain, tachypnea, nausea and vomiting.
- *Nervous system*: Nervous system side effects have included lethargy and somnolence. Higher doses may be associated with mental confusion and/or excitement. The elderly appear to be more prone to the anticholinergic effects of hyoscyamine on the CNS.
- *Ocular*: Ocular side effects due to the anticholinergic activity of hyoscyamine have included inhibition of the iris sphincter muscle (possibly resulting in mydriasis), follicular conjunctivitis, and inhibition of the ciliary muscle (which can produce blurred vision). All muscarinic antagonists can precipitate glaucoma.
- *Endocrine*: Endocrine side effects have included inhibition of exocrine sweat glands. This is usually not clinically significant except when perspiration becomes a major factor in body temperature control.

## Chapter 2

# Steroid

A steroid is a terpenoid lipid characterized by its sterane core and additional functional groups. The core is a carbon structure of four fused rings: three cyclohexane rings and one cyclopentane ring. The steroids vary by the functional groups attached to these rings and the oxidation state of the rings.

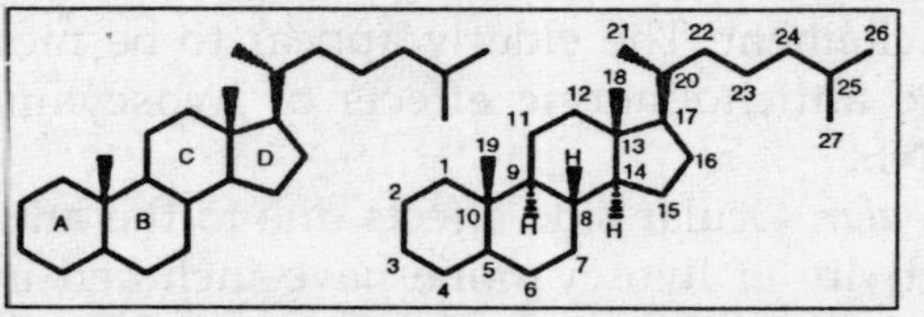


**Fig.** IUPAC Recommended Ring Lettering (Left) and Atom Numbering (Right) of the Steroid Skeleton.

Hundreds of distinct steroids are found in plants, animals, and fungi. All steroids are made in cells either from the sterols lanosterol (animals and fungi) or cycloartenol (plants). Both, lanosterol and cycloartenol, are derived from the cyclization of the triterpene squalene. Sterols are special forms of steroids, with a hydroxyl group at the atom C-3 and a skeleton derived from cholestane. Cholesterol is one of the best known sterols.

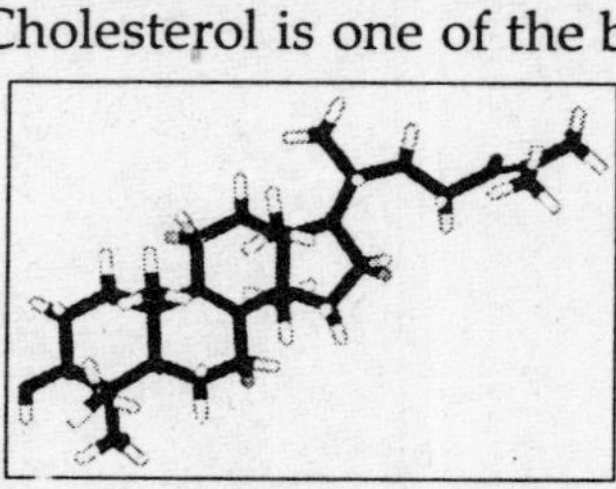

**Fig.** Stick Model of the Steroid Lanosterol. The Total Number of Carbons (30) Reflects its Triterpenoid Origin.

## CLASSIFICATION

### Taxonomical/Functional

*Some of the common categories of steroids:*

- Animal steroids.
  - Insect steroids.
    - (a) Ecdysteroids such as ecdysterone.
  - Vertebrate steroids.
    - (a) Steroid hormones.
    - (b) Sex steroids are a subset of sex hormones that produce sex differences or support reproduction. They include androgens, estrogens, and progestagens.
    - (c) Corticosteroids include glucocorticoids and mineralocorticoids. Glucocorticoids regulate many aspects of metabolism and immune function, whereas mineralocorticoids help maintain blood volume and control renal excretion of electrolytes. Most medical 'steroid' drugs are corticosteroids.
    - (d) Anabolic steroids are a class of steroids that interact with androgen receptors to increase muscle and bone synthesis. There are natural and synthetic anabolic steroids. In popular language, the word "steroids" usually refers to anabolic steroids.
    - (e) Cholesterol, which modulates the fluidity of cell membranes and is the principal constituent of the plaques implicated in atherosclerosis.
- Plant steroids.
  - Phytosterols.
  - Brassinosteroids.
- Fungus steroids.
  - Ergosterols.

### Structural

It is also possible to classify steroids based upon their

chemical composition. Examples from this classification include:

| Class | Examples | Number of carbon atoms |
|---|---|---|
| Cholestanes | cholesterol | 27 |
| Cholanes | cholic acid | 24 |
| Pregnanes | progesterone | 21 |
| Androstanes | testosterone | 19 |
| Estranes | estradiol | 18 |

*Gonane* (or steroid nucleus) is the hypothetic parent (17-carbon tetracyclic) hydrocarbon molecule without any alkyl sidechains.

## Metabolism

Steroids include estrogen, cortisol, progesterone, and testosterone. Estrogen and progesterone are made primarily in the ovary and in the placenta during pregnancy, and testosterone in the testes.

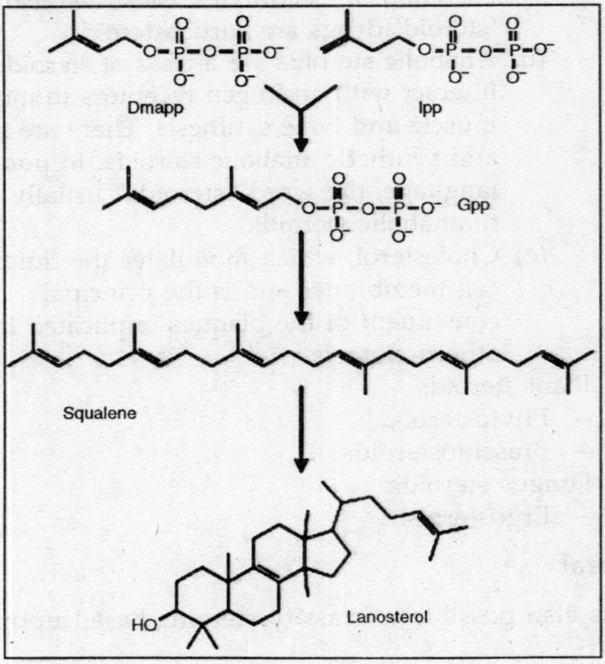

Testosterone is also converted into estrogen to regulate the supply of each, in the bodies of both females and males. Certain neurons and glia in the central nervous system (CNS) express the enzymes that are required for the local synthesis of pregnane neurosteroids, either *de novo* or from peripherally-derived sources.

The rate-limiting step of steroid synthesis is the conversion of cholesterol to pregnenolone, which occurs inside the mitochondrion.

Steroid metabolism is the complete set of chemical reactions in organisms that produce, modify and consume steroids.

*These metabolic pathways include*:

- *Steroid synthesis*: The manufacture of steroids from simpler precursors.
- *Steroidogenesis*: The interconversion of different types of steroids.
- Steroid degradation.

## Steroid Biosynthesis

Steroid biosynthesis is an anabolic metabolic pathway that produces steroids from simple precursors. This pathway is carried out in different ways in animals than in many other organisms, making the pathway a common target for antibiotics and other anti-infective drugs. In addition, steroid metabolism in humans is the target of cholesterol-lowering drugs such as statins.

It starts in the mevalonate pathway in humans, with Acetyl-CoA as building blocks, which form DMAPP and IPP. In following steps, DMAPP and IPP form lanosterol, the first steroid. Further modification belongs to the succeeding steroidogenesis.

### *Mevalonate Pathway*

The mevalonate pathway or HMG-CoA reductase pathway starts with and ends with dimethylallyl pyrophosphate (DMAPP) and isopentenyl pyrophosphate (IPP).

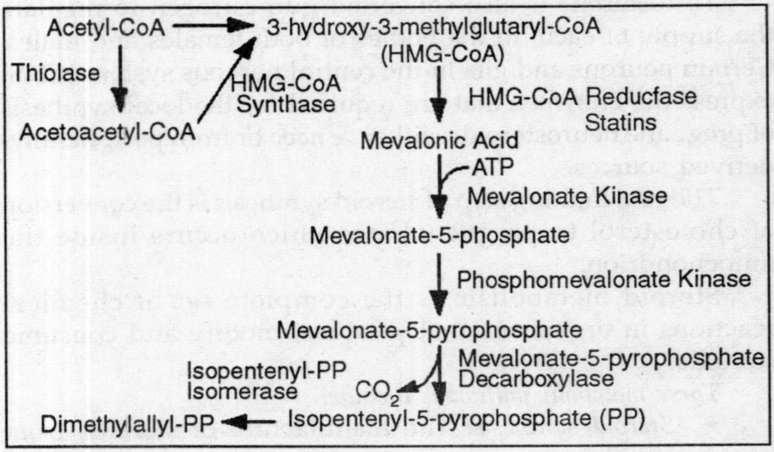


## *Regulation and Feedback*

Several key enzymes can be activated through DNA transcriptional regulation on activation of SREBP (Sterol Regulatory Element-Binding Protein-1 and -2). This intracellular sensor detects low cholesterol levels and stimulates endogenous production by the HMG-CoA reductase pathway, as well as increasing lipoprotein uptake by up-regulating the LDL receptor. Regulation of this pathway is also achieved by controlling the rate of translation of the mRNA, degradation of reductase and phosphorylation.

## *Pharmacology*

A number of drugs target the *mevalonate pathway*:

- Statins (used for elevated cholesterol levels).
- Bisphosphonates (used in treatment of various bone-degenerative diseases).

Plants and bacteria:In plants and bacteria, the non-mevalonate pathway uses pyruvate and glyceraldehyde 3-phosphate as substrates.

## DMAPP to Lanosterol

Isopentenyl pyrophosphate and dimethylallyl pyrophosphate donate isoprene units, which are assembled and modified to form terpenes and isoprenoids, which are a large class of lipids that include the carotenoids, and form the largest class of plant natural products.

Here, the isoprene units are joined together to make squalene and then folded up and formed into a set of rings to make lanosterol. Lanosterol can then be converted into other steroids such as cholesterol and ergosterol.

### Steroidogenesis

Steroidogenesis is the process wherein desired forms of steroids are generated by transformation of other steroids (The formation of steroids; commonly referring to the biological synthesis of steroid hormones, but not to the production of such compounds in a chemical laboratory). The pathways of steroidogenesis can differ from organism to organism, but the pathways of human steroidogenesis are shown in the figure.

Products of steroidogenesis include:

- Androgens
  - Testosterone
- Estrogens and progesterone
- Corticoids
  - Cortisol
  - Aldosterone

### Elimination

Steroids are mainly oxidized by cytochrome P450 oxidase enzymes, such as CYP3A4. These reactions introduce oxygen into the steroid ring and allows the structure to be broken up by other enzymes, to form bile acids as final products. These bile acids can then be eliminated through secretion from the liver in the bile.

The expression of this oxidase gene can be upregulated by the steroid sensor PXR when there is a high blood concentration of steroids.

## BATRACHOTOXIN

Batrachotoxins (BTX) are extremely potent cardiotoxic and neurotoxic steroidal alkaloids found in certain species of frogs (poison dart frog), Melyridae beetles, and birds (*Pitohui, Ifrita kowaldi, Colluricincla megarhyncha*).

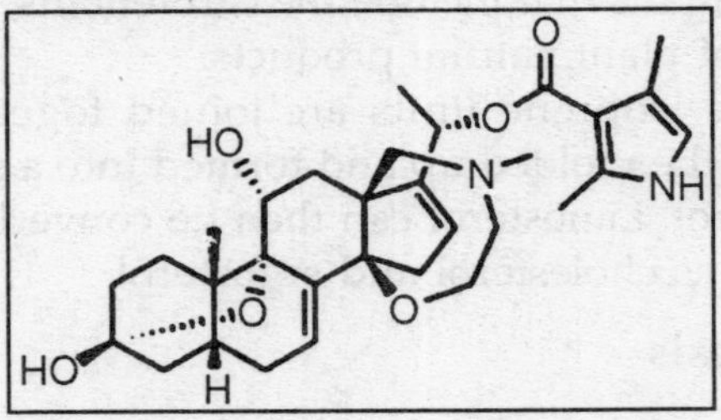


## Chemistry

Batrachotoxin comes from the Greek words "batrachos" (βÜôñα÷ïò), meaning frog, and "toxine" (ôïîßíç), meaning poison. It was named by scientists John Daly and Bernard Witkop, who isolated the pure alkaloid and determined its structure and chemical properties. Its chemical formula is $C_{31}H_{42}N_2O_6$.

More than 100 toxins have been identified from the skin secretions of members of the Dendrobatidae family of frogs, especially *Dendrobates* and *Phyllobates*. Members of the genus *Dendrobates* (of which there are at least 44 known species) are also known as "poison dart" or "poison arrow" frogs. However, only frogs of the genus *Phyllobates* produce the highly lethal batrachotoxin.

Batrachotoxin was successfully synthesized in a laboratory in 1998.

## Toxicity

Extrapolating from the lethal dosage $LD_{50}$ in rats, the lethal dose of this alkaloid in humans is estimated to be 1 to 2 μg/kg. Thus, the lethal dose for a 68 kg (150 pound) person would be approximately 100 micrograms, or equivalent to the weight of two grains of ordinary (fine) table salt (NaCl). Batrachotoxin is thus around fifteen times more potent than curare (another arrow poison used by South American Indians and derived from plants of the genera *Strychnos* and *Curarea*), and about ten times more potent than tetrodotoxin, from the puffer fish. It is far less potent than botulinum toxin.

The toxin is released through colourless or milky secretions from glands located on the back and behind the ears of frogs from the genus *Phyllobates*. When one of these frogs is agitated, feels threatened or is in pain, the toxin is reflexively released through several canals.

As a neurotoxin it affects the nervous system. Neurological function depends on depolarization of nerve and muscle fibres due to increased sodium ion permeability of the excitable cell membrane. Lipid-soluble toxins such as batrachotoxin act directly on sodium ion channels involved in action potential generation and by modifying both their ion selectivity and voltage sensitivity.

This has a direct effect on the peripheral nervous system (PNS). Batrachotoxin in the PNS produces increased permeability (selective and irreversible) of the resting cell membrane to sodium ions, without changing potassium or calcium concentration. This influx of sodium depolarizes the formerly polarized cell membrane. Batrachotoxin also alters the ion selectivity of the ion channel by increasing the permeability of the channel toward larger cations. Voltage-sensitive sodium channels become persistently active at the resting membrane potential. Batrachotoxin kills by permanently blocking nerve signal transmission to the muscles.

Although generally classified as a neurotoxin, batrachotoxin has marked effects on heart muscles. These effects are similar to the cardiotoxic effects of digitalis (digoxin), a poison found in the foxglove plant. Batrachotoxin interferes with heart conduction, causing arrhythmias, extrasystoles, ventricular fibrillation and other changes which lead to cardiac arrest. Batrachotoxin induces a massive release of acetylcholine in nerves and muscles and destruction of synaptic vesicles, as well. Batrachotoxin R is more effective than related batrachotoxin A.

Structural changes in nerves and muscles are due to a massive influx of sodium ions, which produces osmotic alterations. It has been suggested that there may also be an effect on the central nervous system, although it is not currently known what such an effect may be.

Batrachotoxin activity is temperature-dependent, with a maximum activity at 37 degrees Celsius (98.6 degrees Fahrenheit). Its activity is also more rapid at an alkaline pH, which suggests that the unprotonated form may be more active.

## Treatment

Currently no effective antidote exists for the treatment of batrachotoxin poisoning. Veratridine, aconitine and grayanotoxin - like batrachotoxin - are lipid-soluble poisons which similarly alter the ion selectivity of the sodium channels, suggesting a common site of action. Due to these similarities, treatment for batrachotoxin poisoning might best be modeled after, or base7d on, treatments for one of these poisons. Treatment may also be modeled after that for digitalis, which produces somewhat similar cardiotoxic effects.

While it is not an antidote, the membrane depolarization can be prevented or reversed by either tetrodotoxin (from puffer fish), which is a noncompetitive inhibitor, or saxitoxin ("red tide"). These both have effects antagonistic to those of batrachotoxin on sodium flux. Certain anesthetics may act as receptor antagonists to the action of this alkaloid poison, while other local anesthetics block its action altogether by acting as competitive antagonists.

## Source

The "poison dart" (or "poison arrow") frog does not produce batrachotoxin itself. It is believed that the frogs get the poison from eating beetles or other insects in their native habitat, and the insects obtain the poison from a plant source. The toxin has been recently discovered in Melyrid beetles (*Choresine*), making them the likely source of the toxin in birds and frogs. Frogs raised in captivity do not produce batrachotoxin, and thus may be handled without the risk of death.

The native habitat of poison dart frogs is the warm regions

of Central America and South America in which the humidity is around 80 per cent.

Of the three so-called "poison dart" frogs which contain batrachotoxin - *Phyllobates terribilis, Phyllobates aurotaenia,* and *Phyllobates bicolor* - the most toxic is the most recently discovered *Phyllobates terribilis.*

*Phyllobates terribilis* generally contains 27 times more batrachotoxin than its close relatives and is 20-fold more toxic.

Also in 1990 it was discovered that the skin and feathers of some bird species in New Guinea, such as the Hooded Pitohui, contain the toxin on their skin and feathers. Like the dart frogs, it is believed they ingest the toxin from a food source and then secrete it.

## Use

The most common use of this toxin is by the Noanamα Chocσ and Emberα Chocσ Indians of western Colombia for poisoning blowgun darts for use in hunting.

Poison darts are prepared by the Chocσ Amerindians by first impaling a frog on a piece of wood. By some accounts, the frog is then held over or roasted alive over a fire until it cries in pain. Bubbles of poison form as the frog's skin begins to blister. The dart tips are prepared by touching them to the toxin, or the toxin can be caught in a container and allowed to ferment. Poison darts made from either fresh or fermented batrachotoxin are enough to drop monkeys and birds in their tracks. Nerve paralysis is almost instantaneous.

Other accounts say that a stick siurukida ("bamboo tooth") is put through the mouth of the frog and passed out through one of its hind legs. This causes the frog to perspire profusely on its back, which becomes covered with a white froth. The darts are dipped or rolled in the froth, preserving their lethal power for up to a year.

## ANABOLIC STEROID

Anabolic steroids officially known as anabolic-androgenic steroids (AAS), are drugs which mimic the effects of the male steroids testosterone and dihydrotestosterone. They increase protein synthesis within cells, which results in the buildup of cellular tissue (anabolism), especially in muscles.

Anabolic steroids also have androgenic and virilizing properties, including the development and maintenance of masculine characteristics such as the growth of the vocal cords and body hair.

The word *anabolic* comes from the Greek *anabolein*, "to build up", and the word *androgenic* from the Greek *andros*, "man" + *genein*, "to produce".

**Fig.** Crystal structure of human sex hormone-binding globulin, transporting 5a-dihydrotestosterone

Anabolic steroids were first isolated, identified and synthesized in the 1930s, and are now used therapeutically in medicine to stimulate bone growth and appetite, induce male puberty, and treat chronic wasting conditions, such as cancer and AIDS. The American College of Sports Medicine acknowledges that AAS, in the presence of adequate diet, can contribute to increases in body weight, often as lean mass increases, and that the gains in muscular strength achieved through high-intensity exercise and proper diet can be additionally increased by the use of AAS in some individuals.

Some health risks can be produced by long-term use or excessive doses of anabolic steroids. These effects include harmful changes in cholesterol levels (increased low-density lipoprotein and decreased high-density lipoprotein), acne, high blood pressure, liver damage, and dangerous changes in the structure of the left ventricle of the heart.

Ergogenic uses for anabolic steroids in sports and bodybuilding is controversial, because of their adverse effects and the potential to gain an advantage conventionally considered "cheating." Their use is referred to as doping and banned by all major sporting bodies.

For many years the AAS have been by far the most detected doping substances in IOC-accredited laboratories. In countries where AAS are controlled substances, there is often a black market in which smuggled or even counterfeit drugs are sold to users.

## Isolation of Gonadal AAS

The use of gonadal steroids pre-dates their identification and isolation. Medical use of testicle extract began in the late 19th century while its effects on strength were still being studied. The isolation of gonadal steroids can be traced back to 1931 when Adolf Butenandt, a chemist in Marburg, purified 15 milligrams of the male hormone androstenone from tens of thousands of litres of urine. This steroid was subsequently synthesized in 1934 by Leopold Ruzicka, a chemist in Zurich.

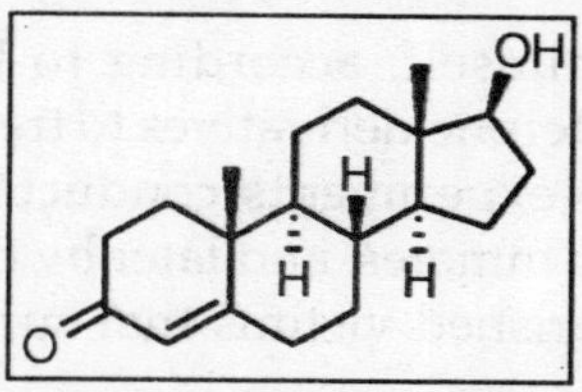


**Fig.** Chemical Structure of the Natural Anabolic Hormone Testosterone, 17β-hydroxy-4-androsten-3-one

In the 1930s it was already known that the testes contained a more powerful androgen than androstenone, and three groups of scientists, funded by competing pharmaceutical companies in the Netherlands, Nazi Germany and Switzerland, raced to isolate it. This hormone was first identified by Karoly Gyula David, E. Dingemanse, J. Freud and Ernst Laqueur in a May 1935 paper"On Crystalline Male Hormone from Testicles (Testosterone)."

They named the hormone testosterone, from the stems of testicle and sterol, and the suffix of ketone. The chemical synthesis of testosterone was achieved in August that year, when Butenandt and G. Hanisch published a paper describing"A Method for Preparing Testosterone from Cholesterol." Only a week later, the third group, Ruzicka and A. Wettstein, announced a patent application in a paper"On the Artificial Preparation of the Testicular Hormone Testosterone (Androsten-3-one-17-ol)."

Ruzicka and Butenandt were offered the 1939 Nobel Prize for Chemistry for their work, but the Nazi government forced Butenandt to decline the honour, although he accepted the prize after the end of World War II.

Clinical trials on humans, involving either oral doses of methyltestosterone or injections of testosterone propionate, began as early as 1937. Testosterone propionate is mentioned in a letter to the editor of Strength and Health magazine in 1938; this is the earliest known reference to an anabolic steroid in a U.S. weightlifting or bodybuilding magazine. There are often reported rumors that German soldiers were administered anabolic steroids during the Second World War, the aim being to increase their aggression and stamina, but these are, as yet, unproven.

Adolf Hitler himself, according to his physician, was injected with testosterone derivatives to treat various ailments. AAS were used in experiments conducted by the Nazis on concentration camp inmates, and later by the allies attempting to treat the malnourished victims that survived Nazi camps.

## Development of synthetic AAS

The development of muscle-building properties of testosterone was pursued in the 1940s, in the Soviet Union and in Eastern Bloc countries such as East Germany, where steroid programs were used to enhance the performance of Olympic and other amateur weight lifters. In response to the success of Russian weightlifters, the U.S. Olympic Team physician Dr. John Ziegler worked with synthetic chemists to develop an anabolic steroid with reduced androgenic effects.

Ziegler's work resulted in the production of methandrostenolone, which Ciba Pharmaceuticals marketed as Dianabol. The new steroid was approved for use in the U.S. by the Food and Drug Administration (FDA) in 1958. It was most commonly administered to burn victims and the elderly.

The drug's off-label users were mostly bodybuilders and weight lifters. Although Ziegler prescribed only small doses to athletes, he soon discovered that those who abused Dianabol suffered from enlarged prostates and atrophied testes. AAS were placed on the list of banned substances of the IOC in 1976, and a decade later the committee introduced'out-of-competition' doping tests because many athletes used AAS in their training period rather than during competition.

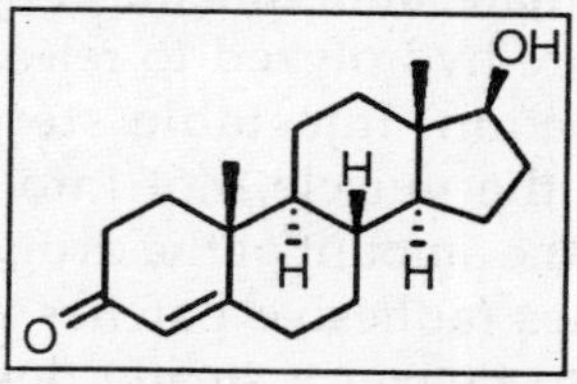


**Fig.** Chemical Structure of the Synthetic Steroid Methandrostenolone (Dianabol). 17α-methylation (Upper Right Corner) Enhances Oral Bioavailability.

Three major ideas governed modifications of testosterone into a multitude of AAS: alkylation at 17-alpha position with methyl or ethyl group created orally active compounds because it slows the degradation of the drug by the liver, esterification of testosterone and nortestosterone at the 17-beta position allows the substance to be administered parenterally and increases the duration of effectiveness because agents soluble in oily liquids may be present in the body for several months, and finally alterations of the ring structure were applied for both oral and parenteral agents to seeking to obtain different anabolic to androgenic effect ratios.

## PHARMACOLOGY

### Routes of Administration

There are three common forms in which anabolic steroids

are administered: oral pills, injectable steroids, and skin patches. Oral administration is the most convenient. Testosterone administered by mouth is rapidly absorbed, but it is largely converted to inactive metabolites, and only about 1/6 is available in active form. In order to be sufficiently active when given by mouth, testosterone derivatives are alkylated at the 17 position, e.g. methyltestosterone and fluoxymesterone. This modification reduces the liver's ability to break down these compounds before they reach the systemic circulation.

Testosterone can be administered parenterally, but it has more irregular prolonged absorption time and greater activity in propionate, enanthate, undecanoate or cypionate ester form. These derivatives are hydrolyzed to release free testosterone at the site of injection. Injectable steroids are typically administered into the muscle, not into the vein, to avoid sudden changes in the amount of the drug in the bloodstream. Transdermal patches (adhesive patches placed on the skin) may also be used to deliver a steady dose through the skin and into the bloodstream. Injection is the most common method used by individuals administering anabolic steroids for non-medical purposes.

The traditional routes of administration do not have differential effects on the efficacy of the drug. Studies indicate that the anabolic properties of anabolic steroids are relatively similar despite the differences in pharmacokinetic principles such as first-pass metabolism. However, the orally available forms of AAS may cause liver damage in high doses.

## Mechanism of Action

The pharmacodynamics of anabolic steroids are unlike peptide hormones. Water-soluble peptide hormones cannot penetrate the fatty cell membrane and only indirectly affect the nucleus of target cells through their interaction with the cell's surface receptors. Conversely, as fat-soluble hormones, anabolic steroids are membrane permeable and influence the nucleus of cells by direct action. The pharmacodynamic action of anabolic steroids begin when the exogenous hormone penetrates the membrane of the target cell and binds to an androgen receptor located in the cytoplasm of that cell. From there, the compound hormone-receptor diffuses into the nucleus, where it either alters the expression of genes or activates processes that send signals to other parts of the cell. Different types of anabolic steroids bind to the androgen receptor with different affinities, depending on their chemical structure. Some anabolic steroids such as methandrostenolone bind weakly to this receptor in vitro, but still exhibit androgenic effects in vivo. The reason for this discrepancy is not known. On the other hand, steroids such as oxandrolone bind tightly to the receptor and act mostly on gene expression.

The effect of anabolic steroids on muscle mass is caused in at least two ways: first, they increase the production of proteins; second, they reduce recovery time by blocking the effects of stress hormone cortisol on muscle tissue, so that catabolism of muscle is greatly reduced. It has been hypothesized that this reduction in muscle breakdown may occur through anabolic steroids inhibiting the action of other steroid hormones called glucocorticoids that promote the breakdown of muscles. Anabolic steroids also affect the number of cells that develop into fat-storage cells, by favouring cellular differentiation into muscle cells instead. Anabolic steroids can also decrease fat by increasing basal metabolic rate (BMR), since an increase in muscle mass increases BMR.

## Anabolic and Androgenic Effects

**Table. Relative androgenic:anabolic activity in animals**

| Preparation | Ratio |
|---|---|
| Testosterone | 1:1 |
| Methyltestosterone | 1:1 |
| Fluoxymesterone | 1:2 |
| Oxymetholone | 1:3 |
| Oxandrolone | 1:3–1:13 |
| Nandrolone decanoate | 1:2.5–1:4 |

*As the name suggests, anabolic-androgenic steroids have two different, but overlapping, types of effects*: *Anabolic*, meaning that they promote anabolism (cell growth), and *androgenic* (or *virilizing*), meaning that they affect the development and maintenance of masculine characteristics.

Some examples of the anabolic effects of these hormones are increased protein synthesis from amino acids, increased appetite, increased bone remodeling and growth, and stimulation of bone marrow, which increases the production of red blood cells. Through a number of mechanisms anabolic steroids stimulate the formation of muscles cells and hence cause an increase in the size of skeletal muscles leading to increased strength.

The androgenic effects of AAS are numerous. Processes affected include pubertal growth, sebaceous gland oil production, and sexuality (especially in fetal development). Some examples of virilizing effects are growth of the clitoris in females and the penis in male children (the adult penis does not grow even when exposed to high doses of androgens), increased growth of androgen-sensitive hair (pubic, beard, chest, and limb hair), increased vocal cord size, deepening the voice, increased libido, suppression of natural sex hormones, and impaired production of sperm.

The androgenic:anabolic ratio of an AAS is an important factor when determining the clinical application of these compounds. Compounds with a high ratio of androgenic to a anabolic effects are the drug of choice in androgen-replacement therapy (e.g. treating hypogonadism in males), whereas compounds with a reduced androgenic:anabolic ratio are preferred for anemia, osteoporosis, and to reverse protein loss following trauma, surgery or prolonged immobilization.

Determination of androgenic:anabolic ratio is typically performed in animal studies, which has led to the marketing of some compounds claimed to have anabolic activity with weak androgenic effects. This disassociation is less marked in humans, where all anabolic steroids have significant androgenic effects.

A commonly used protocol for determining the androgenic:anabolic ratio, dating back to the 1950s, uses the relative weights of ventral prostate (VP) and levator ani muscle (LA) of male rats. The VP weight is an indicator of the androgenic effect, while the LA weight is an indicator of the anabolic effect. Two or more batches of rats are castrated and given no treatment and respectively some AAS of interest.

The *LA/VP ratio* for an AAS is calculated as the ratio of LA/VP weight gains produced by the treatment with that compound using castrated but untreated rats as baseline: $(LA_{c,t}-LA_c)/(VP_{c,t}-VP_c)$. The LA/VP weight gain ratio from rat experiments is not unitary for testosterone (typically 0.3–0.4), but it's normalized for presentation purposes, and used as basis of comparison for other AAS, which have their androgenic:anabolic ratios scaled accordingly. In the early 2000s this procedure was standardized and generalized throughout OECD in what is now known as the Hershberger assay.

## Body Composition and Strength Improvements

A review spanning more than three decades of experimental studies in men found that body weight may increase by 2–5 kg as a result of short term (<10 weeks) AAS use, which may be attributed mainly to an increase of lean mass. Animal studies also found that fat mass was reduced, but most studies in humans failed to elucidate significant fat mass decrements.

The effects on lean body mass have been shown to be dose dependent. Both muscle hypertrophy and the formation of new muscle fibers have been observed. The hydration of lean mass remains unaffected by AAS use, although small increments of blood volume cannot be ruled out.

The upper region of the body (thorax, neck, shoulders and upper arm) seems to be more susceptible for AAS than other body regions because of predominance of androgen receptors in the upper body.

The largest difference in muscle fibre size between AAS users and non-users was observed in type I muscle fibres of the vastus lateralis and the trapezius muscle as a result of long-term AAS self-administration. After drug withdrawal the effects fade away slowly, but may persist for more than 6–12 weeks after cessation of AAS use.

The same review observed strength improvements in the range of 5-20% of baseline strength, largely depending on the drugs and dose used as well as the administration period. Overall, the exercise where the most significant improvements were observed was the bench press. For almost two decades it was assumed that AAS only exerted significant effects in experienced strength athletes, particularly based on the studies of Hervey and coworkers.

In 1996 a randomized controlled trial published in the *New England Journal of Medicine* demonstrated however that even in novice athletes a 10-week strength training programme accompanied by testosterone enanthate at 600 mg/week may improve strength more than training alone does. The same study found that dose was sufficient to significantly improve lean muscle mass relative to placebo even in subjects that did not exercise at all. A 2001 study by the same first author, showed that the anabolic effects of testosterone enanthate were highly dose dependent.

## Adverse Effects

Anabolic steroids can cause many adverse effects. Most of these side effects are dose-dependent, the most common being elevated blood pressure, especially in those with pre-existing hypertension, and harmful changes in cholesterol levels: some steroids cause an increase in LDL cholesterol and a decrease in HDL cholesterol. Anabolic steroids have been shown to alter fasting blood sugar and glucose tolerance tests.

Anabolic steroids such as testosterone also increase the risk of cardiovascular disease or coronary artery disease. Acne is fairly common among anabolic steroid users, mostly due to stimulation of the sebaceous glands by increased testosterone levels. Conversion of testosterone to dihydrotestosterone (DHT) can accelerate the rate of premature baldness for males who are genetically predisposed, but testosterone itself can produce baldness in females.

High doses of oral anabolic steroid compounds can cause

liver damage, as the steroids are metabolized (17α-alkylated) in the digestive system to increase their bioavailability and stability.

There are also sex-specific side effects of anabolic steroids. Development of breast tissue in males, a condition called gynecomastia (which is usually caused by high levels of circulating estrogen), may arise because of increased conversion of testosterone to estrogen by the enzyme aromatase. Reduced sexual function and temporary infertility can also occur in males.

Another male-specific side effect which can occur is testicular atrophy, caused by the suppression of natural testosterone levels, which inhibits production of sperm (most of the mass of the testes is developing sperm). This side effect is temporary: the size of the testicles usually returns to normal within a few weeks of discontinuing anabolic steroid use as normal production of sperm resumes.

Female-specific side effects include increases in body hair, deepening of the voice, enlarged clitoris, and temporary decreases in menstrual cycles. When taken during pregnancy, anabolic steroids can affect fetal development by causing the development of male features in the female fetus and female features in the male fetus. A number of severe side effects can occur if adolescents use anabolic steroids.

For example, the steroids may prematurely stop the lengthening of bones (premature epiphyseal fusion through increased levels of estrogen metabolites), resulting in stunted growth. Other effects include, but are not limited to, accelerated bone maturation, increased frequency and duration of erections, and premature sexual development. Anabolic steroid use in adolescence is also correlated with poorer attitudes related to health.

Other side effects can include alterations in the structure of the heart, such as enlargement and thickening of the left ventricle, which impairs its contraction and relaxation. Possible effects of these alterations in the heart are hypertension, cardiac arrhythmias, congestive heart failure, heart attacks, and sudden cardiac death. These changes are also seen in non-drug using athletes, but steroid use may accelerate this process. However, both the connection between changes in the structure of the left ventricle and decreased cardiac function, as well as the connection to steroid use have been disputed.

**Psychiatric Effects**

A 2005 review in *CNS Drugs* determined that "significant psychiatric symptoms including aggression and violence, mania, and less frequently psychosis and suicide have been associated with steroid abuse.

Long-term steroid abusers may develop symptoms of dependence and withdrawal on discontinuation of AAS". High concentrations of AAS, comparable to those likely sustained by many recreational AAS users, produce apoptotic effects on neurons, raising the specter of possibly irreversible neuropsychiatric toxicity.

Recreational AAS use appears to be associated with a range of potentially prolonged psychiatric effects, including dependence syndromes, mood disorders, and progression to other forms of substance abuse, but the prevalence and severity of these various effects remains poorly understood.

There is no evidence that steroid dependence develops from *therapeutic* use of anabolic steroids to treat medical disorders, but instances of AAS dependence have been reported among weightlifters and bodybuilders who chronically administered supraphysiologic doses.

Mood disturbances (e.g. depression, [hypo-]mania, psychotic features) are likely to be dose- and drug-dependent, but AAS dependence or withdrawal effects seem to occur only in a small number of AAS users.

Large scale long term studies of psychiatric effects on AAS users are generally not available. In 2003, the first naturalistic long term study on ten users, seven of which completed the study, found a high incidence of mood disorders and substance abuse, but few clinically relevant changes in physiological parameters or laboratory measures were noted throughout the study, and these changes were not clearly related to periods of reported AAS use.

A 13-month study, published in 2006 and which involved 320 body builders and athletes suggests that the wide range of psychiatric side effects induced by the use of AAS is correlated to the severity of abuse.

### *Aggression and Hypomania*

From the mid-1980s onwards the popular press has been reporting "roid rage" as a side effect of AAS.

A 2005 review determined that some, but not all, randomized controlled studies have found that anabolic steroid use correlates with hypomania and increased aggressiveness, but pointed out that attempts to determine whether AAS use triggers violent behaviour have failed, primarily because of high rates of non-participation.

A 2008 study on a nationally representative sample of young adult males in the United States found an association between lifetime and past-year self-reported anabolic-androgenic steroid use and involvement in violent acts.

Compared with individuals who did not use steroids, young adult males who used anabolic-androgenic steroids reported greater involvement in violent behaviors even after controlling for the effects of key demographic variables, previous violent behaviour, and polydrug use.

A 1996 review examining the blind studies available at that time also found that these had demonstrated a link between aggression and steroid use, but pointed out that with estimates of over one million past or current steroid users in the United States at that time, an extremely small percentage of those using steroids appear to have experienced mental disturbance severe enough to result in clinical treatments or medical case reports.

A 1996 randomized controlled trial, which involved 43 men, did not find an increase in the occurrence of angry behaviour during 10 weeks of administration of testosterone enanthate at 600 mg/week, but this study screened out subjects that had previously abused steroids or had any psychiatric antecedents. A trial conducted in 2000 using testosterone cypionate at 600 mg/week found that treatment significantly increased manic scores on the YMRS, and aggressive responses on several scales.

The drug response was highly variable, however: 84% of subjects exhibited minimal psychiatric effects, 12% became mildly hypomanic, and 4% (2 subjects) became markedly hypomanic. The mechanism of these variable reactions could not be explained by demographic, psychological, laboratory, or physiological measures.

A 2006 study of two pairs of identical twins, in which one twin used anabolic steroids and the other did not, found that in both cases the steroid-using twin exhibited high levels of aggressiveness, hostility, anxiety and paranoid ideation not found in the "control" twin. A small scale study of 10 AAS users found that cluster B personality disorders were confounding factors for aggression.

## Depression and Suicide

The relationship between AAS use and depression is inconclusive. There have been anecdotal reports of depression and suicide in teenage steroid users, but little systematic evidence. A 1992 review found that anabolic-androgenic steroids may both relieve and cause depression, and that cessation or diminished use of anabolic-androgenic steroids may also result in depression, but called for additional studies due to disparate data.

## Addiction Potential

In an animal study male rats developed a conditioned place preference to testosterone injections into the nucleus accumbens, an effect blocked by dopamine antagonists, which suggests that androgen reinforcement is mediated by the brain. Moreover, testosterone appears to act through the mesolimbic dopamine system, a common substrate for drugs of abuse. Nonetheless, androgen reinforcement is not comparable to that of cocaine, nicotine or heroin. Instead, testosterone resembles other mild reinforcers, such as caffeine, or benzodiazepines. The potential for androgen addiction remains to be determined.

## MEDICAL AND ERGOGENIC USES

### Medical uses

Since the discovery and synthesis of testosterone in the 1930s, anabolic steroids have been used by physicians for many purposes, with varying degrees of success.

- *Bone marrow stimulation*: For decades, anabolic steroids were the mainstay of therapy for hypoplastic anemias due to leukemia or kidney failure, especially aplastic anemia. Anabolic steroids have largely been replaced in this setting by synthetic protein hormones (such as epoetin alfa) that selectively stimulate growth of blood cell precursors.
- *Growth stimulation*: Anabolic steroids can be used by pediatric endocrinologists to treat children with growth failure. However, the availability of synthetic growth hormone, which has fewer side effects, makes this a secondary treatment.
- Prophylaxis for hereditary angioedema (HAE), a deficiency of the blood component that prevents swelling.
- *Stimulation of appetite and preservation and increase of muscle mass*: Anabolic steroids have been given to people with chronic wasting conditions such as cancer and AIDS.
- *Induction of male puberty*: Androgens are given to many boys distressed about extreme delay of puberty. Testosterone is now nearly the only androgen used for this purpose and has been shown to increase height, weight, and fat-free mass in boys with delayed puberty.
- Testosterone enanthate has frequently been used as a male contraceptive and it is thought that in the near future it could be used as a safe, reliable, and reversible male contraceptive.
- Anabolic steroids have been found in some studies to increase lean body mass and prevent bone loss in elderly men. However, a 2006 placebo-controlled trial

of low-dose testosterone supplementation in elderly men with low levels of testosterone found no benefit on body composition, physical performance, insulin sensitivity, or quality of life.

- Used in hormone replacement therapy for men with low levels of testosterone and is also effective in improving libido for elderly males.
- Used to treat Gender Identity Disorder by producing secondary male characteristics, such as a deeper voice, increased bone and muscle mass, facial hair, increased levels of red blood cells and clitoral enlargement in female-to-male patients.

## Ergogenic use and Abuse

Between 1 million and 3 million people (1% of the population) are thought to have misused AAS in the United States. Studies in the United States have shown anabolic steroid users tend to be mostly middle-class heterosexual men with a median age of about 25 who are noncompetitive bodybuilders and non-athletes and use the drugs for cosmetic purposes. Another study found that non-medical use of AAS among college students was at or less than 1%.

According to a recent survey, 78.4% of steroid users were noncompetitive bodybuilders and non-athletes while about 13% reported unsafe injection practices such as reusing needles, sharing needles, and sharing multidose vials, though a 2007 study found that sharing of needles was extremely uncommon among individuals using anabolic steroids for non-medical purposes, less than 1%. Another 2007 study found that 74% of non-medical anabolic steroid users had secondary college degrees and more had completed college and less had failed to complete high school than is expected from the general populace.

The same study found that individuals using anabolic steroids for non-medical purposes had a higher employment rate and a higher household income than the general population. Anabolic steroid users tend to research the drugs they are taking more than other controlled-substance users;

however, the major sources consulted by steroid users include friends, non-medical handbooks, internet-based forums, blogs and fitness magazines, which can provide questionable or inaccurate information.

Anabolic steroid users tend to be disillusioned by the portrayal of anabolic steroids as deadly in the media and in politics. According to one study, AAS users also distrust their physicians and in the sample 56% had not disclosed their AAS use to their physicians. Another 2007 study had similar findings, showing that while 66% of individuals using anabolic steroids for non-medical purposes were willing to seek medical supervision for their steroid use, 58% lacked trust in their physicians, 92% felt that the medical community's knowledge of non-medical anabolic steroid use was lacking and 99% felt that the public has an exaggerated view of the side effects of anabolic steroid use. A recent study has also shown that long term AAS users were more likely to have symptoms of muscle dysmorphia and also showed stronger endorsement of more conventional male roles.

Anabolic steroids have been used by men and women in many different kinds of professional sports to attain a competitive edge or to assist in recovery from injury. These sports include bodybuilding, weightlifting, shot put and other track and field, cycling, baseball, wrestling, mixed martial arts, boxing, football, and cricket. Such use is prohibited by the rules of the governing bodies of most sports. Anabolic steroid use occurs among adolescents, especially by those participating in competitive sports. It has been suggested that the prevalence of use among high-school students in the U.S. may be as high as 2.7%. Male students used anabolic steroids more frequently than female students and, on average, those who participated in sports used steroids more often than those who did not.

## Legal and Sport Restrictions

The use of anabolic steroids is banned by all major sporting bodies, including the International Olympic Committee, Major League Baseball, the National Football League, the National Basketball Association, the National

Hockey League, World Wrestling Entertainment, ICC, ITF, FIFA, FINA, UEFA, the European Athletic Association, and the Brazilian Football Confederation. Anabolic steroids are controlled substances in many countries, including Argentina, Australia, Brazil, Canada, the Netherlands (NL), the United Kingdom (UK) and the United States (U.S.), while in other countries, such as Mexico and Thailand, they are readily available over-the-counter.

## Legal status

The legal status of anabolic steroids varies from country to country: some have stricter controls on their use or prescription than others though in many countries they are not illegal. In the U.S., anabolic steroids are currently listed as Schedule III controlled substances under the Controlled Substances Act, which makes the first offense simple possession of such substances without a prescription a federal crime punishable by up to one year in prison, and the unlawful distribution or possession with intent to distribute anabolic steroids punishable as a first offense by up to ten years in prison.

In Canada, anabolic steroids and their derivatives are part of the Controlled drugs and substances act and are Schedule IV substances, meaning that it is illegal to obtain or sell them without a prescription; however, possession is not punishable, a consequence reserved for schedule I, II or III substances. Those guilty of buying or selling anabolic steroids in Canada can be imprisoned for up to 18 months.

Import and export also carry similar penalties. Anabolic steroids are also illegal without prescription in Australia, Argentina, Brazil and Portugal, and are listed as Class C Controlled Drugs in the United Kingdom. On the other hand, anabolic steroids are readily available without a prescription in some countries such as Mexico and Thailand.

## United States

The history of the U.S. legislation on anabolic steroids goes back to the late 1980s, when the U.S. Congress considered placing anabolic steroids under the Controlled Substances Act following the controversy over Ben Johnson's victory at the 1988 Summer Olympics in Seoul. During deliberations, the American Medical Association (AMA), Drug Enforcement Administration (DEA), Food and Drug Administration (FDA) as well as the National Institute on Drug Abuse (NIDA) all opposed listing anabolic steroids as controlled substances, citing the fact that use of these hormones does not lead to the physical or psychological dependence required for such scheduling under the Controlled Substance Act. Nevertheless, anabolic steroids were added to Schedule III of the Controlled Substances Act in the Anabolic Steroid Control Act of 1990.

The same act also introduced more stringent controls with higher criminal penalties for offenses involving the illegal distribution of anabolic steroids and human growth hormone. By the early 1990s, after anabolic steroids were scheduled in the U.S., several pharmaceutical companies stopped manufacturing or marketing the products in the U.S., including Ciba, Searle, Syntex and others.

In the Controlled Substances Act, anabolic steroids are defined to be any drug or hormonal substance chemically and pharmacologically related to testosterone (other than estrogens, progestins, and corticosteroids) that promote muscle growth. The act was amended by the Anabolic Steroid Control Act of 2004, which added prohormones to the list of controlled substances, with effect from January 20, 2005.

## Movement for Decriminalization

After the Anabolic Steroid Control Act of 1990 listed anabolic steroids as Schedule III controlled substances in the U.S., a small movement has arisen that is highly critical of current laws concerning anabolic steroids. On June 21, 2005, *Real Sports* aired a segment discussing the legality and prohibition of anabolic steroids in America. The show featured Gary I. Wadler, M.D., chairman of the U.S. Anti-Doping Agency and a prominent anti-steroid activist.

When pressed for scientific evidence by correspondent Armen Keteyian that anabolic steroids are as "highly fatal" as is often claimed, Wadler admitted there was no evidence. Bryant Gumbel concluded the "hoopla" concerning the dangers of anabolic steroids in the media was "all smoke and no fire". The show also featured John Romano, a pro-steroid activist who wrote "The Romano Factor", a pro-steroid column for bodybuilding magazine *Muscular Development*.

**United Kingdom**

In the United Kingdom, anabolic steroids are classified as class C drugs for their illegal abuse potential, which puts them in the same class as benzodiazepines. Anabolic steroids are in Schedule 4, which is divided in 2 parts; Part 1 contains most of the benzodiazepines and Part 2 contains the anabolic and androgenic steroids. There are no special controls on Schedule 4 drugs.

**Status in Sports**

Anabolic steroids are banned by all major sports bodies including Fédération Internationale de Football Association the Olympics, the National Basketball Association, the National Hockey League, as well as the National Football League. The World Anti-Doping Agency (WADA) maintains the list of performance-enhancing substances used by many major sports bodies and includes all anabolic agents, which includes all anabolic steroids and precursors as well as all hormones and related substances. Spain has passed an anti-doping law creating a national anti-doping agency.

Italy passed a law in 2000 where penalties range up to three years in prison if an athlete has tested positive for banned substances. In 2006, Russian President Vladimir Putin signed into law ratification of the International Convention Against Doping in Sport which would encourage cooperation with WADA. Many other countries have similar legislation prohibiting anabolic steroids in sports including Denmark, France, the Netherlands and Sweden.

**Illegal Trade**

Anabolic steroids are frequently produced in

pharmaceutical laboratories, but in nations where stricter laws are present, they are also produced in small home made underground laboratories, usually from raw substances imported from abroad. In these countries the majority of steroids are obtained illegally through black market trade. These steroids are usually manufactured in other countries, and therefore must be smuggled across international borders. Like most significant smuggling operations, organized crime is involved.

In the late 2000s the worldwide trade in illicit AAS increased significantly, and authorities announced record captures on three continents. In 2006 Finnish authorities announced a record seizure of 11.8 million AAS tablets. A year later the DEA seized 11.4 million units of AAS in the largest U.S seizure ever. In first three months of 2008, Australian customs reported a record 300 seizures of AAS shipments.

In the U.S., Canada and Europe, illicit steroids are sometimes purchased just like any other illegal drug, through dealers who are able to obtain the drugs from a number of sources. Illegal anabolic steroids are sometimes sold at gyms, competitions, and through the mail, but may also be obtained through pharmacists, veterinarians, and physicians. In addition, a significant number of counterfeit products are sold as anabolic steroids, particularly via mail order from websites posing as overseas pharmacies. Individuals also produce fake steroids and attempt to sell them over the Internet, causing a wide variety of health concerns. In the U.S., black market importation continues from Mexico, Thailand, and other countries where steroids are more easily available as they are legal.

## DIOSGENIN

Diosgenin, a steroid sapogenin, is the product of hydrolysis by acids, strong bases, or enzymes of saponins, extracted from the tubers of Dioscorea wild yam, such as the Kokoro. The sugar-free (aglycone), diosgenin is used for the commercial synthesis of cortisone, pregnenolone, progesterone, and other steroid products.

It is present in Costus speciosus, Smilax menispermoidea, species of Paris, Trigonella, and Trillium, and many species of Dioscorea - D. althaeoides, colletti, futschauensis, gracillima, hispida, hypoglauca, mexicana nipponica, panthaica, parviflora, septemloba, and zingiberensis.

## Clinical uses

Diosgenin is the precursor for the semisynthesis of progesterone which in turn was used in early combined oral contraceptive pills. The unmodified steroid has estrogenic activity and can reduce the level of serum cholesterol.

## Chemistry

The glycoside dioscin from the Mexican wild yam root, *Dioscorea,* constituted the first plant source for steroid drugs.

Hydrolysis of this saponin leads to scission of the trisaccharide at the 3-position and the formation of the aglycone, diosgenin. Treatment of this acetal with hot acetic anhydride in the presence of toluenesulfonic acid leads initially to protonation of one of the acetal oxygens followed by elimination to form an enol ether.

Oxidation by means of chromium trioxide leads to preferential attack at the electron-rich enol ether double bond. In effect, this transformation converts the side chain at C-17 in diosgenin to the acetyl group required for many steroid drugs. Heating that intermediate in with alcoholic sodium hydroxide leads to the elimination of the ester grouping beta to the ketone; there is thus obtained 16-dehydropregnenolone acetate. The presence of the olefin at C-17 allows ready entry to C-19 androstanes and provides the necessary function for the synthesis of potent C-16- and C-16,17-substituted corticosteroids.

## Guggulsterone

Guggulsterone is a plant steroid found in the resin of the guggul plant, *Commiphora mukul*. Guggulsterone can exists as either of two stereoisomer, *E*-guggulsterone and *Z*-guggulsterone. In humans it acts as an antagonist of the farnesoid X receptor, which was once believed to result in decreased cholesterol synthesis in the liver.

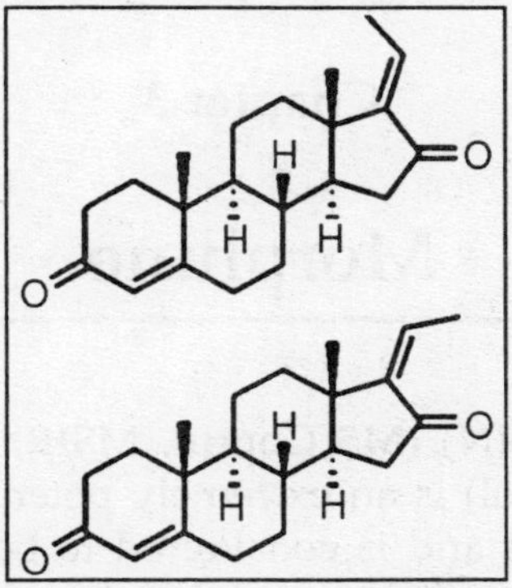

**Fig**. *E*-Guggulsterone (Top) and *Z*-Guggulsterone (Bottom)

Several studies have been published that indicate no overall reduction in total cholesterol occurs using various dosages of guggulsterone, and levels of low-density lipoprotein ("bad cholesterol") increased in many people. Nevertheless, guggulsterone is an ingredient in many nutritional supplements.

## Chapter 3

# Morphine

Morphine (INN) (MS Contin, MSIR, Avinza, Kadian, Oramorph, Roxanol) is an extremely potent opiate analgesic psychoactive drug and is considered to be the prototypical opioid. In clinical medicine, morphine is regarded as the gold standard, or benchmark, of analgesics used to relieve severe or agonizing pain and suffering. Like other opioids, e.g. oxycodone (OxyContin, Percocet, Percodan), hydromorphone (Dilaudid, Palladone), and diacetylmorphine (heroin), morphine acts directly on the central nervous system (CNS) to relieve pain. Morphine has a high potential for addiction; tolerance and both physical and psychological dependence develop rapidly.

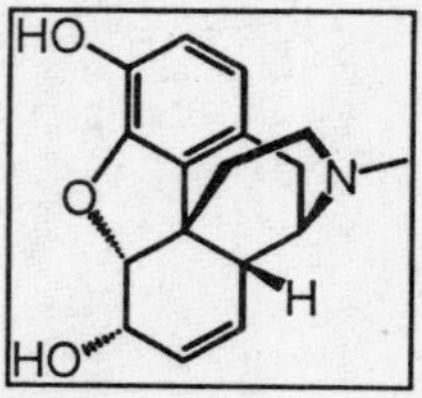


**Fig.** Morphine

An opium-based elixir has been ascribed to alchemists of Byzantine times, but the specific formula was supposedly lost during the Ottoman conquest of Constantinople. Around 1522, Paracelsus made reference to an opium-based elixir which he called, *laudanum* from the Latin word *laudare* meaning "to praise." He described it as a potent pain killer, but recommended that it be used sparingly. In the late eighteenth century, after the British conquest of Bengal in 1757 gave the

East India Company a direct interest in the opium trade, another opiate recipe called 'laudanum' became very popular among physicians and their patients.

Morphine was discovered as the first active alkaloid extracted from the opium poppy plant in December 1804 in Paderborn, Germany by Friedrich Sertürner. The drug was first marketed to the general public by Sertürner and Company in 1817 as an analgesic, and also as a treatment for opium and alcohol addiction. Later it was found that morphine was more addictive than either alcohol or opium, and its extensive use during the American Civil War allegedly resulted in over 400,000 sufferers from the "soldier's disease" of morphine addiction. This idea has been a subject of controversy, as there have been suggestions that such a disease was in fact a fabrication; the first documented use of the phrase "soldier's disease" was in 1915.

Diacetylmorphine (better known as heroin) was synthesized from morphine in 1874 and brought to market by Bayer in 1898. Heroin is approximately 1.5–2 times more potent than morphine on a milligram-for-milligram basis. Using a variety of subjective and objective measures, one study estimated the relative potency of heroin to morphine administered intravenously to post-addicts to be 1.80–2.66 mg of morphine sulfate to 1 mg of diamorphine hydrochloride (heroin).

Morphine became a controlled substance in the US under the Harrison Narcotics Tax Act of 1914, and possession without a prescription in the US is a criminal offense.

Morphine was the most commonly abused narcotic analgesic in the world until heroin was synthesized and came into use.

Until the synthesis of dihydromorphine (ca. 1900), the dihydro-morphinone class of opioids (1920s), and oxycodone (1916) and similar drugs, there generally were no other drugs in the same efficacy range as opium, morphine, and heroin, with synthetics still several years away (pethidine was invented in Germany in 1937) and opioid agonists amongst the semi-synthetics were analogues and derivatives of codeine such as dihydrocodeine (Paracodin), ethylmorphine (Dionine), and benzylmorphine (Peronine).

Even today, morphine is the most sought after prescription narcotic by heroin addicts when heroin is scarce, all other things being equal; local conditions and user preference may cause hydromorphone, oxymorphone, high-dose oxycodone, or methadone as well as dextromoramide in specific instances such as 1970s Australia, to top that particular list. The stop-gap drugs used by the largest absolute number of heroin addicts is probably codeine, with significant use also of dihydrocodeine, poppy straw derivatives like poppy pod and poppy seed tea, propoxyphene, and tramadol.

The structural formula of morphine was determined by 1925. At least three methods of total synthesis of morphine from starting materials such as coal tar and petroleum distillates have been patented, the first of which was announced in 1952, by Dr. Marshall D. Gates, Jr. at the University of Rochester. Still, the vast majority of morphine is derived from the opium poppy by either the traditional method of gathering latex from the scored, unripe pods of the poppy, or processes using poppy straw, the dried pods and stems of the plant, the most widespread of which was invented in Hungary in 1925 and announced in 1930 by the chemist Janos Kabay.

In 2003, there was discovery of endogenous morphine occurring naturally in the human body. Thirty years of speculation were made on this subject because there was a receptor that apparently only reacted to morphine: the mu3 opiate receptor in human tissue. Human cells that form in reaction to cancerous neuroblastoma cells have been found to contain trace amounts of endogenous morphine.

## Indications

*Morphine can be used as an analgesic to relieve:*

- Pain in myocardial infarction.
- Pain in sickle cell crisis.
- Pain associated with surgical conditions, pre- and postoperatively.

- Pain associated with trauma.
- Severe chronic pain, e.g., cancer.
- Pain from kidney stones (renal colic, ureterolithiasis).
- Severe back pain.

*Morphine can also be used:*

- as an adjunct to general anesthesia
- in epidural anesthesia or intrathecal analgesia
- for palliative care (i.e., to alleviate pain without curing the underlying reason for it, usually because the latter is found impossible)
- as an antitussive for severe cough
- in nebulized form, for treatment of dyspnea, although the evidence for efficacy is slim. Evidence is better for other routes.
- as an antidiarrheal in chronic conditions (e.g., for diarrhea associated with AIDS, although loperamide (a non-absorbed opioid acting only on the gut) is the most commonly used opioid for diarrhea).
- for remarkable relief of acute pulmonary edema through an unknown mechanism

## SIDE EFFECTS

### Constipation

Like loperamide and other opioids, morphine acts on the myenteric plexus in the intestinal tract, reducing gut motility, causing constipation. The gastrointestinal effects of morphine are mediated primarily by μ-opioid receptors in the bowel. By inhibiting gastric emptying and reducing propulsive peristalsis of the intestine, morphine decreases the rate of intestinal transit. Reduction in gut secretion and increases in intestinal fluid absorption also contribute to the constipating effect. Opioids also may act on the gut indirectly through tonic gut spasms after inhibition of nitric oxide generation. This effect was shown in animals when a nitric oxide precursor, L-Arginine, reversed morphine-induced changes in gut motility.

### Addiction

In controlled studies comparing the physiological and

subjective effects of injected heroin and morphine in individuals formerly addicted to opiates, subjects showed no preference for one drug over the other. Equipotent, injected doses had comparable action courses, with no difference in subjects' self-rated feelings of euphoria, ambition, nervousness, relaxation, drowsiness, or sleepiness. Short-term addiction studies by the same researchers demonstrated that tolerance developed at a similar rate to both heroin and morphine. When compared to the opioids hydromorphone, fentanyl, oxycodone, and pethidine/meperidine, former addicts showed a strong preference for heroin and morphine, suggesting that heroin and morphine are particularly susceptible to abuse and addiction. Morphine and heroin were also much more likely to produce euphoria and other positive subjective effects when compared to these other opioids.

Other studies, such as the Rat Park experiments, suggest that morphine is less physically addictive than others suggest, and most studies on morphine addiction merely show that "severely distressed animals, like severely distressed people, will relieve their distress pharmacologically if they can." In these studies, rats with a morphine "addiction" overcome their addiction themselves when placed in decent living environments with enough space, good food, companionship, areas for exercise, and areas for privacy. More recent research has shown that an enriched environment may decrease morphine addiction in mice.

Morphine is a potentially highly addictive substance. It can cause psychological dependence and physical dependence as well as tolerance, with an addiction potential identical to that of heroin. When used illicitly, a very serious narcotic habit can develop in a matter of weeks, whereas iatrogenic morphine addiction rates have, according to a number of studies, remained nearly constant at one case in 150 to 200 for at least two centuries. In the presence of pain and the other disorders for which morphine is indicated, a combination of psychological and physiological factors tend to prevent true addiction from developing, although physical dependence and tolerance will develop with protracted opioid therapy. These two factors do *not* add up to addiction without psychological dependence which manifests primarily as a morbid seek orientation for the drug.

## Tolerance

Tolerance to the analgesic effects of morphine is fairly rapid. There are several hypotheses about how tolerance develops, including opioid receptor phosphorylation (which would change the receptor conformation), functional decoupling of receptors from G-proteins (leading to receptor desensitization), mu-opioid receptor internalization and/or receptor down-regulation (reducing the number of available receptors for morphine to act on), and upregulation of the cAMP pathway (a counterregulatory mechanism to opioid effects) CCK might mediate some counter-regulatory pathways responsible of opioid tolerance. CCK-antagonist drugs, specifically proglumide, have been shown to slow the development of tolerance to morphine.

## Withdrawal

The withdrawal symptoms associated with morphine addiction are usually experienced shortly before the time of the next scheduled dose, sometimes within as early as a few hours (usually between 6–12 hours) after the last administration. Early symptoms include watery eyes, insomnia, diarrhea, runny nose, yawning, dysphoria, sweating and in some cases a strong drug craving. Severe headache, restlessness, irritability, loss of appetite, body aches, severe abdominal pain, nausea and vomiting, tremors, and even stronger and more intense drug craving appear as the syndrome progresses.

Severe depression and vomiting are very common. During the acute withdrawal period systolic and diastolic blood pressure increase, usually beyond pre-morphine levels, and heart rate increases, which could potentially cause a heart attack, blood clot, or stroke.

Chills or cold flashes with goose bumps ("cold turkey") alternating with flushing (hot flashes), kicking movements of the legs ("kicking the habit") and excessive sweating are also characteristic symptoms. Severe pains in the bones and muscles of the back and extremities occur, as do muscle spasms.

At any point during this process, a suitable narcotic can be administered that will dramatically reverse the withdrawal symptoms. Major withdrawal symptoms peak between 48 and 96 hours after the last dose and subside after about 8 to 12 days. Sudden withdrawal by heavily dependent users who are in poor health is very rarely fatal. Morphine withdrawal is considered less dangerous than alcohol, barbiturate, or benzodiazepine withdrawal.

The psychological dependence associated with morphine addiction is complex and protracted. Long after the physical need for morphine has passed, the addict will usually continue to think and talk about the use of morphine (or other drugs) and feel strange or overwhelmed coping with daily activities without being under the influence of morphine. Psychological withdrawal from morphine is a very long and painful process. Addicts often suffer severe depression, anxiety, insomnia, mood swings, amnesia (forgetfulness), low self-esteem, confusion, paranoia, and other psychological disorders.

The psychological dependence on morphine can, and usually does, last a lifetime. There is a high probability that relapse will occur after morphine withdrawal when neither the physical environment nor the behavioral motivators that contributed to the abuse have been altered. Testimony to morphine's addictive and reinforcing nature is its relapse rate. Abusers of morphine (and heroin), have one of the highest relapse rates among all drug users.

## Hepatitis C

Researchers at the University of Pennsylvania have demonstrated that morphine withdrawal complicates hepatitis C by suppressing IFN-alpha-mediated immunity and enhancing virus replication. Hepatitis C virus (HCV) is common among intravenous drug users. This high association has piqued interest in determining the effects of drug abuse, specifically morphine and heroin, on progression of the disease. The discovery of such an association would impact treatment of both HCV infection and drug abuse.

## Overdose

A morphine overdose occurs by intentionally or accidentally taking too much of it. A large overdose can cause asphyxia and death by respiratory depression if the person does not get medical attention or an antidote (Naloxone) immediately.

Treatments include administration of activated charcoal, intravenous fluids, laxatives and naloxone. The latter is an antidote to reverse the effect of the poison. Multiple doses of it may be needed.

## Contraindications

*The following conditions are relative contraindications for morphine*:

- Acute respiratory depression.
- Renal failure (due to accumulation of the metabolites morphine-3-glucuronide and morphine-6-glucuronide).
- Chemical toxicity (potentially lethal in low tolerance subjects).
- Raised intracranial pressure, including head injury (risk of worsening respiratory depression).
- Biliary colic.

Although it has previously been thought that morphine was contraindicated in acute pancreatitis, a review of the literature shows no evidence for this.

## Pharmacology

Endogenous opioids include endorphins, enkephalins, dynorphins, and even morphine itself. Morphine appears to mimic endorphins. Endogenous endorphins are responsible for analgesia (reducing pain), causing sleepiness, and feelings of pleasure. They can be released in response to pain, strenuous exercise, orgasm, or excitement.

Morphine is the prototype narcotic drug and is the standard against which all other opioids are tested. It interacts predominantly with the μ-opioid receptor. These μ-binding sites are discretely distributed in the human brain, with high densities in the posterior amygdala, hypothalamus, thalamus, nucleus caudatus, putamen, and certain cortical areas. They are also found on the terminal axons of primary afferents within laminae I and II (substantia gelatinosa) of the spinal cord and in the spinal nucleus of the trigeminal nerve.

Morphine is a phenanthrene opioid receptor agonist – its main effect is binding to and activating the μ-opioid receptors in the central nervous system.

In clinical settings, morphine exerts its principal pharmacological effect on the central nervous system and gastrointestinal tract. Its primary actions of therapeutic value are analgesia and sedation. Activation of the μ-opioid receptors is associated with analgesia, sedation, euphoria, physical dependence, and respiratory depression.

Morphine is a rapid-acting narcotic, and it is known to bind very strongly to the μ-opioid receptors, and for this reason, it often has a higher incidence of euphoria/dysphoria, respiratory depression, sedation, pruritus, tolerance, and physical and psychological dependence when compared to other opioids at equianalgesic doses. Morphine is also a κ-opioid and δ-opioid receptor agonist, κ-opioid's action is associated with spinal analgesia, miosis (pinpoint pupils) and psychotomimetic effects. δ-opioid is thought to play a role in analgesia. Although morphine does not bind to the σ-receptor, it has been shown that sigma agonists, such as (+)pentazocine, antagonize morphine analgesia, and sigma antagonists enhance morphine analgesia, suggesting some interaction between morphine and the σ-opioid receptor.

The effects of morphine can be countered with opioid antagonists such as naloxone and naltrexone; the development of tolerance to morphine may be inhibited by NMDA antagonists such as ketamine or dextromethorphan. The rotation of morphine with chemically dissimilar opioids in the long-term treatment of pain will slow down the growth of tolerance in the longer run, particularly agents known to have significantly incomplete cross-tolerance with morphine such as levorphanol, ketobemidone, piritramide, and methadone and its derivatives; all of these drugs also have NMDA antagonist properties. It is believed that the strong opioid with the most incomplete cross-tolerance with morphine is either methadone or dextromoramide.

## Gene Expression

Studies have shown that morphine can alter the expression of a number of genes. A single injection of morphine has been shown to alter the expression of two major groups of genes, for proteins involved in mitochondrial respiration and for cytoskeleton-related proteins.

## Effects on the Immune System

Morphine has long been known to act on receptors expressed on cells of the central nervous system resulting in pain relief and analgesia. In the 1970s and '80s, evidence suggesting that opiate drug addicts show increased risk of infection (such as increased pneumonia, tuberculosis, and HIV) led scientists to believe that morphine may also affect the immune system. This possibility increased interest in the effect of chronic morphine use on the immune system.

The first step of determining that morphine may affect the immune system was to establish that the opiate receptors known to be expressed on cells of the central nervous system are also expressed on cells of the immune system. One study successfully showed that dendritic cells, part of the innate immune system, display opiate receptors. Dendritic cells are responsible for producing cytokines, which are the tools for communication in the immune system.

This same study showed that dendritic cells chronically treated with morphine during their differentiation produce more interleukin-12 (IL–12), a cytokine responsible for promoting the proliferation, growth, and differentiation of T-cells (another cell of the adaptive immune system) and less interleukin-10 (IL-10), a cytokine responsible for promoting a

B-cell immune response (B cells produce antibodies to fight off infection).

This regulation of cytokines appear to occur via the p38 MAPKs (mitogen activated protein kinase) dependent pathway. Usually, the p38 within the dendritic cell expresses TLR 4 (toll-like receptor 4), which is activated through the ligand LPS (lipopolysaccharide). This causes the p38 MAPK to be phosphorylated.

This phosphorylation activates the p38 MAPK to begin producing IL-10 and IL-12. When the dendritic cell is chronically exposed to morphine during their differentiation process then treated with LPS, the production of cytokines is different. Once treated with morphine, the p38 MAPK does not produce IL-10, instead favoring production of IL-12. The exact mechanism through which the production of one cytokine is increased in favour over another is not known.

Most likely, the morphine causes increased phosphorylation of the p38 MAPK. Transcriptional level interactions between IL-10 and IL-12 may further increase the production of IL-12 once IL-10 is not being produced. Future research may target the exact mechanism that increases the production of IL-12 in morphine treated dendritic cells. This increased production of IL-12 causes increased T-cell immune response. This response is due to the ability of IL-12 to cause T helper cells to differentiate into the Th1 cell, causing a T cell immune response.

Further studies on the effects of morphine on the immune system have shown that morphine influences the production of neutrophils and other cytokines. Since cytokines are produced as part of the immediate immunological response (inflammation), it has been suggested that they may also influence pain. In this way, cytokines may be a logical target for analgesic development.

Recently, one study has used an animal model (hind-paw incision) to observe the effects of morphine administration on the acute immunological response. Following hind-paw incision, pain thresholds and cytokine production were measured. Normally, cytokine production in and around the wounded area increases in order to fight infection and control healing (and, possibly, to control pain), but pre-incisional morphine administration (0.1-10.0 mg/kg) reduced the number of cytokines found around the wound in a dose-dependent manner. The authors suggest that morphine administration in the acute post-injury period may reduce resistance to infection and may impair the healing of the wound.

## PHARMACOKINETICS

### Absorption and Metabolism

Morphine can be taken orally, rectally, subcutaneously, intravenously, intrathecally or epidurally. On the streets, it is becoming more common to inhale ("chasing the dragon"), but for medicinal purposes, intravenous (IV) injection is the most common method of administration. Morphine is subject to extensive first-pass metabolism (a large proportion is broken down in the liver), so if taken orally, only 40-50% of the dose reaches the central nervous system. Resultant plasma levels after subcutaneous (SC), intramuscular (IM), and IV injection are all comparable.

After IM or SC injections, morphine plasma levels peak in approximately 20 minutes, and after oral administration levels peak in approximately 30 minutes. Morphine is metabolised primarily in the liver and approximately 87% of a dose of morphine is excreted in the urine within 72 hours of administration. Morphine is primarily metabolized into morphine-3-glucuronide (M3G) and morphine-6-glucuronide (M6G) via glucuronidation by phase II metabolism enzyme UDP-glucuronosyl transferase-2B7 (UGT2B7). About 60% of morphine is converted to M3G, and 6–10% is converted to M6G. The cytochrome P450 (CYP) family of enzymes involved in phase I metabolism plays a lesser role.

Not only does the metabolism occur in the liver but it may also take place in the brain and the kidneys. M3G does not undergo opioid receptor binding and has no analgesic effect. M6G binds to mu-receptors and is a more potent analgesic than morphine. Morphine may also be metabolized into small amounts of normorphine, codeine, and hydromorphone.

Metabolism rate is determined by gender, age, diet, genetic makeup, disease state (if any) and use of other medications.

The elimination half-life of morphine is approximately 120 minutes, though there may be slight differences between men and women. Morphine can be stored in fat, and thus can be detectable even after death. Morphine is able to cross the blood-brain barrier but because of poor lipid solubility, protein binding, rapid conjugation with glucuronic acid and ionization, it does not cross easily. Diacetylmorphine, which is derived from morphine, crosses the blood-brain barrier more easily, making it more potent.

## Detection in Biological Fluids

Morphine and its major metabolites, morphine-3-glucuronide and morphine-6-glucuronide, may be quantitated in blood, plasma or urine to monitor for abuse, confirm a diagnosis of poisoning or assist in a medicolegal death investigation. Most commercial opiate screening tests based on immunoassays cross-react appreciably with these metabolites. However, chromatographic techniques can easily distinguish and measure each of these substances. When interpreting the results of a test, it is important to consider the morphine usage history of the individual, since a chronic user can develop tolerance to doses that would incapacitate an opiate-naive individual, and the chronic user often has high baseline values of these metabolites in his system.

Furthermore, some testing procedures employ a hydrolysis step prior to quantitation that converts the metabolic products to morphine, yielding a result that may be many times larger than with a method that examines each product individually. Interpretation can be confounded by usage of codeine or ingestion of poppy seed foods, either of which leads to the presence of morphine and its conjugated metabolites in a person's biofluids.

## Effects on Human Performance

Most reviews conclude that opioids produce minimal impairment of human performance on tests of sensory, motor, or attentional abilities. However, recent studies have been able to show some impairments caused by morphine, which is not surprising given that morphine is a central nervous system depressant. Morphine has resulted in impaired functioning on critical flicker frequency (a measure of overall CNS arousal) and impaired performance on the Maddox Wing test (a measure of deviation of the visual axes of the eyes). Few studies have investigated the effects of morphine on motor abilities; a high dose of morphine can impair finger tapping and the ability to maintain a low constant level of isometric force (i.e. fine motor control is impaired), though no studies have shown a correlation between morphine and gross motor abilities.

In terms of cognitive abilities, one study has shown that morphine may have a negative impact on anterograde and retrograde memory, but these effects are minimal and are transient. Overall, it seems that acute doses of opioids in non-tolerant subjects produce minor effects in some sensory and motor abilities, and perhaps also in attention and cognition. It is likely that the effects of morphine will be more pronounced in opioid-naive subjects than chronic opioid users.

In chronic opioid users, such as those on Chronic Opioid Analgesic Therapy (COAT) for managing severe, chronic pain, behavioural testing has shown normal functioning on perception, cognition, coordination and behaviour in most cases. One recent study analysed COAT patients in order to determine whether they were able to safely operate a motor vehicle.

The findings from this study suggest that stable opioid use does not significantly impair abilities inherent in driving (this includes physical, cognitive and perceptual skills). COAT patients showed rapid completion of tasks which require speed of responding for successful performance (e.g. Rey Complex Figure Test) but made more errors than controls. COAT patients showed no deficits in visual-spatial perception and organization (as shown in the WAIS-R Block Design Test) but did show impaired immediate and short-term visual memory

These patients showed no impairments in higher order

cognitive abilities (i.e. Planning). COAT patients appeared to have difficulty following instructions and showed a propensity towards impulsive behaviour, yet this did not reach statistical significance.

Importantly, this study reveals that COAT patients have no domain-specific deficits, which supports the notion that chronic opioid use has minor effects on psychomotor, cognitive, or neuropsychological functioning.

It is difficult to study the performance effects of morphine without considering why a person is taking morphine. Opioid-naive subjects are volunteers in a pain-free state. However, most chronic-users of morphine use it to manage pain.

Pain is a stressor and so it can confound performance results, especially on tests that require a large degree of concentration. Pain is also variable, and will vary over time and from person to person. It is unclear to what extent the stress of pain may cause impairments, and it is also unclear whether morphine is potentiating or attenuating these impairments.

## Chemistry

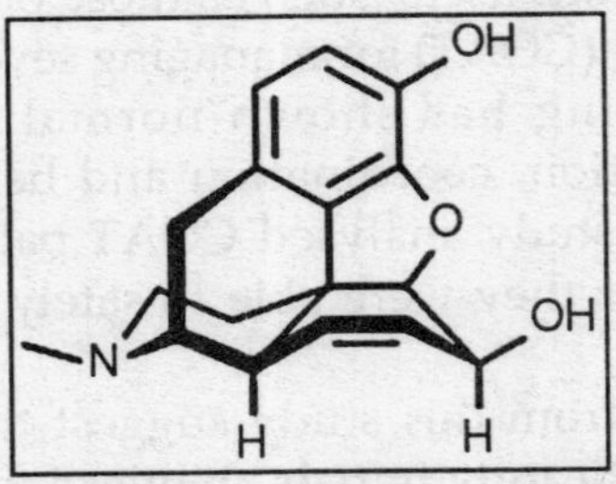


Chemical structure of morphine in correct 3D configuration. The benzylisoquinoline backbone is shown in blue.

Morphine is a benzylisoquinoline alkaloid with two additional ring closures.

Most of the licit morphine produced is used to make codeine by methylation. It is also a precursor for many drugs including heroin (diacetylmorphine), hydromorphone, and oxymorphone. Replacement of the N-methyl group of morphine with an N-phenylethyl group results in a product that is 18 times more powerful than morphine in its opiate agonist potency. Combining this modification with the replacement of the 6-hydroxyl with a 6-methylene produces a compound some 1,443 times more potent than morphine, stronger than the Bentley compounds such as etorphine.

The structure-activity relationship of morphine has been extensively studied. The structural formula of morphine was determined in 1925 and confirmed in 1952 when two methods of total synthesis were also published. As a result of the extensive study and use of this molecule, more than 200 morphine derivatives (also counting codeine and related drugs) have been developed since the last quarter of the 19th Century.

These drugs range from 25 per cent the strength of codeine or a little over 2 per cent of the strength of morphine, to several hundred times the strength of morphine to several powerful opioid antagoinsts including naloxone (Narcan), naltrexone (Trexan), and nalorphine (Nalline) for human use and also the amongst strongest antagonists known, such as diprenorphine (M5050), the reversing agent in the Immobilon large animal tranquilliser dart kit; the tranquilliser is another ultra-potent morphine derivative/structural analogue, viz., etorphine (M99). Morphine-derived agonist-antagonist drugs have also been developed. Elements of the morphine structure have been used to create completely synthetic drugs such as the morphinan family (levorphanol, dextromethorphan and others) and other groups which have many members with morphine-like qualities.

The modification of morphine and the aforementioned synthetics has also given rise to non-narcotic drugs with other uses such as emetics, stimulants, antitussives, anticholinergics, muscle relaxants, local anaesthetics, general anaesthetics, and others.

*Most semi-synthetic opioids, both of the morphine and codeine subgroups, are created by modifying one or more of the following*:

- Halogenating or making other modifications at positions 1 and/or 2 on the morphine carbon skeleton.

- The methyl group which makes morphine into codeine can be removed or added back, or replaced with another functional group like ethyl and others to make codeine analogues of morphine-derived drugs and vice versa. Codeine analogues of morphine-based drugs often serve as prodrugs of the stronger drug, as in codeine & morphine, hydrocodone & hydromorphone, oxycodone & oxymorphone, nicocodeine & nicomorphine, dihydrocodeine and dihydromorphine, &c. &c.
- Saturating, opening, or other changes to the bond betwixt positions 7 and 8, as well as adding, removing, or modifying functional groups to these positions; saturating, reducing, eliminating, or otherwise modifying the 7-8 bond and attaching a functional group at 14 yields hydromorphinol; the oxidation of the hydroxyl group to a carbonyl and changing the 7-8 bond to single from double changes codeine into oxycodone.
- Attachment, removal or modification of functional groups to positions 3 and/or 6 (dihydrocodeine and related, hydrocodone, nicomorphine); in the case of moving the methyl functional group from position 3 to 6, codeine becomes heterocodeine which is 72 times stronger, and therefore six times stronger than morphine
- Attachment of functional groups or other modification at position 14 (oxymorphone, oxycodone, naloxone)
- Modifications at positions 2, 4, 5 or 17, usually along with other changes to the molecule elsewhere on the morphine skeleton. Often this is done with drugs produced by catalytic reduction, hydrogenation, oxidation, or the like, producing strong derivatives of morphine and codeine.

Both morphine and its hydrated form, $C_{17}H_{19}NO_3H_2O$, are sparingly soluble in water. In five liters of water, only one gram of the hydrate will dissolve. For this reason, pharmaceutical companies produce sulfate and hydrochloride salts of the drug, both of which are over 300 times more water-soluble than their parent molecule. Whereas the pH of a saturated morphine hydrate solution is 8.5, the salts are acidic. Since they derive from a strong acid but weak base, they are both at about pH = 5; as a consequence, the morphine salts are mixed with small amounts of NaOH to make them suitable for injection.

A number of salts of morphine are used, with the most common in current clinical use being the hydrochloride, sulphate, tartrate, acetate, citrate; less commonly methobromide, hydrobromide, hydroiodide, lactate, chloride, and bitartrate and the others listed below. Morphine meconate is a major form of the alkaloid in the poppy, as is morphine pectinate, nitrate and some others.

Like codeine, dihydrocodeine and other, especially older, opiates, morphine has been used as the salicylate salt by some suppliers and can be easily compounded, imparting the therapeutic advantage of both the opioid and the NSAID; multiple barbiturate salts of morphine were also used in the past, as was/is morphine valerate, the salt of the acid being the active principle of valerian. Calcium morphenate is the intermediate in various latex and poppy-straw methods of morphine production.

Morphine ascorbate and other salts such as the tannate, citrate, and acetate, phosphate, valerate and others may be present in poppy tea depending on the method of preparation. Morphine valerate produced industrially was one ingredient of a medication available for both oral and parenteral administration popular many years ago in Europe and elsewhere called Trivalin (not to be confused with the curremt, unrelated herbal preparation of the same name) which also included the valerates of caffeine and cocaine, with a version containing codeine valerate as a fourth ingredient being distributed under the name Tetravalin.

Closely related to morphine are the opioids morphine-N-oxide (genomorphine) which is a pharmaceutical which is no longer in common use; and pseudomorphine, an alkaloid which exists in opium, form as degradation products of morphine.

*The salts listed by the United States Drug Enforcement Administration for reporting purposes, in addition to a few others, are as follows:*

**Table. [show]Forms of Morphine, Salts & Chemical form to Freebase Conversion Ratios**

| Salt or drug | CSA schedule | ACSCN | Free base conversion ratio |
|---|---|---|---|
| Morphine (base) | II | 9300 | 1 |
| Morphine acetate | II | 9300 | 0.71 |
| Morphine citrate | II | 9300 | 0.81 |
| Morphine bitartrate | II | 9300 | 0.66 |
| Morphine stearate | II | 9300 | 0.51 |
| Morphine phthalate | II | 9300 | 0.89 |
| Morphine hydrobromide | II | 9300 | 0.78 |
| Morphine hydrobromide (2 $H_2O$) | II | 9300 | 0.71 |
| Morphine hydrochloride | II | 9300 | 0.89 |
| Morphine hydrochloride (3 $H_2O$) | II | 9300 | 0.76 |
| Morphine hydriodide (2 $H_2O$) | II | 9300 | 0.64 |
| Morphine lactate | II | 9300 | 0.76 |
| Morphine monohydrate | II | 9300 | 0.94 |
| Morphine meconate (5 $H_2O$) | II | 9300 | 0.66 |
| Morphine mucate | II | 9300 | 0.57 |
| Morphine nitrate | II | 9300 | 0.82 |
| Morphine phosphate (1/2 $H_2O$) | II | 9300 | 0.73 |
| Morphine phosphate (7 $H_2O$) | II | 9300 | 0.73 |
| Morphine salicylate | II | 9300 | |
| Morphine phenyl-propionate | II | 9300 | 0.65 |
| Morphine methyliodide | II | 9300 | 0.67 |

| | | | |
|---|---|---|---|
| Morphine isobutyrate | II | 9300 | 0.76 |
| Morphine hypophosphite | II | 9300 | 0.81 |
| Morphine sulfate (5 $H_2O$) | II | 9300 | 0.75 |
| Morphine tannate | II | 9300 | |
| Morphine tartrate ($3H_2O$) | II | 9300 | 0.74 |
| Morphine valerate | II | 9300 | 0.74 |
| Morphine methylbromide | I | 9305 | 0.75 |
| Morphine methylsulfonate | I | 9306 | 0.75 |
| Morphine-N-oxide | I | 9307 | 1 |
| Morphine-N-oxide quinate | I | 9307 | 0.60 |
| Pseudomorphine | I | not mentioned | |

## Production

A Hungarian chemist, Janos Kabay, found and internationally patented a method to extract morphine from poppy straw. In the opium poppy the alkaloids are bound to meconic acid. The method is to extract from the crushed plant with diluted sulfuric acid, which is a stronger acid than meconic acid, but not so strong to react with alkaloid molecules.

The extraction is performed in many steps (one amount of crushed plant is at least six to ten times extracted, so practically every alkaloid goes into the solution). From the solution obtained at the last extraction step, the alkaloids are precipitated by either ammonium hydroxide or sodium carbonate.

The last step is purifying and separating morphine from other opium alkaloids. Opium poppy contains at least 40 different alkaloids, but most of them are of very low concentration. Morphine is the principal alkaloid in raw opium and constitutes ~8-19% of opium by dry weight (depending on growing conditions). In the 1950s and 1960s, Hungary supplied nearly 60% of Europe's total medication-purpose morphine production. To this day, poppy farming is legal in

Hungary, but poppy farms are limited by law to 2 acres (8,100 $m^2$). It is also legal to sell dried poppy in flower shops for use in floral arrangements.

It was announced in 1973 that a team at the National Institutes of Health in the United States had developed a method for total synthesis of morphine, codeine, and thebaine using coal tar as a starting material. A shortage in codeine-hydrocodone class cough suppressants (all of which can be made from morphine in one or more steps, as well as from codeine or thebaine) was the initial reason for the research.

The UN Office On Drugs & Crime *Bulletin On Narcotics*, issue II of 1952, describes the process which led to the final determination of the structural formula of morphine in 1925 and the invention of two methods of total synthesis of morphine.

Most morphine produced for pharmaceutical use around the world is actually converted into codeine as the concentration of the latter in both raw opium and poppy straw is much lower than that of morphine; in most countries the usage of codeine (both as end-product and precursor) is at least an order of magnitude greater than that of morphine on a weight basis and codeine is by far the most commonly-used opioid in the world. Whilst strains of poppies have been engineered to produce much higher yields of the other useful opioid pharmaceutical precursors thebaine and oripavine, no known strain of *P. somniferum* will produce more codeine than morphine under most or all possible conditions.

**Extraction and Detection**

Morphine can be isolated from whole blood samples by Solid Phase Extraction (SPE) and detected using Liquid Chromatography-Mass Spectrometry (LC-MS)

**Illicit use**

The euphoria, comprehensive alleviation of distress and therefore all aspects of suffering, promotion of sociability and empathy, "body high", and anxiolysis provided by narcotic drugs including the opioids can cause the use of high doses in the absence of pain for a protracted period, which can impart a morbid craving for the drug in the user. Being the prototype of the entire opioid class of drugs means that morphine has properties that may lend it to misuse. Morphine addiction is the model upon which the current perception of addiction is based.

Animal and human studies and clinical experience back up the contention that morphine is one of the most euphoric of drugs, and via all but the IV route heroin and morphine cannot be distinguished according to studies.

Chemical changes to the morphine molecule yield other powerful euphorigenics such as dihydromorphine, hydromorphone (Dilaudid, Hydal) and oxymorphone (Numorphan, Opana) as well as the latter three's methylated equivalents dihydrocodeine, hydrocodone and oxycodone respectively; in addition to heroin, there are dipropanoylmorphine, diacetyldihydromorphine and other members of the 3,6 morphine diester category like nicomorphine and other similar semi-synthetic opiates like desomorphine, hydromorphinol &c. used clinically in many countries of the world but in many cases also produced illicitly in rare instances.

Misuse of morphine generally entails taking more than prescribed or outside of medical supervision, injecting oral formulations, mixing it with unapproved potentiators such as alcohol, cocaine, and the like, and/or defeating the extended-release mechanism by chewing the tablets or turning into a powder for snorting or preparing injectables.

The latter method can be every bit as time-consuming and involved as traditional methods of smoking opium. This and the fact that the liver destroys a large percentage of the drug on the first pass impacts the demand side of the equation for clandestine re-sellers, as many customers are not needle users and may have been disappointed with ingesting the drug orally. As morphine is generally as hard or harder to divert than oxycodone in a lot of cases, morphine in any form is uncommon on the street, although ampoules and phials of morphine injection, pure pharmaceutical morphine powder, and soluble multi-purpose tablets are very popular where available.

Morphine is also available in a paste which is used in the production of heroin which can be smoked by itself or turned to a soluble salt and injected; the same goes for the penultimate products of the Kompot (Polish Heroin) and black tar processes. Poppy straw as well as opium can yield morphine of purity levels ranging from poppy tea to near-pharmaceutical grade morphine by itself or with all of the more than 50 other alkaloids. It also is the active narcotic ingredient in opium and all of its forms, derivatives, and analogues as well as forming from breakdown of heroin and otherwise being present in many batches of illicit heroin as the result of incomplete acetylation.

## Precursor to other Opioids, in a Pharmaceutical Manufacturing Setting

Morphine is a precursor in the manufacture in a large number of opioids such as dihydromorphine, hydromorphone, nicomorphine, and heroin as well as codeine, which itself has a large family of semi-synthetic derivatives. Morphine is commonly treated with acetic anhydride and ignited to yield heroin. The pharmacology of heroin and morphine is identical except the two acetyl groups increase the lipid solubility of the heroin molecule, causing it to cross the blood-brain barrier and enter the brain more rapidly. Once in the brain, these acetyl groups are removed to yield morphine, which causes the subjective effects of heroin. Thus, heroin may be thought of as a more rapidly acting form of morphine.

## Precursor to other Opioids, in an Underground and Illicit Setting

Illicit morphine is rarely produced from codeine found in over the counter cough and pain medicines. This demethylation reaction is often performed using pyridine and hydrochloric acid.

Another source of illicit morphine comes from the extraction of morphine from extended release morphine products, such as MS-Contin. Morphine can be extracted from these products with simple extraction techniques to yield a morphine solution that can be injected.

Alternatively, the tablets can be crushed and snorted, injected or swallowed, although this provides much less euphoria although retaining some of the extended-release effect and the extended-release property is why MS-Contin is used in some countries alongside methadone, dihydrocodeine, buprenorphine, dihydroe-torphine, piritramide, levo-alpha-acetylmethadol (LAAM) and special 24-hour formulations of hydromor-phone for maintenance and detoxification of those physically dependent on opioids.

Another means of using or misusing morphine is to use chemical reactions to turn it into heroin or another stronger opioid.

Morphine can, using a technique reported in New Zealand (where the initial precursor is codeine) and elsewhere known as home-bake, be turned into what is usually a mixture of morphine, heroin, 3-monoacety-lmorphine, 6-monoace-tylmorphine, and codeine derivatives like acetylcodeine if the process is using morphine made from demethylating codeine by mixing acetic anhydride or acetyl chloride with the morphine and cooking it in an oven between 80 and 85°C for several hours.

Since heroin is one of a series of 3,6 diesters of morphine, it is possible to convert morphine to nicomorphine (Vilan) using nicotinic anhydride, dipropanoylmorphine with propionic anhydride, dibutanoylmorphine and disalicyloy-lmorphine with the respective acid anhydrides. Glacial Acetic acid can be used to obtain a mixture high in 6-monoa-cetylmorphine, nicotinic acid (Vitamin B3) in some form would be precursor to 6-nicotinylmorphine, salicylic acid may yield the salicyoyl analogue of 6-MAM, and so on.

Homebake or other clandestinely-produced heroin produced from extended-release morphine tablets may be known as Blue Heroin because of the blue colour of some of these tablets, even though the coloured coating of the tablet is usually removed before processing, many strengths of the tablets are not blue, bluish or a related colour like purple, and the final product tends not to be blue. A writer of a 2006 description of producing heroin from 100 mg as well as some 30 and 15 mg MS-Contin type tablets coined the term Blue Heroin to distinguish his, her or their product from New Zealand-style homebake as the process was shorter and began with uncoated tablets which in the case of the 100 mg tablet was at or above 35 per cent morphine sulphate by weight, resulting in a final liquid injectable which was brown-purple and quite potent.

The clandestine conversion of morphine to ketones of the hydromorphone class or other derivatives like dihydromorphine (Paramorfan), desomorphine (Permonid), metopon &c. and codeine to hydrocodone (Dicodid), dihydrocodeine (Paracodin) &c. is more involved, time consuming, requires lab equipment of various types, and usually requires expensive catalysts and large amounts of morphine at the outset and is less common but still has been discovered by authorities in various ways during the last 20 years or so.

Dihydromorphine can be acetylated into another 3,6 morphine diester, namely diacetyldihydro-morphine (Paralaudin), and hydrocodone into thebacon.

## Legal Classification

- In the United Kingdom, morphine is listed as a Class A drug under the Misuse of Drugs Act 1971 and a Schedule 2 Controlled Drug under The Misuse of Drugs Regulations 2001.
- In the United States, morphine is classified as a Schedule II drug under the Controlled Substances Act.
- In Canada, morphine is classified as a Schedule I drug under the Controlled Drugs and Substances Act.
- In Australia, morphine is classified as a Schedule 8 drug under the variously titled State and Territory Poisons Acts.
- In the Netherlands, morphine is classified as a List 1 drug under the Opium Law.

- In Japan, morphine is classified as a narcotic under the Narcotics and Psychotropics Control Act.
- Internationally, morphine is a Schedule I drug under the Single Convention on Narcotic Drugs.

### Access to Morphine in Poor Countries

Although morphine is cheap, people in poorer countries often do not have access to it. According to a 2005 estimate by the International Narcotics Control Board, six countries (Australia, Britain, Canada, France, Germany, and the United States) consume 79 per cent of the world's morphine.

The less affluent countries, accounting for 80 per cent of the world's population, consumed only about 6 per cent of the global morphine supply. Some countries import virtually no morphine, and in others the drug is rarely available even for relieving severe pain while dying.

Experts in pain management attribute the under-distribution of morphine to an unwarranted fear of the drug's potential for addiction and abuse. While morphine is clearly addictive, Western doctors believe it is worthwhile to use the drug and then wean the patient off when the treatment is over.

## ERGOMETRINE

Ergometrine (other names include ergonovine and d-lysergic acid beta-propanolamide), is an ergoline (and lysergamide) derivative, and one of the primary ergot and morning glory alkaloids. It is chemically similar to LSD, ergine, and lysergic acid.

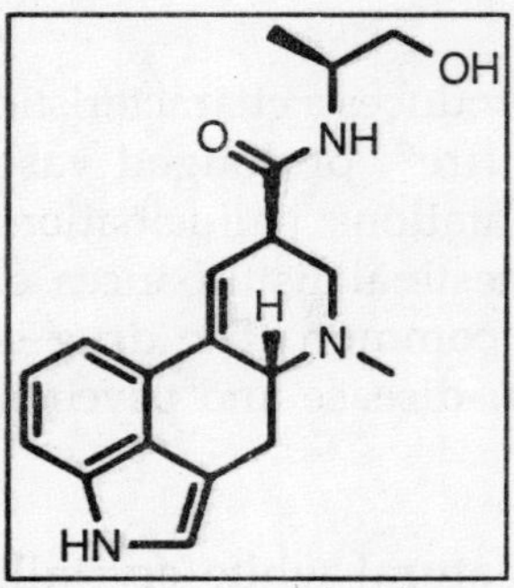

## Mechanism of Action

While it acts at alpha-adrenergic, dopamine and serotonin (5-HT2) receptors, it exerts on the uterus and other smooth muscle a powerful stimulant effect not clearly associated with a specific receptor type.

## Medical Use

It has a medical use in obstetrics to facilitate delivery of the placenta and to prevent bleeding after childbirth by causing smooth muscle tissue in the blood vessel walls to narrow, thereby reducing blood flow. It is usually combined with oxytocin (Syntocinon) as syntometrine.

It can induce spasm of the coronary arteries. This is sometimes used in the differential diagnosis of angina.

## Recreational Use

According to TIHKAL by Alexander Shulgin, ergonovine has LSD-like action at levels of 2-10 milligrams. Clinical dosages are about ten times lower.

## Legal status

Ergometrine is listed as Table I precursors under the United Nations Convention Against Illicit Traffic in Narcotic Drugs and Psychotropic Substances, as possible precursor compound for LSD. As an N-alkyl derivative of lysergamide, ergonovine is also covered by the Misuse of Drugs Act 1971, effectively rendering it illegal in the United Kingdom.

## Side Effects

An overdose produces a characteristic poisoning, ergotism or "St. Anthony's fire": prolonged vasospasm resulting in gangrene and amputations; hallucinations and dementia; and abortions. Gastrointestinal disturbances, e.g. diarrhoea, nausea and vomiting, are common. The drug is contraindicated in pregnancy, vascular disease and psychosis.

## QUININE

Quinine is a natural white crystalline alkaloid having

antipyretic (fever-reducing), antimalarial, analgesic (painkilling), and anti-inflammatory properties and a bitter taste. It is a stereoisomer of quinidine which, unlike quinine, is an anti-arrhythmic.

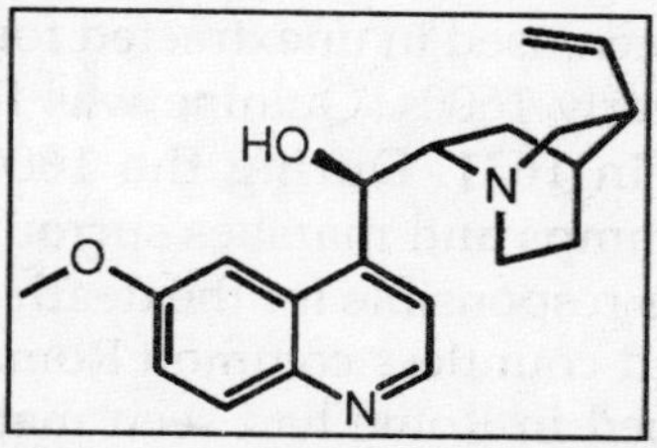

Though it has been synthesized in the lab, the bark of the cinchona tree is the only natural source of quinine. The medicinal properties of the cinchona tree were originally discovered by the Quechua Indians of Peru and Bolivia; later, the Jesuits were the first to bring the cinchona to Europe.

Quinine was the first effective treatment for malaria caused by *Plasmodium falciparum*, appearing in therapeutics in the 17th century. It remained the antimalarial drug of choice until the 1940s, when other drugs replaced it. Since then, many effective antimalarials have been introduced, although quinine is still used to treat the disease in certain critical situations. Quinine is available with a prescription in the United States and over-the-counter, in very small quantities, in tonic water. Quinine is also used to treat lupus, nocturnal leg cramps and arthritis.

*Chemical structure*:Quinine contains two major fused-ring systems: the aromatic quinoline and the bicyclic quinuclidine.

## Mechanism of Action Against P. Falciparum

As with other quinoline anti-malarial drugs, the action of quinine has not been fully resolved. The most widely accepted hypothesis of quinine action is based on the well-studied and closely related quinoline drug, chloroquine. This model involves the inhibition of hemozoin biocrystallization, which facilitates the aggregation of cytotoxic heme. Toxic free heme accumulates in the parasites, leading to their death.

Quinine is an effective muscle relaxant, long used by the

Quechua Indians of Peru to halt shivering due to low temperatures. The Peruvians would mix the ground bark of cinchona trees with sweetened water to offset the bark's bitter taste, thus producing tonic water.

Quinine has been used in unextracted form by Europeans since at least the early 1600s. Quinine was first used to treat malaria in Rome in 1631. During the 1600s, malaria was endemic to the swamps and marshes surrounding the city of Rome. Malaria was responsible for the death of several popes, many cardinals and countless common Roman citizens. Most of the priests trained in Rome had seen malaria victims and were familiar with the shivering brought on by the febrile phase of the disease.

The Jesuit brother Agostino Salumbrino (1561-1642), an apothecary by training who lived in Lima, observed the Quechua using the bark of the cinchona tree for that purpose. While its effect in treating malaria (and hence malaria-induced shivering) was unrelated to its effect in controlling shivering from rigors, it was still a successful medicine for malaria. At the first opportunity, Salumbrino sent a small quantity to Rome to test as a malaria treatment.

In the years that followed, cinchona bark was known as Jesuit's bark and became one of the most valuable commodities shipped from Peru to Europe.

The form of quinine most effective in treating malaria was found by Charles Marie de La Condamine in 1737. Quinine was isolated and named in 1820 by French researchers Pierre Joseph Pelletier and Joseph Bienaimé Caventou. The name was derived from the original Quechua (Inca) word for the cinchona tree bark, "quina" or "quina-quina", which roughly means "bark of bark" or "holy bark". Prior to 1820, the bark was first dried, ground to a fine powder and then mixed into a liquid (commonly wine) which was then drunk. Large scale use of quinine as a prophylaxis started around 1850.

Quinine also played a significant role in the colonization of Africa by Europeans. It has been said that quinine was the prime reason that Africa ceased to be known as the "white man's grave". A historian has stated that "it was quinine's efficacy that gave colonists fresh opportunities to swarm into the Gold Coast, Nigeria and other parts of west Africa".

To maintain their monopoly on cinchona bark, Peru and surrounding countries began outlawing the export of cinchona seeds and saplings beginning in the early 19th century. The Dutch government persisted in its attempt to smuggle the seeds, and by the 1930s Dutch plantations in Java were producing 22 million pounds of cinchona bark, or 97% of the world's quinine production. During World War II, Allied powers were cut off from their supply of quinine when the Germans conquered Holland and the Japanese controlled the Philippines and Indonesia. The United States, however, had managed to obtain four million cinchona seeds from the Philippines and began operation of cinchona plantations in Costa Rica. Nonetheless, such supplies came too late; tens of thousands US troops in Africa and the South Pacific died due to the lack of quinine. Despite controlling the supply, the Japanese did not make effective use of quinine, and thousands of Japanese troops in the Southwest Pacific died as a result.

## Synthetic Quinine

Cinchona trees remain the only economically practical source of quinine. However, under wartime pressure, research towards its synthetic production was undertaken. A formal chemical synthesis was accomplished in 1944 by American chemists R.B. Woodward and W.E. Doering. Since then, several more efficient quinine total syntheses have been achieved, but none of them can compete in economic terms with isolation of the alkaloid from natural sources. The first synthetic organic dye, mauveine, was discovered by William Henry Perkin in 1856 while he was attempting to synthesize quinine.

## Dosing and Indication

As of 2006, quinine is no longer recommended by the WHO as first line treatment for malaria and should only be used when artemesinins are not available.

Quinine is a basic amine and is therefore always presented as a salt. Various preparations that exist include the hydrochloride, dihydrochloride, sulfate, bisulfate and gluconate. This makes quinine dosing complicated since each of the salts has a different weight.

*The following amounts of each form are equal:*

- Quinine base 100 mg.
- Quinine bisulfate 169 mg.
- Quinine dihydrochloride 122 mg.
- quinine hydrochloride 111 mg.
- quinine sulfate (actually (quinine)$_2H_2SO_4 \cdot 2H_2O$) 121 mg.
- quinine gluconate 160 mg.

All quinine salts may be given orally or intravenously (IV); quinine gluconate may also be given intramuscularly (IM) or rectally (PR). The main problem with the rectal route is that the dose can be expelled before it is completely absorbed; this can be corrected by giving a half dose again.

The IV dose of quinine is 8 mg/kg of quinine base every eight hours; the IM dose is 12.8 mg/kg of quinine base twice daily; the PR dose is 20 mg/kg of quinine base twice daily. Treatment should be given for seven days.

The preparations available in the UK are quinine sulfate (200 mg or 300 mg tablets) and quinine hydrochloride (300 mg/ml for injection). Quinine is not licensed for IM or PR use in the UK. The adult dose in the UK is 600 mg quinine dihydrochloride IV or 600 mg quinine sulfate orally every eight hours. For nocturnal leg cramps, the dosage is 200–300 mg at night.

In the United States, quinine sulfate is commercially available in 324-mg tablets under the brand name Qualaquin; the adult dose is two tablets every eight hours. There is no injectable preparation of quinine licensed in the U.S.: quinidine is used instead.

### Side-effects

It is usual for quinine in therapeutic doses to cause cinchonism; in rare cases, it may even cause death (usually by pulmonary edema). The development of mild cinchonism is not a reason for stopping or interrupting quinine therapy and the patient should be reassured. Blood glucose levels and electrolyte concentrations must be monitored when quinine is given by injection. The patient should ideally be in cardiac monitoring when the first quinine injection is given (these precautions are often unavailable in developing countries where malaria is endemic).

Cinchonism is much less common when quinine is given by mouth, but oral quinine is not well tolerated (quinine is exceedingly bitter and many patients will vomit after ingesting quinine tablets): Other drugs such as Fansidar (sulfadoxine (sulfonamide antibiotic) with pyrimethamine) or Malarone (proguanil with atovaquone) are often used when oral therapy is required. Quinine ethyl carbonate is tasteless and odourless, but is only commercially available in Japan. Blood glucose, electrolyte and cardiac monitoring are not necessary when quinine is given by mouth.

Quinine can cause paralysis if accidentally injected into a nerve. It is extremely toxic in overdose, and the advice of a poisons specialist should be sought immediately.

Quinine in some cases can lead to constipation, erectile dysfunction and diarrhea.

The New York Times Magazine described a case, presenting with fever, hypotension, and blood abnormalities mimicking septic shock.

## Abortifacient

Despite popular belief, quinine is an ineffective abortifacient (in the US, quinine is listed as Pregnancy category D). Pregnant women who take toxic doses of quinine will suffer from renal failure before experiencing any kind of quinine-induced abortion. Indeed, quinine is the only drug recommended by the WHO as firstline treatment for uncomplicated malaria in pregnancy.

## Disease Interactions

Quinine can cause hemolysis in G6PD deficiency, but again this risk is small and the physician should not hesitate to use quinine in patients with G6PD deficiency when there is no alternative. Quinine can also cause drug-induced immune thrombocytopenic purpura (ITP). Symptoms can be severe enough to require hospitalisation and platelet transfusion, with several cases resulting in death.

Quinine can cause abnormal heart rhythms and should be avoided if possible in patients with atrial fibrillation, conduction defects or heart block.

Quinine can worsen hemoglobinuria, myasthenia gravis and optic neuritis.

**Hearing impairment**

Some studies have related the use of quinine and hearing impairment, in particular high-frequency loss, but it has not been conclusively established whether such impairment is temporary or permanent.

**Regulation by the United States Food and Drug Administration**

From 1969 to 1992, the U.S. Food and Drug Administration (FDA) received 157 reports of health problems related to quinine use, including 23 which had resulted in death. In 1994, the FDA banned the use of over-the-counter (OTC) quinine as a treatment for nocturnal leg cramps. Pfizer Pharmaceuticals had been selling the brand name Legatrin for this purpose. Doctors may still prescribe quinine, but the FDA has ordered firms to stop marketing unapproved drug products containing quinine. The FDA is also cautioning consumers about off-label use of quinine to treat leg cramps.

Quinine is approved for treatment of malaria, but is also commonly prescribed to treat leg cramps and similar conditions. Because malaria is life-threatening, the risks associated with quinine use are considered acceptable when used to treat that affliction.

Though Legatrin was banned by the FDA for the treatment of leg cramps, drug manufacturer URL Mutual has branded a quinine containing drug named "Qualaquin". Qualaquin is marketed as a treatment for malaria and is only sold in the United States by prescription. In 2004, the CDC reported only 1,347 confirmed cases of malaria in the United States.

## Non-medical uses of Quinine

Quinine is a flavour component of tonic water and bitter lemon. According to tradition, the bitter taste of anti-malarial quinine tonic led British colonials in India to mix it with gin, thus creating the gin and tonic cocktail, which is still popular today in many parts of the world, especially the U.K., United States, Canada, Australia, New Zealand, and Lhasa, Tibet.

Bark of *Remijia* contains 0.5 - 2 % of quinine. The bark is cheaper than bark of *Cinchona* and as it has an intense taste, it is used for making tonic water.

In some areas, non-medical use of quinine is regulated. For example, in the United States and in Germany, quinine is limited to between 83-85 parts per million.

In France, quinine is an ingredient of an apéritif known as Quinquina or "Cap Corse".

In Italy, the traditional flavored wine Barolo Chinato is infused with quinine and local herbs and is served as a digestive.

Because of its relatively constant and well-known fluorescence quantum yield, quinine is also used in photochemistry as a common fluorescence standard.

Quinine (and quinidine) are used as the chiral moiety for the ligands used in Sharpless asymmetric dihydroxylation.

In Canada and Italy, quinine is an ingredient in the carbonated chinotto beverages Brio and San Pellegrino Chinotto.

In the United Kingdom, Scottish company A.G. Barr's uses quinine as an ingredient in the carbonated and caffeinated beverage Irn-Bru.

In the United Kingdom, Australia, New Zealand and Egypt, quinine is an ingredient in Schweppes and other Indian tonic waters, at a concentration of 0.67 mg/l.

In Uruguay and Argentina, quinine is an ingredient of a Pepsico Inc. Tonic water named Paso de los Toros.

In South Africa, quinine is an ingredient of a Clifton

Instant Drink named Chikree produced by Tiger Food Brands.

As a treatment for *Cryptocaryon irritans* (commonly referred to as white spot, crypto or marine ich) infection of marine aquarium fish.

Quinine is sometimes used as a cutting agent in street drugs such as cocaine and heroin.

## RESERPINE

Reserpine is an indole alkaloid antipsychotic and antihypertensive drug that has been used for the control of high blood pressure and for the relief of psychotic behaviors, although because of the development of better drugs for these purposes and because of its numerous side-effects, it is rarely used today. The antihypertensive actions of Reserpine are a result of its ability to deplete catecholamines (among the others) from peripheral sympathetic nerve endings. These substances are normally involved in controlling heart rate, force of cardiac contraction and peripheral resistance. Reserpine depletion of monoamine neurotransmitters in the synapses is often cited as evidence to the theory that depletion of the neurotransmitters causes subsequent depression in humans. Moreover, reserpine has a peripheral action in many parts of the body, resulting in a preponderance of the cholinergic part of the nervous system (GI-Tract, smooth muscles vessels).

### Mode of Action

Reserpine acts by blocking the vesicular monoamine transporter VMAT, which normally transports free norepinephrine, serotonin, and dopamine from the cytoplasm of the presynaptic nerve into vesicles for subsequent release into the synaptic cleft. The unprotected neurotransmitters are then metabolized by MAO and therefore never reach the synapse.

### Biosynthetic Pathway

Tryptophan is the starting material in the biosynthetic pathway of reserpine, and is converted to tryptamine by tryptophan decarboxylase enzyme. Tryptamine is combined with secologanin in the presence of strictosidine synthetase enzyme and yields strictosidine. Various enzymatic conversion reactions lead to the synthesis of reserpine from strictosidine.

Reserpine was isolated in 1952 from the dried root of *Rauwolfia serpentina* (Indian snakeroot), (which had been known as *Sarpaganda* and had been used for centuries in India for the treatment of insanity, as well as fever and snakebites — even Mahatma Gandhi used it as a tranquilizer during his lifetime. It was first used in the United States by Robert Wallace Wilkins in 1950. Its molecular structure was elucidated in 1953 and natural configuration published in 1955. It was introduced in 1954, two years after chlorpromazine. The first total synthesis was accomplished by R. B. Woodward in 1958.

Reserpine almost irreversibly blocks the uptake (and storage) of norepinephrine (i.e. noradrenaline) and dopamine into synaptic vesicles by inhibiting the Vesicular Monoamine Transporters (VMAT).

Reserpine has been discontinued in the UK for some years due to its numerous interactions and side effects.

## Uses Today

Reserpine is one of the few antihypertensive medications that have been shown in randomized controlled trials to reduce mortality: The Hypertension Detection and Follow-up Programme, the Veterans Administration Cooperative Study Group in Anti-hypertensive Agents, and the Systolic Hypertension in the Elderly Programme.

Reserpine is rarely used in the management of hypertension today. Reserpine is listed as an option by the JNC 7. Reserpine is a second-line adjunct agent for patients who are uncontrolled on a diuretic when cost is an issue.

It is also used to treat symptoms of dyskinesia in patients suffering from Huntington's disease.

In some countries reserpine is still available as part of combination drugs for the treatment of hypertension, in most cases they contain also a diuretic and/or a vasodilator like hydralazine. These combinations are currently regarded as second choice drugs. The daily dose of reserpine in antihypertensive treatment is as low as 0.1 to 0.25 mg. The use of reserpine as an antipsychotic drug had been nearly completely abandoned, but more recently it made a comeback as adjunctive treatment, in combination with other antipsychotics, so that more refractory patients get dopamine blockade from the other antipsychotic, and dopamine depletion from reserpine.

Doses for this kind of adjunctive goal can be kept low, resulting in better tolerability. Originally, doses of 0.5 mg to 40 mg daily were used to treat psychotic diseases. Doses in excess of 3 mg daily often required use of an anticholinergic drug to combat excessive cholinergic activity in many parts of the body as well as parkinsonism. For adjunctive treatment, doses are typically kept at or below 0.25 mg twice a day. Reserpine may be used as a sedative for horses.

### Side Effects

At doses of less than 0.2 mg/day, reserpine has few side effects, most commonly is nasal congestion.

There has been much concern about reserpine causing depression leading to suicide. However, this was reported in uncontrolled studies using doses averaging 0.5 mg per day.

Reserpine can cause: nasal congestion, nausea, vomiting, weight gain, gastric intolerance, gastric ulceration (due to increased cholinergic activity in gastric tissue and impaired mucosal quality), stomach cramps and diarrhea are noted. The drug causes hypotension and bradycardia and may worsen asthma. Congested nose and erectile dysfunction are other consequences of alpha-blockade.

Depression can occur at any dose and may be severe enough to lead to suicide. Other central effects are a high incidence of drowsiness, dizziness, and nightmares. Parkinsonism occurs in a dose dependent manner. General weakness or fatigue is quite often encountered. High dose studies in rodents found reserpine to cause fibroadenoma of the breast and malignant tumors of the seminal vesicles among others. Early suggestions that reserpine causes breast cancer in women (risk approximately doubled) were not confirmed. It may also cause hyperprolactinemia.

Reserpine passes into breast milk and is harmful to breast-fed infants, and should therefore be avoided during breastfeeding if possible.

## STRYCHNINE

Strychnine is a very toxic ($LD_{50}$ = c. 10 mg/kg), colorless crystalline alkaloid used as a pesticide, particularly for killing small vertebrates such as birds and rodents. Strychnine causes muscular convulsions and eventually death through asphyxia or sheer exhaustion. The most common source is from the seeds of the *Strychnos nux vomica* tree. Strychnine is one of the most bitter substances known. Its taste is detectable in concentrations as low as 1 ppm.

### Pharmacology

Strychnine acts as a blocker or antagonist at the inhibitory or strychnine-sensitive glycine receptor (GlyR), a ligand-gated chloride channel in the spinal cord and the brain.

Although it is best known as a poison, small doses of strychnine were once used in medications as a stimulant, as a laxative, and as a treatment for other stomach ailments. A 1934 drug guide for nurses described it as "among the most valuable and widely prescribed drugs". Strychnine's stimulant effects also led to its use historically for enhancing performance in sports. Because of its high toxicity and tendency to cause convulsions, the use of strychnine in medicine was eventually abandoned once safer alternatives became available.

The dosage for medical use was cited as between "1/60th grain–1/10th grain", which is between 1.1 milligrams and 6.4 milligrams in metric measures. In normal circumstances, the maximum dosage used was 3.2 mg, half of a "full dose". A lethal dose was cited as 1/2 a grain (32 mg)

Strychnine was first isolated from the beans of *Strychnos ignatii* by Pierre Joseph Pelletier and Joseph Bienaimé Caventou in 1818. Its structure was determined by Sir Robert Robinson and Herman Leuchs in 1946. In 1952, Robinson wrote that "For its molecular size it is the most complex substance known."

The first total synthesis of this molecule was reported by R. B. Woodward and his coworkers in 1954. X-ray crystallography studies confirmed the natural configuration of the molecule in 1956. In 1963, a complete paper was published by Woodward and his coworkers. K. C. Nicolaou calls the published synthesis "a spectacular achievement of organic synthesis". Other syntheses have been published.

## STRYCHNINE POISONING

Strychnine poisoning can be fatal to humans and other animals and can occur by inhalation, swallowing or absorption through eyes or mouth. It produces some of the most dramatic and painful symptoms of any known toxic reaction. For this reason, strychnine poisoning is often used in literature and film.

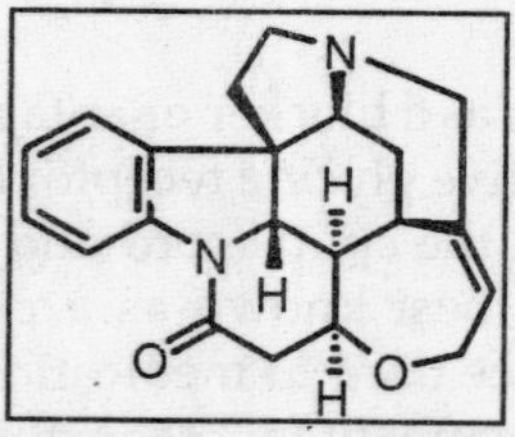

**Fig.** Strychnine Poisoning

### Presentation in Humans

Ten to twenty minutes after exposure, the body's muscles begin to spasm, starting with the head and neck in the form of trismus and risus sardonicus. The spasms then spread to every muscle in the body, with nearly continuous convulsions, and get worse at the slightest stimulus. The convulsions progress, increasing in intensity and frequency until the backbone arches continually. Convulsions lead to lactic acidosis, hyperthermia and rhabdomyolysis. These are followed by postictal depression. Death comes from asphyxiation caused by paralysis of the neural pathways that control breathing, or by exhaustion from the convulsions. The subject dies within 2–3 hours after exposure.

One medical student in 1896 described the experience in a letter to the Lancet: Three years ago I was reading for an examination, and feeling "run down". I took 10 minims of strychnia solution (B.P.) with the same quantity of dilute phosphoric acid well diluted twice a day. On the second day of taking it, towards the evening, I felt a tightness in the "facial muscles " and a peculiar metallic taste in the mouth. There was great uneasiness and restlessness, and I felt a desire to walk about and do something rather than sit still and read. I lay on the bed and the calf muscles began to stiffen and' jerk. My toes drew up under my feet, and as I moved or turned my head flashes of light kept darting across my eyes..

I then knew something serious was developing, so I crawled off the bed and scrambled to a case in my room and got out (fortunately) the bromide of potassium and the chloral. I had no confidence or courage to weigh them, so I guessed the quantity-about 30 gr. bromide of potassium and 10 gr. chloral-put them in a tumbler with some water, and drank it off. My whole body was in a cold sweat, with anginous attacks in the precordial region, and a feeling of "going off." I did not call for medical aid, as I thought the symptoms declining.

I felt better, but my lower limbs. were as cold as ice and the calf muscles kept tense and, jerking. There was no opisthotonos, only a slight stiffness at the back of the neck. Half an hour later, as I could judge, I took the same quantity of bromide of potassium and chloral, and a little time after I lost consciousness and fell into a " profound sleep," awaking in the morning with no unpleasant symptoms, no headache, but a desire " to be on the move " and a slight feeling of stiffness in the jaw. These worked off during the day.

**Treatment**

There is no specific antidote for strychnine. Treatment of strychnine poisoning involves an oral application of an activated charcoal infusion which serves to absorb any poison within the digestive tract that has not yet been absorbed into the blood. Anticonvulsants such as phenobarbital or diazepam are administered to control convulsions, along with muscle relaxants such as dantrolene to combat muscle rigidity. If the patient survives past 24 hours, recovery is probable.

The treatment for strychnine poisoning in the late 19th and early 20th centuries was to administer tannic acid which precipitates the strychnine as an insoluble tannate salt, and then to anaesthetise the patient with chloroform until the effects of the strychnine had worn off.

## Strychnine Toxicity in Animals

Strychnine poisoning in animals occurs usually from ingestion of baits designed for use against rodents (especially gophers and moles) and coyotes. Rodent baits are commonly available over-the-counter, but coyote baits are illegal in the United States. However, since 1990 in the United States most baits containing strychnine have been replaced with zinc phosphide baits.

The most common domestic animal to be affected is the dog, either through accidental ingestion or intentional poisoning. An approximate lethal dose for a dog is 0.75 mg per kg body weight. For a 0.3% strychnine bait, five grams of bait could be enough to kill a 20 kilogram dog.

The onset of symptoms is 10 to 120 minutes after ingestion. Symptoms include seizures, a "sawhorse" stance, and opisthotonus (rigid extension of all four limbs). Death is usually secondary to respiratory paralysis. Treatment is by detoxification using activated charcoal, pentobarbital for the symptoms, and artificial respiration for apnea.

In most western nations a special license is needed to use and possess strychnine for agricultural use.

## Notable Strychnine Poisonings

- Strychnine poisoning (in contaminated wine) is one of the theories concerning the death of Alexander the Great.
- Strychnine was used in several of the murders committed by serial killer Thomas Neill Cream, who poisoned prostitutes on the streets of London.
- Famous Delta Blues legend Robert Johnson's whiskey

bottle was laced with strychnine, resulting in pneumonia.

- A childhood friend of Vincent Van Gogh, Margot Begemann, attempted suicide by ingestion of strychnine.
- Belle Gunness of La Porte, Indiana, also known as *Lady Bluebeard*, reportedly used strychnine to murder her victims at the turn of the last century.
- Hannes Hirtzberger, Mayor of Spitz in Lower Austria was reported to have been poisoned by Helmut Osberger, a local wine producer.
- Jane Stanford, cofounder of Stanford University may have died from strychnine poisoning.

## VINCRISTINE

Vincristine (brand name, Oncovin), also known as leurocristine, is a vinca alkaloid from the *Catharanthus roseus* (Madagascar periwinkle), formerly *Vinca rosea* and hence its name. It is a mitotic inhibitor, and is used in cancer chemotherapy.

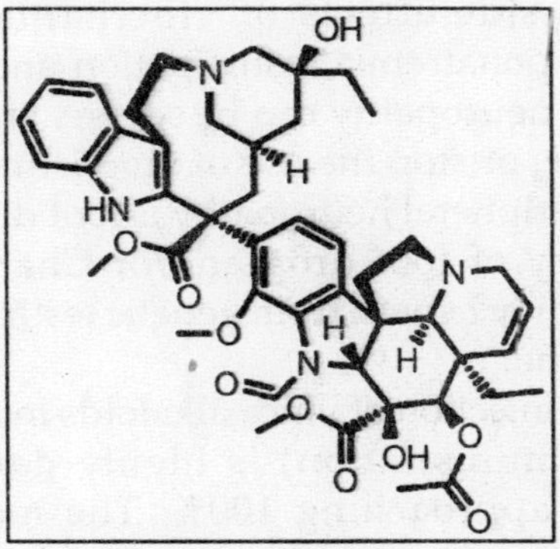

### Mode of Action

*Tubulin* is a structural protein which polymerizes to action microtubules. The cell cytoskeleton and mitotic spindle, amongst other things, are made of microtubules. *Vincristine* binds to tubulin dimers, inhibiting assembly of microtubule structures. Disruption of the microtubules arrests mitosis in metaphase. The *vinca* alkaloids therefore affect all rapidly dividing cell types including cancer cells, but also intestinal epithelium and bone marrow.

**Uses**

Vincristine is delivered via intravenous infusion for use in various types of chemotherapy regimens. Its main uses are in non-Hodgkin's lymphoma as part of the chemotherapy regimen CHOP, Hodgkin's lymphoma as part of MOPP, COPP, BEACOPP, or the less popular Stanford V chemotherapy regimen, in acute lymphoblastic leukemia, and in treatment for nephroblastoma (Wilms tumor, a kidney tumor common in children). It is also used to induce remission in ALL with Dexamethasone and L Asparginase. Vincristine is occasionally used as an immunosuppressant, for example, in treating thrombotic thrombocytopenic purpura (TTP) or chronic idiopathic thrombocytopenic purpura (ITP). It is used in combination with prednisone to treat childhood leukemia.

**Side effects**

The main side-effects of vincristine are peripheral neuropathy, hyponatremia, constipation and hair loss.

Peripheral neuropathy can be severe, and hence a reason to avoid, reduce, or stop the use of vincristine. One of the first symptoms of peripheral neuropathy is foot drop: a person with a family history of foot drop and/or Charcot-Marie-Tooth disease (CMT) may benefit from genetic testing for CMT before taking vincristine.

Accidental injection of vinca alkaloids into the spinal canal (intrathecal administration) is highly dangerous, with a mortality rate approaching 100%. The medical literature documents cases of ascending paralysis due to massive encephalopathy and spinal nerve demyelination, accompanied by intractable pain, almost uniformly leading to death; a handful of survivors were left with devastating neurological damage with no hope of recovery. Rescue treatments consist of washout of the cerebrospinal fluid and administration of protective medications. A significant series of inadvertent intrathecal vincristine administration occurred in China in 2007 when batches of cytarabine and methotrexate (both often used intrathecally) manufactured by the company Shanghai Hualian were found to be contaminated with vincristine.

## PIPERINE

Piperine is the alkaloid responsible for the pungency of black pepper and long pepper, along with chavicine (an isomer of piperine). It has also been used in some forms of traditional medicine and as an insecticide. Piperine forms monoclinic needles, is slightly soluble in water and more so in alcohol, ether or chloroform: the solution in alcohol has a pepper-like taste. It yields salts only with strong acids.

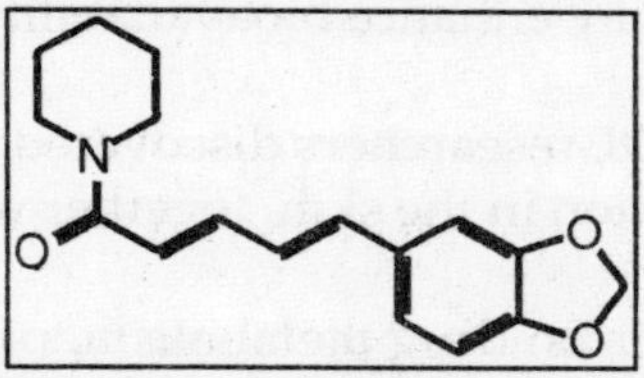

The platinichloride $B_4 \bullet H_2PtCl_6$ forms orange-red needles. ("B" denotes one mole of the alkaloid base in this and the following formulae.) Iodine in potassium iodide added to an alcoholic solution of the base in presence of a little hydrochloric acid gives a characteristic periodide, $B_2 \bullet HI \bullet I_2$, crystallising in steel-blue needles, mp. 145°C. Anderson first hydrolysed piperine by alkalis into a base and an acid, which were later named piperidine and piperic acid respectively. The alkaloid was synthesised by the action of piperoyl chloride on piperidine.

### Preparation

Piperine is commercially available. If desired, it may be extracted from black pepper using dichloromethane. The amount of piperine varies from 1-2% in long pepper, to 5-9% in the white and the black peppers of commerce. Further, it may be prepared by treating the solvent-free residue from an alcoholic extract of black pepper, with a solution of sodium hydroxide to remove resin (said to contain chavicine, an isomer of piperine) and solution of the washed, insoluble residue in warm alcohol, from which the alkaloid crystallises on cooling.

## Biological Activity

The pungency caused by capsaicin and piperine is caused by activation of the heat and acidity sensing TRPV ion channel TRPV1 on nociceptors (pain sensing nerve cells).

Piperine has also been found to inhibit human CYP3A4 and P-glycoprotein, enzymes important for the metabolism and transport of xenobiotics and metabolites. In animal studies, piperine also inhibited other enzymes important in drug metabolism. By inhibiting drug metabolism, piperine may increase the bioavailability of various compounds. Notably, piperine may enhance bioavailability of curcumin by 2000% in humans.

In February 2008, researchers discovered that piperine can stimulate pigmentation in the skin, together with the exposure to UVB light.

Due to its effects on drug metabolism, piperine should be taken cautiously (if at all) by individuals taking some other medications.

Piperine was discovered by Hans Christian Ørsted in 1819, he isolated it from the fruits of Piper nigrum, the source plant of both the black and white pepper grains. Piper longum and Piper officinarum (Miq.) C. DC. (=Piper retrofractum Vahl), two species called "long pepper" also found containing it by Flückiger and Hanbury. West African Pepper also contains it.

## BERBERINE

Berberine is a quaternary ammonium salt from the group of isoquinoline alkaloids. It is found in such plants as *Berberis*, goldenseal (*Hydrastis canadensis*), and *Coptis chinensis*, usually in the roots, rhizomes, stems, and bark. Berberine is strongly yellow colored, which is why in earlier times berberis species were used to dye wool, leather and wood. Wool is still today dyed with berberine in Northern India. Under ultraviolet light, berberine shows a strong yellow fluorescence. Because of this it is used in histology for staining heparin in mast cells. As a natural dye berberin has a Colour Index (CI) of 75160.

## Traditional Use

As a traditional medicine or dietary supplement, berberine has showed some activity against fungal infections, *Candida albicans,* yeast, parasites, and bacterial/viral infections. Berberine seems to exert synergistic effects with fluconazole even in drug-resistant Candida albicans infections. Some research has been undertaken into possible use against MRSA infection.

Berberine is considered an ineffective antibiotic. However, when applied in vitro and in combination with methoxyhydnocarpin, an inhibitor of multidrug resistance pumps, berberine inhibits growth of *Staphylococcus aureus.*

Berberine is a component of some eye drop formulations. There is some evidence that it is useful in the treatment of trachoma, and it has been a standard treatment for leishmaniasis.

Berberine prevents and supresses proinflammatory cytokines, E-selectin, and genes, and increases adiponectin expression which partly explains its versatile health effects. Berberine is a nucleic acid-binding isoquinolone alkaloid with wide potential therapeutic properties.

## Biosynthesis

The alkaloid berberine has a tetracyclic skeleton that is derived from a benzyltetrahydroisoquinoline system with the incorporation of an extra carbon atom provided by S-Adenosyl methionine (SAM) via an N-methyl group. Formation of the berberine bridge is readily rationalized as an oxidative process in which the N-methyl group is oxidized to an iminium ion, and a cyclization to the aromatic ring occurs by virtue of the phenolic group.

It is known that the immediate precursor of protoberberine alkaloids in plants is (S)-reticuline. Berberine is an alkaloid derived from tyrosine. L-DOPA and 4-hydroxypyruvic acid both come from L-Tyr.

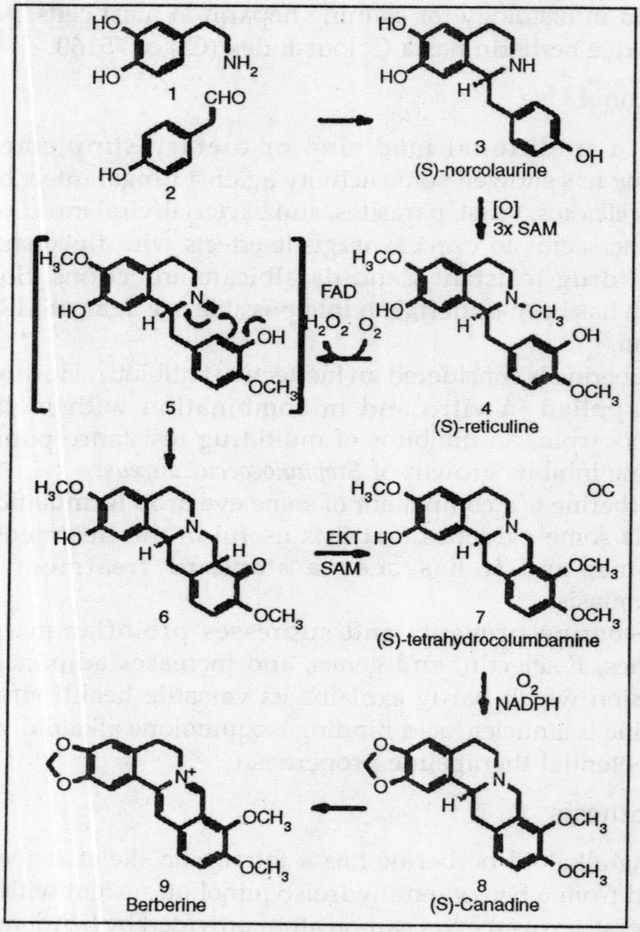


**Fig.** Biosynthesis of Berberine

Although two tyrosine molecules are used in the biosynthetic pathway, only the phenylethylamine fragment of the tetrahydroisoquinoline ring system is formed via DOPA, the remaining carbon atoms come from tyrosine via 4-hydroxyphenylacetaldehyde. L-DOPA loses carbon dioxide to form dopamine 1. Likewise, 4-hydroxypyruvic acid also loses carbon dioxide to form 4-hydroxyphenyl-acetaldehyde 2. Dopamine 1 then reacts with 4-hydroxy-phenylacetaldehyde

2 to form (S)-norcolaurine 3 in a reaction similar to the Mannich reaction. After oxidation and methylation by SAM, (S)-reticuline 4 is formed. (S)-reticuline serves as a pivotal intermediate to other alkaloids. Oxidation of the tertiary amine then occurs and an iminium ion is formed 5. In a Mannich-like reaction the ortho position to the phenol is nucleophilic, and electrons are pushed to form 6. Product 6 then undergoes keto-enol tautomerism to form (S)-scoulerine which is then methylated by SAM to form (S)-tetrahydrocolumbamine 7. Product 7 is then oxidized to form the methylenedioxy ring from the ortho-methoxyphenol, via an $O_2$-, NADPH- and cytochrome P-450-dependent enzyme. giving (S)-canadine 8. (S)-canadine is then oxidized to give the quaternary isoquinolinium system of berberine. This happens in two separate oxidation steps, both requiring molecular oxygen, with $H_2O_2$ and $H_2O$ produced in the successive processes.

## Diabetes, Dyslipidemias and Cardiovascular Conditions

During the last few decades, many studies have shown that berberine has various beneficial effects on the cardiovascular system and significant anti-inflammatory activities. Berberine exerts up-regulating activity on both low-density-lipoprotein receptor (LDLR) and insulin receptor (InsR). This one-drug-multiple-target characteristic might be suitable for the treatment of metabolic syndrome. Berberine has been tested and used successfully in experimental and human diabetes mellitus. Berberine has been shown to lower elevated blood glucose as effectively as metformin.

The mechanisms include inhibition of aldose reductase, inducing glycolysis, preventing insulin resistance through increasing insulin receptor expression and acting like incretins. A new study suggest that berberine may overcome insulin resistance via modulating key molecules in insulin signaling pathway, leading to increased glucose uptake in insulin resistant cells. Berberine inhibits Foxo1, which integrates insulin signaling with mitochondrial function. Inhibition of Foxo1 can improve hepatic metabolism during insulin resistance and the metabolic syndrome. Berberine might exert its insulinotropic effect in isolated rat islets by up-regulating the expression of hepatocyte nuclear factor 4 alpha, which probably acts solely or together with other HNFs to modulate glucokinase activity, rendering ? cell more sensitive to glucose fluctuation and response more effectively to glucose challenge.

Berberine seems to inhibit human dipeptidyl peptidase-4 (DPP IV) as well as the pro-diabetic target human protein tyrosine phosphatase 1B (h-PTP 1B), which explain at least some of its anti-hyperglycemic activities. Berberine suppresses intestinal disaccharidases with beneficial metabolic effects in diabetic states.

A recent comprehensive metabonomics method, applied to 60 type 2 diabetics, suggests that administration of berberine down-regulates the high level of free fatty acids which are known to be toxic to the pancreas and cause insulin resistance. These results suggest that berberine might play a pivotal role in the treatment of type 2 diabetes, conclude the authors.

Berberine has been shown to boost the effects of metformin and 2,4-thiazoiodinedione (THZ) and can partly replace the commercial drugs, which could lead to a reduction in toxicity and side effects of the latter.

Berberine lowers elevated blood total cholesterol, LDL cholesterol, triglycerides and aterogenic apolipoproteins (apo B) (Apo B), but the mechanism of action is distinct from statins. Berberine reduces LDL cholesterol by upregulating LDLR mRNA expression posttranscriptionally while downregulating the transcription of proprotein convertase subtilisin/kexin type 9 (PCSK9), a natural inhibitor of LDL receptor (LDLR), and increasing in the liver the expression of LDL receptors through extracellular signal-regulated kinase (ERK) signaling pathway, while statins inhibit cholesterol synthesis in the liver by blocking HMG-CoA-reduktase. This explains why berberine does not cause side effects typical to statins. Berberine and plant stanols synergistically inhibit cholesterol absorption in hamsters. Berberin seems to improve the arterial endothelial function in humans. Berberine activates AMP-activated protein kinase (AMPK), specifically extracellular signal-regulated kinases (ERK), which plays a central role in glucose and lipid metabolism, suppresses proinflammatory cystokines, and reduces MMP-9 and EMMPRIN expression, which are all beneficial changes for heart health. Morevover, berberine reduces hepatic fat content in the rats of non-alcoholic fatty liver disease (NAFLD). Berberine also prevents proliferation of hepatic stellate cells (HSCs), which are central for the development of fibrosis during liver injury.

Experimental and clinical studies suggest that berberine may be useful for patients with severe congestive heart failure.

According to a Chinese report, combined use of berberine with ciclosporin A (CsA) could markedly increase the blood concentration of CsA in heart transplanted recipients and reduce the dosage of CsA required, save the cost for medical service, and shows no obvious adverse reaction.

## Cancer

Berberine has drawn extensive attention towards its antineoplastic effects. It seems to suppress the growth of a wide variety of tumor cells including breast cancer, leukemia, melanoma, epidermoid carcinoma, hepatoma, oral carcinoma, tongue carcinoma, glioblastoma, prostate carcinoma, gastric carcinoma.

Animal studies have shown that berberine can suppress chemical-induced carcinogenesis, tumor promotion, tumor invasion, prostate cancer, neuroblastoma, and leukemia. It is a radiosensitizer of tumor cells but not of normal cells.

How berberine mediates these effects is not fully understood, but its ability to inhibit angiogenesis and to modulate Mcl-1, Bcl-xL, cyclooxygenase (COX)-2, MDR, tumor necrosis factor (TNF)- and IL-6, iNOS, IL-12, intercellular adhesion molecule-1 and ELAM-1 expression, MCP-1 and CINC-1, cyclin D1, activator protein (AP-1), HIF-1, PPAR-, and topoisomerase II has been shown.

By using yeast mutants, berberine was found to bind and inhibit stress-induced mitogen-activated protein kinase kinase activation. Because apoptotic, carcinogenic, and inflammatory effects and various gene products (such as TNF-, IL-6, COX-2, adhesion molecules, cyclin D1, and MDR) modulated by berberine are regulated by the transcription factor nuclear factor- B (NF- B), it is postulated that this pathway plays a major role in the action of berberine. Berberine suppressed NF-kappaB activation induced by various inflammatory agents and carcinogens.

This alkaloid also suppressed constitutive NF-kappaB activation found in certain tumor cells. It seems to protect against side effects of radiation therapy in lung cancer. Berberine, 300 mg three times a day orally, also seems to inhibit complication of abdominal or pelvic radiation, called radiation-induced acute intestinal symptoms (RIAISs). The studies suggest that its use in clinical development may be more as a cytostatic agent than a cytotoxic compound.

## Mental Health

Berberine seems to act as an herbal antidepressant and a neuroprotector against neurodegenerative disorders. Berberine inhibits prolyl oligopeptidase (POP) in a dose-dependent manner.

Berberine is also known to bind sigma receptors like many synthetic antidepressant drugs. As berberine is a natural compound that has been safely administered to humans, preliminary results suggest the initiation of clinical trials in patients with depression, bipolar affective disorder, schizophrenia, or related diseases in which cognitive capabilities are affected, with either the extract or pure berberine. New experimental results suggest that berberine may have a potential of inhibition and prevention of Alzheimer's disease (AD) mainly through both cholinesterase (ChEs)inhibitory and beta-amyloids pathways, and additionally through antioxidant capacities.

## Intestinal Disorders

Berberine can ameliorate pro-inflammatory cytokines induced intestinal epithelia tight junction damage *in vitro*, and berberine may be one of the targeted therapeutic agents that can restore barrier function in intestinal disease states.

## HIV

A new study identified a key cellular mechanism underlying the protective effect of berberine on HIV PI-induced inflammatory response in macrophages. Modulation of the Endoplasmic reticulum (ER) stress response represents a potential therapeutic target for various inflammatory diseases and metabolic syndrome including HIV PI-associated atherosclerosis. The report shows the potential application of berberine as a complimentary therapeutic agent for HIV infection.

## Chapter 4

# Antibiotic

In common usage, an antibiotic is a substance or compound that kills, or inhibits the growth of, bacteria. Antibiotics belong to the broader group of antimicrobial compounds, used to treat infections caused by micro-organisms, including fungi and protozoa.

The term "antibiotic" was coined by Selman Waksman in 1942 to describe any substance produced by a micro-organism that is antagonistic to the growth of other micro-organisms in high dilution.

This original definition excluded naturally occurring substances that kill bacteria but are not produced by microorganisms (such as gastric juice and hydrogen peroxide) and also excluded synthetic antibacterial compounds such as the sulfonamides.

Many antibiotics are relatively small molecules with a molecular weight less than 2000 Da. With advances in medicinal chemistry, most antibiotics are now semisynthetic—modified chemically from original compounds found in nature, as is the case with beta-lactams (which include the penicillins, produced by fungi in the genus *Penicillium*, the cephalosporins, and the carbapenems).

Some antibiotics are still produced and isolated from living organisms, such as the aminoglycosides, and others have been created through purely synthetic means: the sulfonamides, the quinolones, and the oxazolidinones.

In addition to this origin-based classification into natural, semisynthetic, and synthetic, antibiotics may be divided into two broad groups according to their effect on microorganisms:

those that kill bacteria are bactericidal agents, while those that only impair bacterial growth are known as bacteriostatic agents.

## HISTORY OF ANTIBIOTICS

Many cures for infectious diseases prior to the beginning of the twentieth century were based on medicinal folklore. Cures for infection in ancient Chinese medicine using plants with antibiotic-like properties began to be described over 2,500 years ago. Many other ancient cultures, including the ancient Egyptians, ancient Greeks and medieval Arabs already used molds and plants to treat infections. Cinchona bark was a widely effective treatment of malaria in the 17th century, the disease caused by protozoan parasites of the genus *Plasmodium*.

Scientific endeavours to understand the science behind what caused these diseases, the development of synthetic antibiotic chemotherapy, the isolation of the natural antibiotics marked milestones in antibiotic development

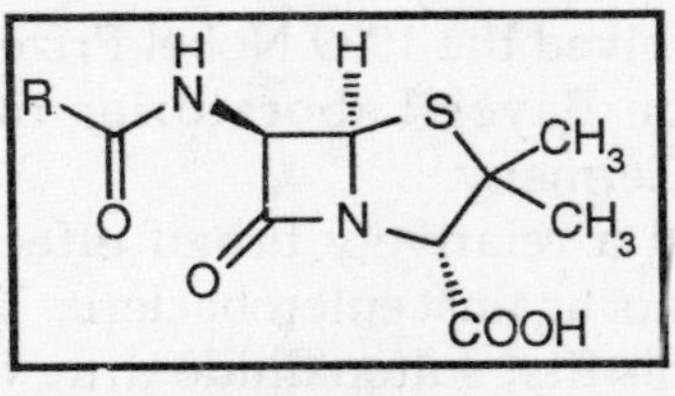


**Fig.** Penicillin, the First Natural Antibiotic Discovered by Alexander Fleming in 1928.

Originally known as antiobiosis, antibiotics were drugs that had actions against bacteria. The term antibiosis which means 'against life' was introduced by the French bacteriologist Vuillemin as a descriptive name of the phenomenon exhibited by these drugs.

Antibiosis was first described in 1877 in bacteria when Louis Pasteur and Robert Koch observed that an airborne bacillus could inhibit the growth of *Bacillus anthracis*. These drugs were later renamed antibiotics by Selman Waksman, an American microbiologist in 1942.

Synthetic antibiotic chemotherapy as a science and the

story of antibiotic development began in Germany with Paul Ehrlich, a German medical scientist in the late 1880s.

Dr. Ehrlich noted that certain dyes would bind to and colour human, animal or bacterial cells, while others did not. He then extended the idea that it might be possible to make certain dyes or chemicals that would act as a magic bullet or selective drug that would bind to and kill bacteria while not harming the human host.

After much experimentation, screening hundreds of dyes against various organisms, he discovered a medicinally useful drug, the man-made antibiotic, Salvarsan. However, the adverse side-effect profile of salvarsan, coupled with the later discovery of the antibiotic penicillin, superseded its use as an antibiotic.

The work of Ehrlich, which marked the birth of the antibiotic revolution, was followed by the discovery of Prontosil by Domagk in 1932.

Prontosil, the first commercially available antibacterial antibiotic was developed by a research team led by Gerhard Domagk (who received the 1939 Nobel Prize for Medicine for his efforts) at the Bayer Laboratories of the IG Farben conglomerate in Germany.

Prontosil had a relatively broad effect against Gram-positive cocci but not against enterobacteria. The discovery and development of this first sulfonamide drug opened the era of antibiotics.

The discovery of natural antibiotics produced by microorganisms stemmed from earlier work on the observation of antibiosis between micro-organisms. Pasteur observed that "if we could intervene in the antagonism observed between some bacteria, it would offer 'perhaps the greatest hopes for therapeutics'".

Bacterial antagonism of *Penicillium spp.* were first described in England by John Tyndall in 1875. However, his work went by without much notice from the scientific community until Alexander Fleming's discovery of Penicillin in 1928.

Even then the therapeutic potential of penicillin was not

pursued. More than ten years later, Ernst Chain and Howard Florey became interested in Fleming's work following the earlier discovery of another natural antibiotic like substance named gramicidin from B. brevis.

In 1939, Rene Dubos isolated gramicidin, one of the first commercially manufactured antibiotics in use during World War II to prove highly effective in treating wounds and ulcers.Florey and Chain succeeded in purifying penicillin. The purified antibiotic displayed antibacterial activity against a wide range of bacteria. It also had low toxicity and could be taken without causing adverse effects.

Furthermore its activity was not inhibited by biological constituents such as pus, unlike the synthetic antibiotic class available at the time the sulfonamides. The discovery of such a powerful antibiotic was unprecedented. The development of penicillin led to renewed interest in the search for antibiotic compounds with similar capabilities. Because of their discovery of penicillin Ernst Chain, Howard Florey and Alexander Fleming shared the 1945 Nobel Prize in Medicine. Florey credited Dubos with pioneering the approach of deliberately, systematically searching for antibacterial compounds. Such a methodology had led to the discovery of gramicidin, which revived Florey's research in penicillin.

## ANTIMICROBIAL PHARMACODYNAMICS

The assessment of the activity of an antibiotic is crucial to the successful outcome of antimicrobial therapy. Non-microbiological factors such as host defence mechanisms, the location of an infection, underlying disease as well as the intrinsic pharmacokinetic and pharmacodynamic properties of the antibiotic.

Fundamentally, antibiotics are classified as either having lethal or bactericidal action against bacteria or are bacteriostatic, preventing bacterial growth. The bactericidal activity of antibiotics may be growth phase dependent and in most but not all cases the action of many bactericidal antibiotics requires ongoing cell activity and cell division for the drugs' killing activity.

These classifications are based on laboratory behaviour; in practice, both of these are capable of ending a bacterial infection.

'In vitro' characterisation of the action of antibiotics to evaluate activity measure the minimum inhibitory concentration and minimum bactericidal concentration of an antimicrobial and are excellent indicators of antimicrobial potency.

However, in clinical practice, these measurements alone are insufficient to predict clinical outcome. By combining the pharmacokinetic profile of an antibiotic with the antimicrobial activity, several pharmacological parameters appear to be significant markers of drug efficacy.

The activity of antibiotics may be concentration-dependent and their characteristic antimicrobial activity increases with progressively higher antibiotic concentrations. They may also be time-dependent, where their antimicrobial activity does not increase with increasing antibiotic concentrations; however, it is critical that a minimum inhibitory serum concentration is maintained for a certain length of time.

A laboratory evaluation of the killing kinetics of the antibiotic using kill curves is useful to determine the time- or concentration-dependence of actimicrobial activity.

## Antibiotic classes

Antibiotics are commonly classified based on their mechanism of action, chemical structure or spectrum of activity. Most antibiotics target bacterial functions or growth processes.

Antibiotics which target the bacterial cell wall (penicillins, cephalosporins), or cell membrane (polymixins), or interfere with essential bacterial enzymes (quinolones, sulfonamides) usually are bactericidal in nature. Those which target protein synthesis, such as the aminoglycosides, macrolides and tetracyclines, are usually bacteriostatic.

Further categorization is based on their target specificity: "narrow-spectrum" antibiotics target particular types of bacteria, such as Gram-negative or Gram-positive bacteria, while broad-spectrum antibiotics affect a wide range of bacteria. In the last few years three new classes of antibiotics have been brought into clinical use.

This follows a 40-year hiatus in discovering new classes of antibiotic compounds. These new antibiotics are of the following three classes: cyclic lipopeptides (daptomycin), glycylcyclines (tigecycline), and oxazolidinones (linezolid). Tigecycline is a broad-spectrum antibiotic, while the two others are used for Gram-positive infections. These developments show promise as a means to counteract the bacterial resistance to existing antibiotics.

### *Production*

Since the first pioneering efforts of Florey and Chain in 1939, the importance of antibiotics to medicine has led to much research into discovering and producing them. The process of production usually involves the screening of wide ranges of microorganisms, and their testing and modification. Production is carried out using fermentation, usually in strongly aerobic form.

### *Administration*

Oral antibiotics are simply ingested, while intravenous antibiotics are used in more serious cases, such as deep-seated systemic infections. Antibiotics may also sometimes be administered topically, as with eye drops or ointments.

### *Side Effects*

Although antibiotics are generally considered safe and well tolerated, they have been associated with a wide range of adverse effects. Side effects are many, varied and can be very serious depending on the antibiotics used and the microbial organisms targeted.

The safety profiles of newer medications may not be as well established as those that have been in use for many years. Adverse effects can range from fever and nausea to major allergic reactions including photodermatitis and anaphylaxis.

One of the more common side effects is diarrhea, sometimes caused by the anaerobic bacterium *Clostridium difficile*, which results from the antibiotic disrupting the normal balance of the intestinal flora, Such overgrowth of pathogenic bacteria may be alleviated by ingesting probiotics during a course of antibiotics.

An antibiotic-induced disruption of the population of the bacteria normally present as constituents of the normal vaginal flora may also occur, and may lead to overgrowth of yeast species of the genus *Candida* in the vulvo-vaginal area. Other side effects can result from interaction with other drugs, such as elevated risk of tendon damage from administration of a quinolone antibiotic with a systemic corticosteroid.

**Drug-drug Interactions**

***Contraceptive Pills***

Hypothetically, interference of some antibiotics with the efficiency of birth control pills is thought to occur in two ways. Modification of the intestinal flora may result in reduced absorption of estrogens.

Secondly, induction of hepatic liver enzymes causing them to metabolize the pill's active ingredients faster may affect the pill's usefulness.

However, the majority of studies indicate that antibiotics do not interfere with contraception. Even though a small percentage of women may experience decreased effectiveness of birth control pills while taking an antibiotic, the failure rate is comparable to those taking the pill.

Moreover, there have been no studies that have conclusively demonstrated that disruption of the gut flora affects contraception.

Interaction with the combined oral contraceptive pill through induction of hepatic enzymes by the antifungal medication griseofulvin and the broad-spectrum antibiotic rifampicin has been shown to occur. It is recommended that extra contraceptive measures are applied during antimicrobial therapy using these antimicrobials.

### *Alcohol*

Alcohol can interfere with the activity or metabolization of antibiotics. It may affect the activity of liver enzymes, which break down the antibiotics.

Moreover, certain antibiotics, including metronidazole, tinidazole, cephamandole, ketoconazole, latamoxef, cefoperazone, cefmenoxime, and furazolidone, chemically react with alcohol, leading to serious side effects, which include severe vomiting, nausea, and shortness of breath. Alcohol consumption while taking such antibiotics is therefore not recommended. Additionally, serum levels of doxycycline and erythromycin succinate may, in certain circumstances, be significantly reduced by alcohol consumption.

## CLASSIFICATIONS OF ANTIBIOTIC

Chemical substance that in dilute solutions can inhibit the growth of microorganisms or destroy them with little or no harm to the infected host.

Early antibiotics were natural microbial products, but chemists have modified the structures of many to produce semisynthetic and even wholly synthetic ones. Since the discovery of penicillin (1928), antibiotics have revolutionized the treatment of bacterial, fungal, and some other diseases.

They are produced by many actinomycetes (e.g., streptomycin, tetracycline) and other bacteria (e.g., polypeptides such as bacitracin) and by fungi (e.g., penicillin). Antibiotics may be broad-spectrum (active against a wide range of pathogens) or specific (active against one, or one class). Drawbacks include activity against beneficial microorganisms, often causing diarrhea; allergies; and development of drug-resistant strains of the targeted microorganisms.

Antibiotics may be informally defined as the sub-group of anti-infectives that are derived from bacterial sources and are used to treat bacterial infections. Other classes of drugs, most notably the sulfonamides, may be effective antibacterials. Similarly, some antibiotics may have secondary uses, such as the use of demeclocycline (Declomycin, a tetracycline derivative) to treat the syndrome of inappropriate antidiuretic hormone (SIADH) secretion. Other antibiotics may be useful in treating protozoal infections.

Although there are several classification schemes for antibiotics, based on bacterial spectrum (broad versus narrow) or route of administration (injectable versus oral versus topical), or type of activity (bactericidal vs. bacteriostatic), the most useful is based on chemical structure.

Antibiotics within a structural class will generally show similar patterns of effectiveness, toxicity, and allergic potential.

- *Penicillins*: The penicillins are the oldest class of antibiotics, and have a common chemical structure which they share with the cephalopsorins. The two groups are classed as the beta-lactam antibiotics, and are generally bacteriocidal—that is, they kill bacteria rather than inhibiting growth. The penicillins can be further subdivided. The natural pencillins are based on the original penicillin G structure; penicillinase-resistant penicillins, notably methicillin and oxacillin, are active even in the presence of the bacterial enzyme that inactivates most natural penicillins. Aminopenicillins such as ampicillin and amoxicillin have an extended spectrum of action compared with the natural penicillins; extended spectrum penicillins are effective against a wider range of bacteria. These generally include coverage for *Pseudomonas aeruginaosa* and may provide the penicillin in combination with a penicillinase inhibitor.
- *Cephalosporins*: Cephalosporins and the closely related cephamycins and carbapenems, like the pencillins, contain a beta-lactam chemical structure. Consequently, there are patterns of cross-resistance and cross-allergenicity among the drugs in these classes. The "cepha" drugs are among the most diverse classes of antibiotics, and are themselves subgrouped into 1st, 2nd and 3rd generations. Each generation has a broader spectrum of activity than the one before. In addition, cefoxitin, a cephamycin,

is highly active against anaerobic bacteria, which offers utility in treatment of abdominal infections. The 3rd generation drugs, cefotaxime, ceftizoxime, ceftriaxone and others, cross the blood-brain barrier and may be used to treat meningitis and encephalitis. Cephalopsorins are the usually preferred agents for surgical prophylaxis.

- *Fluroquinolones*: The fluroquinolones are synthetic antibacterial agents, and not derived from bacteria. They are included here because they can be readily interchanged with traditional antibiotics. An earlier, related class of antibacterial agents, the quinolones, was not well absorbed, and could be used only to treat urinary tract infections.

  The fluroquinolones, which are based on the older group, are broad-spectrum bacteriocidal drugs that are chemically unrelated to the penicillins or the cephaloprosins. They are well distributed into bone tissue, and so well absorbed that in general they are as effective by the oral route as by intravenous infusion.
- *Tetracyclines*: Tetracyclines got their name because they share a chemical structure that has four rings. They are derived from a species of *Streptomyces* bacteria. Broad-spectrum bacteriostatic agents, the tetracyclines may be effective against a wide variety of microorganisms, including rickettsia and amebic parasites.
- *Macrolides*: The macrolide antibiotics are derived from *Streptomyces* bacteria, and got their name because they all have a macrocyclic lactone chemical structure. Erythromycin, the prototype of this class, has a spectrum and use similar to penicillin. Newer members of the group, azithromycin and clarithyromycin, are particularly useful for their high level of lung penetration. Clarithromycin has been widely used to treat *Helicobacter pylori* infections, the cause of stomach ulcers.

- *Others*: Other classes of antibiotics include the aminoglycosides, which are particularly useful for their effectiveness in treating *Pseudomonas aeruginosa* infections; the lincosamindes, clindamycin and lincomycin, which are highly active against anaerobic pathogens. There are other, individual drugs which may have utility in specific infections.

## RECOMMENDED DOSAGE

Dosage varies with drug, route of administration, pathogen, site of infection, and severity. Additional considerations include renal (kidney) function, age of patient, and other factors. Patients should consult manufac turers' recommendations or ask their doctors.

### Side Effects

All antibiotics cause risk of overgrowth by non-susceptible bacteria. Manufacturers list other major hazards by class; however, the health care provider should review each drug individually to assess the degree of risk.

Generally, breastfeeding is not recommended while taking antibiotics because of risk of alteration to infant's intestinal flora, and risk of masking infection in the infant. Excessive or inappropriate use may promote growth of resistant pathogens.

- *Penicillins*: Hypersensitivity may be common, and cross allergenicity with cephalosporins has been reported. Penicillins are classed as category B during pregnancy.
- *Cephalosporins*: Several cephalosporins and related compounds have been associated with seizures. Cefmetazole, cefoperazone, cefotetan and ceftriaxone may be associated with a fall in prothrombin activity and coagulation abnormalities. Pseudomembranous colitis (inflammation of the colon) has been reported with cephalosporins and other broad spectrum antibiotics. Some drugs in this class may cause renal toxicity. Pregnancy category B.
- *Fluoroquinolones*: Lomefloxacin has been associated

with increased photosensitivity. All drugs in this class have been associated with convulsions. Pregnancy category C.

- *Tetracyclines*: Demeclocycline may cause increased photosensitivity. Minocycline may cause dizziness. hildren under the age of eight should not use tetracyclines, and specifically during periods of tooth development. Oral tetracyclines bind to anions such as calcium and iron. Although doxycycline and minocycline may be taken with meals, patients are advised to take other tetracycline antibiotics on an empty stomach, and not to take the drugs with milk or other calcium-rich foods. Expired tetracycline should never be administered. Pregnancy category D; use during pregnancy may cause alterations in bone development.
- *Macrolides*: Erythromycin may aggravate the weakness of patients with myasthenia gravis. Azithromycin has, rarely, been associated with allergic reactions, including angioedema, anaphylaxis, and dermatologic reactions, including Stevens-Johnson syndrome and toxic epidermal necrolysis. Oral erythromycin may be highly irritating to the stomach and may cause severe phlebitis (inflammation of the vein) when given by injection. These drugs should be used with caution in patients with liver dysfunction. Pregnancy category B: Azithromycin, erythromycin. Pregnancy category C: Clarithromycin, dirithromycin, troleandomycin.
- *Aminoglycosides*: This class of drugs causes kidney and hearing problems. These problems can occur even with normal doses. Dosing should be based on renal function, with periodic testing of both kidney function and hearing. Pregnancy category D.

### Interactions

Use of all antibiotics may temporarily reduce the

effectiveness of birth control pills; alternative birth control methods should be used while taking these medications. Antacids should be avoided while on tetracyclines as the calcium can impair absorption of this antibiotic class.

For this reason, tetracyclines should not be taken just before or after consuming foods rich in calcium or iron. Consult specialized references for additional interactions to specific antibiotics.

### *Recommended Usage*

To minimize risk of adverse reactions and development of resistant strains of bacteria, antibiotics should be restricted to use in cases where there is either known or a reasonable presumption of bacterial infection. The use of antibiotics in viral infections is to be avoided. Avoid use of fluroquinolones for trivial infections. In severe infections, presumptive therapy with a broad-spectrum antibiotic such as a third generation cephalosporin may be appropriate. Treatment should be changed to a narrow spectrum agent as soon as the pathogen has been identified. After 48 hours of treatment, if there is clinical improvement, an oral antibiotic should be considered.

When the pathogen is known or suspected to be *Pseudomonas*, a suitable beta-lactam drug is often prescribed in combination with an aminoglycoside. A single agent cannot be relied upon for treatment of *Pseudomonas*. When the patient has renal insufficiency, azactam should be considered in place of the aminoglycoside. In treatment of children with antibiotic suspensions, caregivers should be instructed in use of oral syringes or measuring teaspoons. Household teaspoons are not standardized and will give unreliable doses.

## ONCOLOGY ANTIBIOTICS

Antibiotics are drugs that are used to treat infections caused by bacteria and other organisms, including protozoa, parasites, and fungi.

### Purpose

Many treatments for cancer destroy disease-fighting white

blood cells, thereby reducing the body's ability to fight infection.

For example, bladder, pulmonary, and urinary tract infections may occur with chemotherapy. Single-celled organisms called protozoa are rarely a problem for healthy individuals.

However, they can cause serious infections in individuals with low white blood cell counts. Because of the dangers that infections present for cancer patients, antibiotic treatment often is initiated before the exact nature of the infection has been determined; instead, the choice of antibiotic may depend on the site of the infection and the organism that is likely to be the cause. Often, an antibiotic that kills a broad spectrum of bacteria is chosen and several antibiotics may be used together.

*The common antibiotics that are used during cancer treatment include*:

- *Atovaquone (Mapren)*: antiprotozoal drug used to prevent and treat a very serious type of pneumonia called *Pneumocystis carinii* pneumonia (PCP), in individuals who experience serious side effects with SMZ-TMP (Sulfamethoxazole/Trimethoprim, brand name Bactrim).
- *Aztreonam (Azactam)*: monobactam antibiotic used to treat gram-negative bacterial infections of the urinary and lower respiratory tracts and the female organs, and infections that are present throughout the body (systemic infections or septicemia).
- Cefepime (Maxipime), ceftazidime (Ceptaz, Fortaz, Tazicef, Tazidime), and ceftriaxone sodium (Rocephin): members of a group of antibiotics called cephalosporins used to treat bacterial infections of the urinary and lower respiratory tracts, and infections of the skin, bones, joints, pelvis, and abdomen.
- *Ciprofloxacin (Cipro)*: fluoroquinolone antibiotic used to treat certain gram-negative and gram-positive bacteria and some mycobacteria.
- *Clindamycin phosphate (Cleocin)*: used to treat gram-

positive and gram-negative bacterial infections and, in individuals who are allergic to sulfadiazine, toxoplasmosis caused by a parasitic protozoa.

- Gentamicin (gentamycin) sulfate (generic name product, Garamycin, G-Mycin, Jenamicin): aminoglycoside antibiotic used to treat serious infections by many gram-negative bacteria that cannot be treated with other medicines.
- Metronidazole hydrochloride (Flagyl, Metric 21, Metro I.V., Protostat): used for anaerobic bacteria and protozoa.
- Pentamidine (generic name product, Pentam 300): used to treat PCP if serious side effects develop with SMZ-TMP.
- *Pyrimethamine (Daraprim)*: antiprotozoal medicine used together with sulfadiazine to treat toxoplasmosis; or in combination with other medicines for treating mild to moderate PCP, in individuals who cannot tolerate the standard treatment.
- *Sulfadiazine (generic name product)*: sulfonamide antibiotic used with pyrimethamine to treat toxoplasmosis.
- *Sulfamethoxazole*: Trimethoprim (SMZ-TMP) (generic name product, Bactrim, Cofatrim Forte, Cotrim, Septra, Sulfatrim): the sulfonamide antibiotic, sulfamethoxazole, used in combination with trimethoprim, to prevent and treat PCP and bacterial infections, such as bronchitis and middle ear and urinary tract infections.
- Trimethoprim (generic name product, Proloprim, Trimpex): primarily used to prevent or treat urinary tract infections.
- Vancomycin hydrochloride (generic name product, Vancocin): glycopeptide antibiotic used to treat a variety of serious gram-positive bacterial infections for which other medicines are ineffective, including strains of *Staphylococcus* that are resistant to most oral antibiotics.

Most of these antibiotics kill bacteria by preventing them from making protein for their cell walls. Ciprofloxacin and metronidazole prevent bacteria from reproducing by interfering with their ability to make new DNA. All of these drugs are approved for prescription by the U.S. Food and Drug Administration.

### *Recommended Dosage*

Dosages of antibiotics depend on the individual, the infection that is being treated, and the presence of other medical conditions.

For children, the dosage usually is based on body weight and is lower than the adult dosage. To be effective, an entire treatment with antibiotics must be completed, even if the symptoms of infection have disappeared.

Furthermore, it is important to keep the level of antibiotic in the body at a constant level during treatment. Therefore, the drug should be taken on a regular schedule.

If a dose is missed, it should be taken as soon as possible. If it is almost time for the next dose, the missed dose should be skipped. Doubling up doses is generally not recommended.

*Average adult dosages of common antibiotics for cancer patients are as follows*:

- *Atovaquone*: For PCP treatment, 750 mg oral suspension twice a day, or tablets three times per day, for 21 days; for PCP prevention, 1,500 mg oral suspension, once a day; must be taken with balanced meals.
- *Aztreonam*: 1–2 gm every 6–12 hours, injected into a vein, over a 20–60 minute-period.
- *Cefepime*: 500 mg to 2 gm, injected into a vein or muscle, every 8–12 hours for 7–10 days.
- *Ceftazidime*: 250 mg to 2 gm, injected into a vein or muscle, every 8–12 hours.
- *Ceftriaxone*: 1–2 gm, injected into a vein or muscle, every 24 hours.
- *Ciprofloxacin*: 500–750 mg of the tablet or suspension, every 12 hours, for 3–28 days, taken two hours after

meals with 8 oz of water; bone and joint infections usually are treated for at least 4–6 weeks; 200–400 mg injected every 8–12 hours.

- *Clindamycin*: 150–300 mg of capsule or solution, every six hours; 300–600 mg every six to eight hours or 900 mg every eight hours, injected into a vein or muscle.
- *Gentamicin*: Dosage determined by body weight, every 8–24 hours for at least 7–10 days, injected into a vein or muscle.
- *Metronidazole*: For bacterial infections, 7.5 mg per kg (3.4 mg per lb) of body weight up to a maximum of 1 gm, every six hours for at least seven days (capsules or tablets); 15 mg per kg (6.8 mg per lb) for the first dose, followed by half that dosage every six hours for at least seven days (injected into a vein); for protozoal infections caused by amebas, 500–750 mg of oral medicine, three times per day for 5–10 days; for trichomoniasis, 2 gm for one day or 250 mg three times per day for seven days (oral medicine); extended-release tablets for vaginal bacterial infections, 750 mg once a day for seven days.
- *Pentamidine*: For treating PCP, 4 mg per kg (1.8 mg per lb) of body weight, once per day for 14–21 days, injected into a vein over one to two hours, while lying down.
- *Pyrimethamine*: For toxoplasmosis, 25–200 mg tablets, taken with other medicine, for several weeks.
- *Sulfadiazine*: For bacterial and protozoal infections, 2–4 gm for the first dose, followed by 1 gm every four to six hours (tablets).
- *SMZ-TMP*: 800 mg of sulfamethoxazole and 160 mg of trimethoprim, (tablet or oral suspension), every 12 hours for bacterial infections and every 24 hours for prevention of PCP; dosage based on body weight for PCP treatment; injections based on body weight, every six, eight or 12 hours for bacterial infections and every six hours for PCP treatment.

- *Trimethoprim*: 100 mg tablet every 12 hours for 10 days; for prevention of urinary tract infections, once a day for a long period.
- *Vancomycin*: 7.5 mg per kg (3.4 mg per lb) of body weight, or 500 mg–1 gram, injected or taken orally, every 6–12 hours.

## Precautions

*Stomach or intestinal problems or colitis (inflammation of the colon) may affect the use of*:

- Atovaquone
- Cephalosporins
- Clindamycin

*Kidney or liver disease may affect the use of*:

- Aztreonam
- Cefepime
- Ceftazidime
- Ciprofloxacin
- Clindamycin
- Gentamicin
- Metronidazole
- Pentamidine
- Pyrimethamine
- Sulfadiazine
- SMZ-TMP
- Trimethoprim
- Vancomycin

*Central nervous system or seizure disorders may affect the use of*:

- Ciprofloxacin
- Metronidazole
- Pyrimethamine

*Anemia (low red blood cell count) or other blood disorders may affect the use of*:

- Metronidazole
- Pentamidine
- Pyrimethamine
- Sulfadiazine
- SMZ-TMP

- Trimethoprim

Ciprofloxacin may not be suitable for individuals with tendinitis or with skin sensitivities to sunlight. Gentamicin may not be suitable for people with hearing problems, myasthenia gravis, or Parkinson's disease.

Metronidazole may not be suitable for individuals with heart disease, oral or vaginal yeast infections, or a history of alcoholism. Pentamidine may not be suitable for individuals with heart disease, bleeding disorders, or low blood pressure. Pentamidine may affect blood sugar levels, making control of diabetes mellitus or hypoglycemia (low blood sugar) difficult. Vancomycin may not be appropriate for individuals with hearing problems.

Many antibiotics should not be taken during pregnancy or while breast-feeding. Older individuals may be more susceptible to the side effects of sulfadiazine, SMZ-TMP, or trimethoprim.

**Side Effects**

Some individuals may have allergic reactions to antibiotics. If symptoms of an allergic reaction (such as rash, shortness of breath, swelling of the face and neck), severe diarrhea, or abdominal cramping occur, the antibiotic should be stopped and the individual should seek medical advice.

Because antibiotics can affect bacteria that are beneficial, as well as those that are harmful, women may become susceptible to infections by fungi when taking antibiotics. Vaginal itching or discharge may be symptoms of such infections. All patients may develop oral fungal infections of the mouth, indicated by white plaques in the mouth.

Injected antibiotics may result in irritation, pain, tenderness, or swelling in the vein used for injection. Antibiotics used in cancer patients may have numerous side effects, both minor and severe; however, most side effects are uncommon or rare.

The more common side effects of atovaquone, aztreonam, cephalosporins, ciprofloxacin, clindamycin, gentamicin, metronidazole, and SMZ-TMP include:

- Nausea and vomiting
- Diarrhea
- Loss of appetite Eating active cultured yogurt may help counte.act diarrhea, but if a patient has low white blood cells, this remedy is not recommended. For mild diarrhea with cephalosporins, only diarrhea medicines containing kaolin or attapulgite should be taken. With clindamycin, diarrhea medicines containing attapulgite should be taken several hours before or after the oral antibiotic. Diarrhea following antibiotics like clindamycin may indicate a bacterial infection that needs additional therapy, and a physicians hould be consulted.

*Other side effects of atovaquone may include*:

- Fever
- Skin rash
- Cough
- Headache
- Insomnia

*Other side effects of ciprofloxacin may include*:

- Abdominal pain
- Increase in blood tests for kidney function
- Dizziness or light-headedness
- Inflammation or tearing of a tendon
- Drowsiness
- Insomnia

Other common side effects of clindamycin include abdominal pain and fever. Side effects may occur up to several weeks after treatment with this medicine. Gentamicin and vancomycin may cause serious side effects, particularly in elderly individuals and newborn infants. These include kidney damage and damage to the auditory nerve that controls hearing.

*Other, more common side effects of gentamicin may include*:

- Changes in urination
- Increased thirst
- Muscle twitching or seizures
- Headache

- Lethargy

*When gentamicin is injected into a muscle, vein, or the spinal fluid, the following side effects may occur*:

- Leg cramps
- Skin rash
- Fever
- Seizures Side effects from gentamicin may develop up to several weeks after the medicine is stopped.

*More common side effects of metronidazole include*:

- Mouth dryness
- Unpleasant or metallic taste
- Dizziness or light-headedness
- Headache
- Stomach pain Sugarless candy or gum, bits of ice, or a saliva substitute may relieve symptoms of dry mouth.

Pentamidine, pyrimethamine, sulfonamides, SMZTMP, and trimethoprim can lower the number of white blood cells, resulting in an increased risk of infection. These drugs also can lower the number of blood platelets that are important for blood clotting. Thus, there is an increased risk of bleeding or bruising while taking these drugs.

*Serious side effects of pentamidine may include*:

- Heart problems
- Low blood pressure
- High or low blood sugar
- Other blood problems
- Decrease in urination
- Sore throat and fever
- Sharp pain in upper abdomen Some of these symptoms may not occur until several months after treatment with pentamidine.

Pyrimethamine and trimethoprim may lower the red blood cell count, causing anemia. Leucovorin or the vitamin folic acid may be prescribed for anemia.

Some individuals become more sensitive to sunlight when taking sulfonamides, SMZ-TMP, or trimethoprim. Other common side effects of sulfonamides and SMZTMP include:

- Dizziness
- Itching
- Skin rash
- Headache
- Mouth sores or swelling of the tongue
- Fatigue

If vancomycin is injected into a vein too quickly, it can cause flushing and a rash over the neck, face, and chest, wheezing or difficulty breathing, and a dangerous decrease in blood pressure.

### *Interactions*

Many prescription and non-prescription medicines can interact with these antibiotics. Therefore, it is important to consult a complete list of known drug interactions.

*Among the more common or dangerous interactions*:

- Antibiotics that lower the number of blood platelets, with blood thinners (anticoagulants), such as warfarin
- Aztreonam and metronidazole with alcohol; it is important nct to consume alcohol until at least three days after treatment with these antibiotics
- Ciprofloxacin with antacids, iron supplements, or caffeine
- Pentamidine or pyrimethamine with previous treatments with x rays or cancer medicines (increased risk of blood cell damage)
- Trimethoprim with diuretics to remove excess fluid in the elderly

Many medicines can increase the risk of hearing or kidney damage from gentamicin.

*These include*:

- Cisplatin
- Combination pain medicine with acetaminophen and aspirin oı other salicylates (taken regularly in large amounts)
- Cyclosporine
- Inflammation or pain medicine, except narcotics
- Lithium

- Methotrexate
- Other medicines for infection

## MANUFACTURE OF ANTIBIOTIC

Antibiotics are chemical substances that can inhibit the growth of, and even destroy, harmful microorganisms. They are derived from special microorganisms or other living systems, and are produced on an industrial scale using a fermentation process.

Although the principles of antibiotic action were not discovered until the twentieth century, the first known use of antibiotics was by the Chinese over 2,500 years ago. Today, over 10,000 antibiotic substances have been reported. Currently, antibiotics represent a multibillion dollar industry that continues to grow each year.

Antibiotics are used in many forms-each of which imposes somewhat different manufacturing requirements. For bacterial infections on the skin surface, eye, or ear, an antibiotic may be applied as an ointment or cream. If the infection is internal, the antibiotic can be swallowed or injected directly into the body. In these cases, the antibiotic is delivered throughout the body by absorption into the bloodstream.

Antibiotics differ chemically so it is under-standable that they also differ in the types of infections they cure and the ways in which they cure them. Certain antibiotics destroy bacteria by affecting the structure of their cells. This can occur in one of two ways.

First, the antibiotic can weaken the cell walls of the infectious bacteria, which causes them to burst. Second, antibiotics can cause the contents of the bacterial cells to leak out by damaging the cell membranes. Another way in which antibiotics function is by interfering with the bacteria's metabolism. Some antibiotics such as tetracycline and erythromycin interfere with protein synthesis. Antibiotics like rifampin inhibit nucleic acid biosynthesis. Still other antibiotics, such as sulfonamide or trimethoprim have a general blocking effect on cell metabolism.

The commercial development of an antibiotic is a long and

costly proposal. It begins with basic research designed to identify organisms, which produce antibiotic compounds. During this phase, thousands of species are screened for any sign of antibacterial action.

When one is found, the species is tested against a variety of known infectious bacteria. If the results are promising, the organism is grown on a large scale so the compound responsible for the antibiotic effect can be isolated.

This is a complex procedure because thousands of antibiotic materials have already been discovered. Often, scientists find that their new antibiotics are not unique. If the material passes this phase, further testing can be done.

This typically involves clinical testing to prove that the antibiotic works in animals and humans and is not harmful. If these tests are passed, the Food and Drug Administration (FDA) must then approve the antibiotic as a new drug. This whole process can take many years.

The large-scale production of an antibiotic depends on a fermentation process. During fermentation, large amounts of the antibiotic-producing organism are grown. During fermentation, the organisms produce the antibiotic material, which can then be isolated for use as a drug.

For a new antibiotic to be economically feasible, manufacturers must be able to get a high yield of drug from the fermentation process, and be able to easily isolate it. Extensive research is usually required before a new antibiotic can be commercially scaled up.

### *History*

While our scientific knowledge of antibiotics has only recently been developed, the practical application of antibiotics has existed for centuries. The first known use was by the Chinese about 2,500 years ago. During this time, they discovered that applying the moldy curd of soybeans to infections had certain therapeutic benefits. It was so effective that it became a standard treatment.

Evidence suggests that other cultures used antibiotic-type substances as therapeutic agents. The Sudanese-Nubian civilization used a type of tetracycline antibiotic as early as 350 A.D.

In Europe during the Middle Ages, crude plant extracts and cheese curds were also used to fight infection. Although these cultures used antibiotics, the general principles of antibiotic action were not understood until the twentieth century.

The development of modern antibiotics depended on a few key individuals who demonstrated to the world that materials derived from microorganisms could be used to cure infectious diseases. One of the first pioneers in this field was Louis Pasteur. In 1877, he and an associate discovered that the growth of disease-causing anthrax bacteria could be inhibited by a saprophytic bacteria.

They showed that large amounts of anthrax bacilli could be given to animals with no adverse affects as long as the saprophytic bacilli were also given. Over the next few years, other observations supported the fact that some bacterially derived materials could prevent the growth of disease-causing bacteria.

In 1928, Alexander Fleming made one of the most important contributions to the field of antibiotics. In an experiment, he found that a strain of green *Penicillium* mold inhibited the growth of bacteria on an agar plate. This led to the development of the first modern era antibiotic, penicillin. A few years later in 1932, a paper was published which suggested a method for treating infected wounds using a penicillin preparation. Although these early samples of penicillin were functional, they were not reliable and further refinements were needed. These improvements came in the early 1940s when Howard Florey and associates discovered a new strain of *Penicillium,* which produced high yields of penicillin. This allowed large-scale production of penicillin, which helped launch the modern antibiotics industry.

After the discovery of penicillin, other antibiotics were sought. In 1939, work began on the isolation of potential antibiotic products from the soil bacteria streptomyces. It was around this time that the term antibiotic was introduced.

Selman Waxman and associates discovered streptomycin in 1944.

Subsequent studies resulted in the discovery of a host of new, different antibiotics including actinomycin, streptothricin, and neomycin all produced by *Streptomyces*. Other antibiotics that have been discovered since include bacitracin, polymyxin, viomycin, chloramphenicol and tetracyclines. Since the 1970s, most new antibiotics have been synthetic modifications of naturally occurring antibiotics.

### *Raw Materials*

The compounds that make the fermentation broth are the primary raw materials required for antibiotic production. This broth is an aqueous solution made up of all of the ingredients necessary for the proliferation of the microorganisms. Typically, it contains a carbon source like molasses, or soy meal, both of which are made up of lactose and glucose sugars. These materials are needed as a food source for the organisms. Nitrogen is another necessary compound in the metabolic cycles of the organisms. For this reason, an ammonia salt is typically used. Additionally, trace elements needed for the proper growth of the antibiotic-producing organisms are included.

These are components such as phosphorus, sulfur, magnesium, zinc, iron, and copper introduced through water soluble salts. To prevent foaming during fermentation, anti-foaming agents such as lard oil, octadecanol, and silicones are used.

## THE MANUFACTURING PROCESS

Although most antibiotics occur in nature, they are not normally available in the quantities necessary for large-scale production. For this reason, a fermentation process was developed. It involves isolating a desired microorganism, fueling growth of the culture and refining and isolating the final antibiotic product. It is important that sterile conditions be maintained throughout the manufacturing process, because contamination by foreign microbes will ruin the fermentation.

## Starting the Culture

- Before fermentation can begin, the desired antibiotic-producing organism must be isolated and its numbers must be increased by many times. To do this, a starter culture from a sample of previously isolated, cold-stored organisms is created in the lab. In order to grow the initial culture, a sample of the organism is transferred to an agar-containing plate. The initial culture is then put into shake flasks along with food and other nutrients necessary for growth. This creates a suspension, which can be transferred to seed tanks for further growth.
- The seed tanks are steel tanks designed to provide an ideal environment for growing microorganisms. They are filled with the all the things the specific microorganism would need to survive and thrive, including warm water and carbohydrate foods like lactose or glucose sugars. Additionally, they contain other necessary carbon sources, such as acetic acid, alcohols, or hydrocarbons, and nitrogen sources like ammonia salts. Growth factors like vitamins, amino acids, and minor nutrients round out the composition of the seed tank contents. The seed tanks are equipped with mixers, which keep the growth medium moving, and a pump to deliver sterilized, filtered air. After about 24-28 hours, the material in the seed tanks is transferred to the primary fermentation tanks.

## Fermentation

- The fermentation tank is essentially a larger version of the steel, seed tank, which is able to hold about 30,000 gallons. It is filled with the same growth media found in the seed tank and also provides an environment inducive to growth. Here the microorganisms are allowed to grow and multiply. During this process, they excrete large quantities of the desired antibiotic. The tanks are cooled to keep the temperature between 73-81° F (23-27.2 ° C). It is constantly agitated, and a continuous stream of sterilized air is pumped into it. For this reason, anti-foaming agents are periodically added. Since pH control is vital for optimal growth, acids or bases are added to the tank as necessary.

## Isolation and purification

- After three to five days, the maximum amount of antibiotic will have been produced and the isolation process can begin. Depending on the specific antibiotic produced, the fermentation broth is processed by various purification methods. For example, for antibiotic compounds that are water soluble, an ion-exchange method may be used for purification. In this method, the compound is first separated from the waste organic materials in the broth and then sent through equipment, which separates the other water-soluble compounds from the desired one. To isolate an oil-soluble antibiotic such as penicillin, a solvent extraction method is used. In this method, the broth is treated with organic solvents such as butyl acetate or methyl isobutyl ketone, which can specifically dissolve the antibiotic. The dissolved antibiotic is then recovered using various organic chemical means. At the end of this step, the manufacturer is typically left with a purified powdered form of the antibiotic, which can be further refined into different product types.

## Refining

- Antibiotic products can take on many different forms. They can be sold in solutions for intravenous bags or syringes, in pill or gel capsule form, or they may be sold as powders, which are incorporated into topical ointments. Depending on the final form of the antibiotic, various refining steps may be taken after the initial isolation. For intravenous bags, the crystalline antibiotic can be dissolved in a solution, put in the bag, which is then hermetically sealed. For gel capsules, the powdered antibiotic is physically filled into the bottom half of a capsule then the top half is mechanically put in place. When used in topical ointments, the antibiotic is mixed into the ointment.

- From this point, the antibiotic product is transported to the final packaging stations. Here, the products are stacked and put in boxes. They are loaded up on trucks and transported to various distributors, hospitals, and pharmacies. The entire process of fermentation, recovery, and processing can take anywhere from five to eight days.

## QUALITY CONTROL

Quality control is of utmost importance in the production of antibiotics. Since it involves a fermentation process, steps must be taken to ensure that absolutely no contamination is introduced at any point during production. To this end, the medium and all of the processing equipment are thoroughly steam sterilized. During manufacturing, the quality of all the compounds is checked on a regular basis. Of particular importance are frequent checks of the condition of the microorganism culture during fermentation.

These are accomplished using various chromatography techniques. Also, various physical and chemical properties of the finished product are checked such as pH, melting point, and moisture content. In the United States, antibiotic production is highly regulated by the Food and Drug Administration (FDA). Depending on the application and type of antibiotic, more or less testing must be completed. For example, the FDA requires that for certain antibiotics each batch must be checked by them for effectiveness and purity. Only after they have certified the batch can it be sold for general consumption.

### The Future

Since the development of a new drug is a costly

proposition, pharmaceutical companies have done very little research in the last decade. However, an alarming development has spurred a revived interest in the development of new antibiotics.

It turns out that some of the disease-causing bacteria have mutated and developed a resistance to many of the standard antibiotics. This could have grave consequences on the world's public health unless new antibiotics are discovered or improvements are made on the ones that are available. This challenging problem will be the focus of research for many years to come.

**Antibiotic Resistance**

The emergence of antibiotic resistance is an evolutionary process that is based on selection for organisms that have enhanced ability to survive doses of antibiotics that would have previously been lethal.

Antibiotics like Penicillin and Erythromycin which used to be one-time miracle cures are now less effective because bacteria have become more resistant. Antibiotics themselves act as a selective pressure which allows the growth of resistant bacteria within a population and inhibits susceptible bacteria.

Antibiotic selection of pre-existing antibiotic resistant mutants within bacterial populations was demonstrated in 1943 by the Luria-Delbrück experiment. Survival of bacteria often results from an inheritable resistance.

Any antibiotic resistance may impose a biological cost and the spread of antibiotic resistant bacteria may be hampered by the reduced fitness associated with the resistance which proves disadvantageous for survival of the bacteria when antibiotic is not present. Additional mutations, however, may compensate for this fitness cost and aids the survival of these bacteria.

The underlying molecular mechanisms leading to antibiotic resistance can vary. Intrinsic resistance may naturally occur as a result of the bacteria's genetic makeup. The bacterial chromosome may fail to encode a protein which the antibiotic targets.

Acquired resistance results from a mutation in the bacterial chromosome or the acquisition of extra-chromosomal DNA. Antibiotic-producing bacteria have evolved resistance mechanisms which have been shown to be similar to and may have been transferred to antibiotic resistant strains.

The spread of antibiotic resistance mechanisms occurs through vertical transmission of inherited mutations from previous generations and genetic recombination of DNA by horizontal genetic exchange. Antibiotic resistance is exchanged between different bacteria by plasmids that carry genes which encode antibiotic resistance which may result in co-resistance to multiple antibiotics.

These plasmids can carry different genes with diverse resistance mechanisms to unrelated antibiotics but because they are located on the same plasmid multiple antibiotic resistance to more than one antibiotic is transferred. Alternatively, cross-resistance to other antibiotics within the bacteria results when the same resistance mechanism is responsible for resistance to more than one antibiotic is selected for.

### *Antibiotic Misuse*

Inappropriate antibiotic treatment and overuse of antibiotics have been a contributing factor to the emergence of resistant bacteria. The problem is further exacerbated by self-prescribing of antibiotics by individuals without the guidelines of a qualified clinician and the non-therapeutic use of antibiotics as growth promoters in agriculture.

Antibiotics are frequently prescribed for indications in which their use is not warranted, an incorrect or sub-optimal antibiotic is prescribed or in some cases for infections likely to resolve without treatment.The overuse of antibiotics like penicillin and erythromycin which used to be one-time miracle cures were associated with emerging resistance since the 1950s.

Therapeutic usage of antibiotics in hospitals has been seen to be associated with increases in multi-antibiotic resistant bacteria.

Common forms of antibiotic misuse include excessive use

of prophylactic antibiotics in travelers, failure to take into account the patient's weight and history of prior antibiotic use when prescribing, since both can strongly affect the efficacy of an antibiotic prescription, failure to take the entire prescribed course of the antibiotic, failure to prescribe or take the course of treatment at fairly precise correct daily intervals (e.g."every 8 hours" rather than merely"3x per day"), or failure to rest for sufficient recovery to allow clearance of the infecting organism.

These practices may facilitate the development of bacterial populations with antibiotic resistance. Inappropriate antibiotic treatment is another common form of antibiotic misuse. A common example is the prescription and use of antibiotics to treat viral infections such as the common cold that have no effect.

One study on respiratory tract infections found"physicians were more likely to prescribe antibiotics to patients who they believed expected them, although they correctly identified only about 1 in 4 of those patients". Multifactorial interventions aimed at both physicians and patients can reduce inappropriate prescribing of antibiotics.

Delaying antibiotics for 48 hours while observing for spontaneous resolution of respiratory tract infections may reduce antibiotic usage; however, this strategy may reduce patient satisfaction.

Several organizations concerned with antimicrobial resistance are lobbying to improve the regulatory climate. Approaches to tackling the issues of misuse and overuse of antibiotics by the establishment of the U.S.

Interagency Task Force on Antimicrobial Resistance which aims actively address the problem antimicrobial resistance are being organised and coordinated by the US Centers for Disease Control and Prevention, the Food and Drug Administration (FDA), and the National Institutes of Health (NIH) and also includes several other federal agencies.

An NGO campaign group is Keep Antibiotics Working. In France, an"Antibiotics are not automatic" government campaign starting in 2002 led to a marked reduction of unnecessary antibiotic prescriptions, especially in children.

In the United Kingdom, there are NHS posters in many doctors surgeries indicating that'unfortunately, no amount of antibiotics will get rid of your cold', following on from many patients specifically requesting antibiotics from their doctor inappropriately, believing they will help treat viral infections.

In agriculture, associated antibiotic resistance with the non-therapeutic use of antibiotics as growth promoters in animals resulted in their restricted use in the UK in the 1970.

Currently there is a EU wide ban on the non-therapeutic use of antibiotics as growth promoters. It is estimated that greater than 70% of the antibiotics used in U.S. are given to feed animals (e.g. chickens, pigs and cattle) in the absence of disease.

Antibiotic use in food animal production has been associated with the emergence of antibiotic-resistant strains of bacteria including Salmonella spp., Campylobacter spp.,

Escherichia coli, and Enterococcus spp. Evidence from some US and European studies suggest that these resistant bacteria cause infections in humans that do not respond to commonly prescribed antibiotics. In response to these practices and attendant problems, several organizations (e.g. The American Society for Microbiology (ASM), American Public Health Association (APHA) and the American Medical Association (AMA)) have called for restrictions on antibiotic use in food animal production and an end to all non-therapeutic uses.

However, delays in regulatory and legislative actions to limit the use of antibiotics are common, and may include resistance to these changes by industries using or selling antibiotics, as well as time spent on research to establish causal links between antibiotic use and emergence of untreatable bacterial diseases. Two federal bills (S.742 and H.R. 2562) aimed at phasing out non-therapeutic antibiotics in US food animal production were proposed but not passed. These bills were endorsed by public health and medical organizations including the American Holistic Nurses' Association, the American Medical Association, and the American Public

Health Association (APHA). The EU has banned the use of antibiotics as growth promotional agents since 2003.

### *Resistance Modifying Agents*

One solution to combat resistance currently being researched is the development of pharmaceutical compounds that would revert multiple antibiotic resistance. These so called resistance modifying agents may target and inhibit MDR mechanisms, rendering the bacteria susceptible to antibiotics to which they were previously resistant.

*These compounds targets include among others:*

- Efflux inhibition(Phe-Arg-β-naphthylamide)
- Beta Lactamase inhibitors - Including Clavulanic acid and Sulbactam

## Beyond Antibiotics: Treating Non-bacterial Infections

The comparative ease of identifying compounds which safely cured bacterial infections was more difficult to duplicate in treatments of fungal and viral infections. Antibiotic research led to great strides in the knowledge of biochemistry, establishing large differences between the cellular and molecular physiology of the bacterial cell and that of the mammalian cell. This explained the observation that many compounds that are toxic to bacteria are non-toxic to human cells. In contrast, the basic biochemistries of the fungal cell and the mammalian cell are much more similar. This restricts the development and use of therapeutic compounds that attack a fungal cell, while not harming mammalian cells.

Similar problems exist in antibiotic treatments of viral diseases. Human viral metabolic biochemistry is very closely similar to human biochemistry, and the possible targets of antiviral compounds are restricted to very few components unique to a mammalian virus.

## Beyond Antibiotics: Treating Multi-drug Resistant Bacteria

Multi-drug resistant organisms (MDRO) generally refer

to bacteria that are not affected by the clinical doses of classical antibiotics, particularly the antibiotics which were being used to treat them until recently. The rise of these organisms has created a need for alternative antibacterial therapies.

Phage therapy, the use of particular viruses to attack bacteria, was in use during the 1920s and 1930s on humans in the US, Western and Eastern Europe. Phage are commonly a part of the ecology surrounding bacteria and provide substantial population control of bacteria in the intestine, the ocean, the soil and other environments.

The success of these therapies are largely anecdotal or otherwise poorly controlled. The original publications are also generally inaccessible, even to persons with Russian language fluency. With the discovery of penicillin in the 1940s, Europe and the US changed therapeutic strategies to the use of antibiotics. However, in the former Soviet Union phage therapies continued to be studied.

In the Republic of Georgia, the Eliava Institute of Bacteriophage, Microbiology & Virology continues to research the use of phage therapy. Various companies (Intralytix, among others), universities, and foundations in North America and Europe are currently researching phage therapies.

However, concerns about genetic engineering in freely released viruses currently limit certain aspects of phage therapy. One result is attempts to use phage in ways other than to directly infect the bacteria. While bacteriophage and related therapies provide a possible solution to aspects of antibiotic resistance, their place in clinical therapy is still in question.

Different classes of bacteriocins have different potential as therapeutic agents. Small molecule bacteriocins (microcins, for example, and lantibiotics) may be similar to the classic antibiotics; colicin-like bacteriocins are more likely to be narrow-spectrum, demanding new molecular diagnostics prior to therapy but also not raising the spectre of resistance to the same degree.

One drawback to the large molecule antibiotics is that they will have relative difficulty crossing membranes and travelling systemically throughout the body.

For this reason, they are most often proposed for application topically or gastrointestinally. Because bacteriocins are peptides, they are more readily engineered than small molecules. This may permit the generation of cocktails and dynamically improved antibiotics that are modified to overcome resistance.

Nutrient withdrawal is a potential strategy for replacing or supplementing antibiotics. The restriction of iron availability is one way the human body limits bacterial proliferation. Mechanisms for freeing iron from the body (such as toxins and siderophores) are common among pathogens.

Building on this dynamic, various research groups are attempting to produce novel chelators which would withdraw iron otherwise available to pathogens (bacterial, fungal and parasitic). This is distinct from chelation therapy for conditions other than bacterial infections - including successful treatment for iron overload.

Vaccines are a commonly suggested method for combating MDRO infections. They actually fit within a larger class of therapies that rely on immune modulation or augmentation. These therapies either excite or reinforce the natural immune competency of the infected or susceptible host, leading to the activity of macrophages, the production of antibodies, inflammation, or other classic immune reactions. Just as the macrophage engulfs and consumes bacteria, various forms of biotherapy have been suggested which employ organisms to consume the pathogens. This includes the employment of protozoa and maggot therapy.

Probiotics are another alternative that goes beyond traditional antibiotics by employing a live culture which may in theory establish itself as a symbiont, competing, inhibiting, or simply interfering with colonization by pathogens.

## ANTIBIOTIC RESISTANCE

Antibiotic resistance is a specific type of drug resistance when a microorganism has the ability of withstanding the effects of antibiotics. Antibiotic resistance evolves via natural selection acting upon random mutation, but it can also be engineered by applying an evolutionary stress on a population. Once such a gene is generated, bacteria can then transfer the genetic information in a horizontal fashion (between individuals) by plasmid exchange.

If a bacterium carries several resistance genes, it is called multiresistant or, informally, a superbug. The term antimicrobial resistance is sometimes used to explicitly encompass organisms other than bacteria.

Antibiotic resistance can also be introduced artificially into a microorganism through transformation protocols. This can aid in implanting artificial genes into the microorganism. If the resistance gene is linked with the gene to be implanted, the antibiotic can be used to kill off organisms that lack the new gene.

## CAUSES

The widespread use of antibiotics both inside and outside of medicine is playing a significant role in the emergence of resistant bacteria. They are often used in animals but also in other industries which at least in the case of agricultural use lead to the spread of resistant strains to human populations.

In some countries antibiotics are sold over the counter without a prescription which compounds the problem. In human medicine the major problem of the emergence of resistant bacteria is due to misuse and overuse of antibiotics by doctors as well as patients. Other practices contributing towards resistance include the addition of antibiotics to the feed of livestock.

Household use of antibacterials in soaps and other products, although not clearly contributing to resistance, is also discouraged (as not being effective at infection control). Also unsound practices in the pharmaceutical manufacturing industry can contribute towards the likelihood of creating antibiotic resistant strains.

Certain antibiotic classes are highly associated with colonisation with superbugs compared to other antibiotic classes.

The risk for colonisation increases if there is a lack of

sensitivity (resistance) of the superbugs to the antibiotic used and high tissue penetration as well as broad spectrum activity against"good bacteria".

In the case of MRSA, increased rates of MRSA infections are seen with glycopeptides, cephalosporins and especially quinolones. In the case of colonisation with C difficile the high risk antibiotics include cephalosporins and in particular quinolones and clindamycin.

## In Medicine

The volume of antibiotic prescribed is the major factor in increasing rates or bacterial resistance rather than compliance with antibiotics.

Inappropriate prescribing of antibiotics has been attributed to a number of causes including: people who insist on antibiotics, physicians simply prescribe them as they feel they do not have time to explain why they are not necessary, physicians who do not know when to prescribe antibiotics or else are overly cautious for medical legal reasons.

A third of people for example believe that antibiotics are effective for the common cold and 22% of people do not finish a course of antibiotics primarily due to that fact that they feel better (varying from 10% to 44% depending on the country). Compliance with once daily antibiotics is better than with twice daily antibiotics.

Sub optimum antibiotic concentrations in critically ill people increase the frequency of antibiotic resistance organisms. While taking antibiotics doses less than those recommended may increase rates of resistance, shortening the course of antibiotics may actually decrease rates of resistance.

Poor hand hygiene by hospital staff has been associated with the spread of resistant organisms and an increase in hand washing compliance results in decreased rates of these organisms.

### *Role of Other Animals*

Drugs are used in animals that are used as human food, such as cows, pigs, chickens, fish, etc, and these drugs can affect the safety of the meat, milk, and eggs produced from those animals and can be the source of superbugs. For example, farm animals, particularly pigs, are believed to be able to infect people with MRSA.

The resistant bacteria in animals due to antibiotic exposure can be transmitted to humans via three pathways, those being through the consumption of meat, from close or direct contact with animals, or through the environment.

The World Health Organization concluded that antibiotics as growth promoters in animal feeds should be prohibited (in the absence of risk assessments).

In 1998, European Union health ministers voted to ban four antibiotics widely used to promote animal growth (despite their scientific panel's recommendations).

Regulation banning the use of antibiotics in European feed, with the exception of two antibiotics in poultry feeds, became effective in 2006. In Scandinavia, there's evidence that the ban has led to a lower prevalence of antimicrobial resistance in (non-hazardous) animal bacterial populations.

In the USA federal agencies do not collect data on antibiotic use in animals but animal to human spread of drug resistant organisms has been demonstrated in research studies. Antibiotics are still used in U.S. animal feed-along with other ingredients which have safety concerns.

Growing U.S. consumer concern about using antibiotics in animal feed has led to a niche market of"antibiotic-free" animal products, but this small market is unlikely to change entrenched industry-wide practices.

In 2001, the Union of Concerned Scientists estimated that greater than 70% of the antibiotics used in the US are given to food animals (e.g. chickens, pigs and cattle) in the absence of disease.

In 2000 the US Food and Drug Administration (FDA) announced their intention to revoke approval of fluoroquinolone use in poultry production because of substantial evidence linking it to the emergence of fluoroquinolone resistant campylobacter infections in humans.

The final decision to ban fluoroquinolones from use in

poultry production was not made until five yea-s later because of challenges from the food animal and pharmaceutical industries. Today, there are two federal bills (S. 549 and H.R. 962) aimed at phasing out"non-therapeutic" antibiotics in US food animal production.

## Mechanisms

The top section represents a population of bacteria before exposure to an antibiotic. The middle section shows the population directly after exposure, the phase in which selection took place. The last section shows the distribution of resistance in a new generation of bacteria. The legend indicates the resistance levels of individuals.

Antibiotic resistance can be a result of horizontal gene transfer, and also of unlinked point mutations in the pathogen genome and a rate of about 1 in $10^8$ per chromosomal replication.

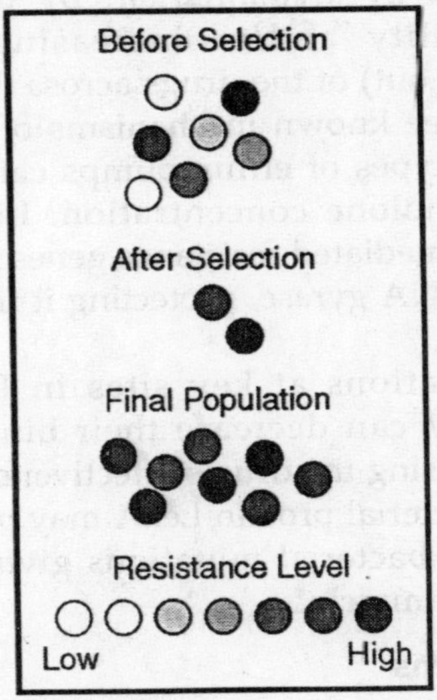


**Fig.** Schematic Representation of How Antibiotic Resistance Evolves Via Natural Selection.

The antibiotic action against the pathogen can be seen as an environmental pressure; those bacteria which have a mutation allowing them to survive will live on to reproduce. They will then pass this trait to their offspring, which will result in a fully resistant colony.

*The four main mechanisms by which microorganisms exhibit resistance to antimicrobials are*:

- *Drug inactivation or modification*: e.g. enzymatic deactivation of *Penicillin* G in some penicillin-resistant bacteria through the production of β-lactamases.
- *Alteration of target site*: e.g. alteration of PBP—the binding target site of penicillins—in MRSA and other penicillin-resistant bacteria.
- *Alteration of metabolic pathway*: e.g. some sulfonamide-resistant bacteria do not require para-aminobenzoic acid (PABA), an important precursor for the synthesis of folic acid and nucleic acids in bacteria inhibited by sulfonamides. Instead, like mammalian cells, they turn to utilizing preformed folic acid.
- *Reduced drug accumulation*: By decreasing drug permeability and/or increasing active efflux (pumping out) of the drugs across the cell surface.

There are three known mechanisms of fluoroquinolone resistance. Some types of efflux pumps can act to decrease intracellular quinolone concentration. In gram-negative bacteria, plasmid-mediated resistance genes produce proteins that can bind to DNA gyrase, protecting it from the action of quinolones.

Finally, mutations at key sites in DNA gyrase or Topoisomerase IV can decrease their binding affinity to quinolones, decreasing the drug's effectiveness. Research has shown that the bacterial protein LexA may play a key role in the acquisition of bacterial mutations giving resistance to quinolones and rifampicin.

## Resistant Pathogens

### Staphylococcus Aureus

*Staphylococcus aureus* (colloquially known as "Staph aureus" or a *Staph infection*) is one of the major resistant pathogens. Found on the mucous membranes and the human skin of around a third of the population, it is extremely adaptable to antibiotic pressure.

It was the first bacterium in which penicillin resistance was found—in 1947, just four years after the drug started being mass-produced. Methicillin was then the antibiotic of choice, but has since been replaced by oxacillin due to significant kidney toxicity. MRSA (methicillin-resistant *Staphylococcus aureus*) was first detected in Britain in 1961 and is now "quite common" in hospitals. MRSA was responsible for 37% of fatal cases of blood poisoning in the UK in 1999, up from 4% in 1991. Half of all *S. aureus* infections in the US are resistant to penicillin, methicillin, tetracycline and erythromycin.

This left vancomycin as the only effective agent available at the time. However, strains with intermediate (4-8 ug/ml) levels of resistance, termed GISA (glycopeptide intermediate *Staphylococcus aureus*) or VISA (vancomycin intermediate *Staphylococcus aureus*), began appearing in the late 1990s.

The first identified case was in Japan in 1996, and strains have since been found in hospitals in England, France and the US. The first documented strain with complete (>16 ug/ml) resistance to vancomycin, termed VRSA (Vancomycin-resistant *Staphylococcus aureus*) appeared in the United States in 2002. A *new* class of antibiotics, oxazolidinones, became available in the 1990s, and the first commercially available oxazolidinone, linezolid, is comparable to vancomycin in effectiveness against MRSA. Linezolid-resistance in *Staphylococcus aureus* was reported in 2003.

CA-MRSA (Community-acquired MRSA) has now emerged as an epidemic that is responsible for rapidly progressive, fatal diseases including necrotizing pneumonia, severe sepsis and necrotizing fasciitis. Methicillin-resistant *Staphylococcus aureus* (MRSA) is the most frequently identified antimicrobial drug-resistant pathogen in US hospitals.

The epidemiology of infections caused by MRSA is rapidly changing. In the past 10 years, infections caused by this organism have emerged in the community. The 2 MRSA clones in the United States most closely associated with community outbreaks, USA400 (MW2 strain, ST1 lineage) and USA300, often contain Panton-Valentine leukocidin (PVL) genes and, more frequently, have been associated with skin and soft tissue infections.

Outbreaks of community-associated (CA)-MRSA infections have been reported in correctional facilities, among athletic teams, among military recruits, in newborn nurseries, and among men who engage in frequent homosexual activities. CA-MRSA infections now appear to be endemic in many urban regions and cause most CA-S. aureus infections.

**Streptococcus *and* Enterococcus**

*Streptococcus pyogenes* (Group A Streptococcus: GAS) infections can usually be treated with many different antibiotics. Early treatment may reduce the risk of death from invasive group A streptococcal disease.

However, even the best medical care does not prevent death in every case. For those with very severe illness, supportive care in an intensive care unit may be needed. For persons with necrotizing fasciitis, surgery often is needed to remove damaged tissue. Strains of *S. pyogenes* resistant to macrolide antibiotics have emerged, however all strains remain uniformly sensitive to penicillin.

Resistance of *Streptococcus pneumoniae* to penicillin and other beta-lactams is increasing worldwide. The major mechanism of resistance involves the introduction of mutations in genes encoding penicillin-binding proteins.

Selective pressure is thought to play an important role, and use of beta-lactam antibiotics has been implicated as a risk factor for infection and colonization. Streptococcus pneumoniae is responsible for pneumonia, bacteremia, otitis media, meningitis, sinusitis, peritonitis and arthritis.

Penicillin-resistant pneumonia caused by *Streptococcus pneumoniae* (commonly known as *pneumococcus*), was first detected in 1967, as was penicillin-resistant gonorrhea. Resistance to penicillin substitutes is also known as beyond *S. aureus*. By 1993 *Escherichia coli* was resistant to five fluoroquinolone variants.

*Mycobacterium tuberculosis* is commonly resistant to isoniazid and rifampin and sometimes universally resistant to the common treatments. Other pathogens showing some resistance include *Salmonella, Campylobacter,* and *Streptococci.*

*Enterococcus faecium* is another superbug found in hospitals. Penicillin-Resistant Enterococcus was seen in 1983, vancomycin-resistant enterococcus (VRE) in 1987, and Linezolid-Resistant Enterococcus (LRE) in the late 1990s.

## Pseudomonas Aeruginosa

*Pseudomonas aeruginosa* is a highly prevalent opportunistic pathogen. One of the most worrisome characteristics of *P. aeruginosa* consists in its low antibiotic susceptibility.

This low susceptibility is attributable to a concerted action of multidrug efflux pumps with chromosomally-encoded antibiotic resistance genes (e.g. *mexAB-oprM, mexXY* etc) and the low permeability of the bacterial cellular envelopes. Besides intrinsic resistance, *P. aeruginosa* easily develop acquired resistance either by mutation in chromosomally-encoded genes, or by the horizontal gene transfer of antibiotic resistance determinants. Development of multidrug resistance by *P. aeruginosa* isolates requires several different genetic events that include acquisition of different mutations and/or horizontal transfer of antibiotic resistance genes.

Hypermutation favours the selection of mutation-driven antibiotic resistance in *P. aeruginosa* strains producing chronic infections, whereas the clustering of several different antibiotic resistance genes in integrons favours the concerted acquisition of antibiotic resistance determinants.

Some recent studies have shown that phenotypic resistance associated to biofilm formation or to the emergence of small-colony-variants may be important in the response of *P. aeruginosa* populations to antibiotics treatment.

## Clostridium Difficile

*Clostridium difficile* is a nosocomial pathogen that causes diarrheal disease in hospitals world wide. Clindamycin-resistant *C. difficile* was reported as the causative agent of large outbreaks of diarrheal disease in hospitals in New York, Arizona, Florida and Massachusetts between 1989 and 1992. Geographically dispersed outbreaks of C. *difficile* strains resistant to fluoroquinolone antibiotics, such as Cipro (ciprofloxacin) and Levaquin (levofloxacin), were also reported in North America in 2005.

### Salmonella *and* E. coli

E. coli and Salmonella come directly from contaminated food. Of the meat that is contaminated with E. coli, eighty per cent of the bacteria are resistant to one or more drugs made; it causes bladder infections that are resistant to antibiotics ("HSUS Fact Sheet").

Salmonella was first found in humans in the 1970s and in some cases is resistant to as many as nine different antibiotics ("HSUS Fact Sheet"). When both bacterium are spread, serious health conditions arise. Many people are hospitalized each year after becoming infected, and some die as a result.

### Acinetobacter Baumannii

On November 5, 2004, the Centers for Disease Control and Prevention (CDC) reported an increasing number of *Acinetobacter baumannii* bloodstream infections in patients at military medical facilities in which service members injured in the Iraq/Kuwait region during Operation Iraqi Freedom and in Afghanistan during Operation Enduring Freedom were treated. Most of these showed multidrug resistance (MRAB), with a few isolates resistant to all drugs tested.

### Alternatives

#### *Prevention*

Rational use of antibiotics may reduce the chances of development of opportunistic infection by antibiotic-resistant bacteria due to dysbacteriosis. In one study the use of fluoroquinolones are clearly associated with *Clostridium difficile* infection, which is a leading cause of nosocomial diarrhea in the United States, and a major cause of death, worldwide.

There is clinical evidence that topical dermatological preparations containing tea tree oil and thyme oil may be effective in preventing transmittal of CA-MRSA. Vaccines do not suffer the problem of resistance because a vaccine enhances the body's natural defenses, while an antibiotic operates separately from the body's normal defenses. Nevertheless, new strains may evolve that escape immunity induced by vaccines.

While theoretically promising, anti-staphylococcal vaccines have shown limited efficacy, because of immunological variation between *Staphylococcus* species, and the limited duration of effectiveness of the antibodies produced. Development and testing of more effective vaccines is under way.

The Australian Commonwealth Scientific and Industrial Research Organization (CSIRO), realizing the need for the reduction of antibiotic use, has been working on two alternatives. One alternative is to prevent diseases by adding cytokines instead of antibiotics to animal feed.

These proteins are made in the animal body "naturally" after a disease and are not antibiotics so they do not contribute to the antibiotic resistance problem. Furthermore, studies on using cytokines have shown that they also enhance the growth of animals like the antibiotics now used, but without the drawbacks of non-therapeutic antibiotic use.

Cytokines have the potential to achieve the animal growth rates traditionally sought by the use of antibiotics without the contribution of antibiotic resistance associated with the widespread non-therapeutic uses of antibiotics currently utilized in the food animal production industries. Additionally, CSIRO is working on vaccines for diseases.

### *Phage Therapy*

Phage therapy, an approach that has been extensively researched and utilized as a therapeutic agent for over 60 years, especially in the Soviet Union, is an alternative that might help with the problem of resistance. Phage therapy was widely used in the United States until the discovery of antibiotics, in the early 1940s.

Bacteriophages or "phages" are viruses that invade bacterial cells and, in the case of lytic phages, disrupt bacterial metabolism and cause the bacterium to lyse. Phage therapy is the therapeutic use of lytic bacteriophages to treat pathogenic bacterial infections.

Bacteriophage therapy is an important alternative to antibiotics in the current era of multidrug resistant pathogens. A review of studies that dealt with the therapeutic use of phages from 1966–1996 and few latest ongoing phage therapy projects via internet showed: phages were used topically, orally or systemically in Polish and Soviet studies.

The success rate found in these studies was 80–95% with few gastrointestinal or allergic side effects. British studies also demonstrated significant efficacy of phages against *Escherichia coli, Acinetobacter* spp., *Pseudomonas* spp and *Staphylococcus aureus*. US studies dealt with improving the bioavailability of phage. Phage therapy may prove as an important alternative to antibiotics for treating multidrug resistant pathogens.

## Research

### *New Medications*

Until recently, research and development (R&D) efforts have provided new drugs in time to treat bacteria that became resistant to older antibiotics. That is no longer the case. The potential crisis at hand is the result of a marked decrease in industry R&D, and the increasing prevalence of resistant bacteria. Infectious disease physicians are alarmed by the prospect that effective antibiotics may not be available to treat seriously ill patients in the near future.

The pipeline of new antibiotics is drying up. Major pharmaceutical companies are losing interest in the antibiotics market because these drugs may not be as profitable as drugs that treat chronic (long-term) conditions and lifestyle issues.

The resistance problem demands that a renewed effort be made to seek antibacterial agents effective against pathogenic bacteria resistant to current antibiotics. One of the possible strategies towards this objective is the rational localization of bioactive phytochemicals. Plants have an almost limitless ability to synthesize aromatic substances, most of which are phenols or their oxygen-substituted derivatives such as tannins. Most are secondary metabolites, of which at least 12,000 have been isolated, a number estimated to be less than 10% of the total. In many cases, these substances serve as plant defence mechanisms against predation by microorganisms, insects, and herbivores.

Many of the herbs and spices used by humans to season food yield useful medicinal compounds including those having antibacterial activity.

Traditional healers have long used plants to prevent or cure infectious conditions. Many of these plants have been investigated scientifically for antimicrobial activity and a large number of plant products have been shown to inhibit growth of pathogenic bacteria.

A number of these agents appear to have structures and modes of action that are distinct from those of the antibiotics in current use, suggesting that cross-resistance with agents already in use may be minimal. For example the combination of 5'-methoxyhydnocarpine and berberine in herbs like Hydrastis canadensis and Berberis vulgaris can block the MDR-pumps that cause multidrug resistance. This has been shown for Staphylococcus aureus.

Archaeocins is the name given to a new class of potentially useful antibiotics that are derived from the Archaea group of organisms. Eight archaeocins have been partially or fully characterized, but hundreds of archaeocins are believed to exist, especially within the haloarchaea. The prevalence of archaeocins is unknown simply because no one has looked for them.

The discovery of new archaeocins hinges on recovery and cultivation of archaeal organisms from the environment. For example, samples from a novel hypersaline field site, Wilson Hot Springs, recovered 350 halophilic organisms; preliminary analysis of 75 isolates showed that 48 were archaeal and 27 were bacterial.

In research published on October 17, 2008 in *Cell*, a team

of scientists pinpointed the place on bacteria where the antibiotic myxopyronin launches its attack, and why that attack is successful. The myxopyronin binds to and inhibits the crucial bacterial enzyme, RNA polymerase.

The myxopyronin changes the structure of the switch-2 segment of the enzyme, inhibiting its function of reading and transmitting DNA code. This prevents RNA polymerase from delivering genetic information to the ribosomes, causing the bacteria to die.

One of the major causes of antibiotic resistance is the decrease of effective drug concentrations at their target place, due to the increased action of ABC transporters. Since ABC transporter blockers can be used in combination with current drugs to increase their effective intracellular concentration, the possible impact of ABC transporter inhibitors is of great clinical interest.

ABC transporter blockers that may be useful to increase the efficacy of current drugs have entered clinical trials and are available to be used in therapeutic regimes.

### *Applications*

Antibiotic resistance is an important tool for genetic engineering. By constructing a plasmid which contains an antibiotic resistance gene as well as the gene being engineered or expressed, a researcher can ensure that when bacteria replicate, only the copies which carry along the plasmid survive. This ensures that the gene being manipulated passes along when the bacteria replicates.

The most commonly used antibiotics in genetic engineering are generally "older" antibiotics which have largely fallen out of use in clinical practice.

*These include*:

- Ampicillin
- Kanamycin
- Tetracycline
- Chloramphenicol

Industrially the use of antibiotic resistance is disfavored since maintaining bacterial cultures would require feeding them large quantities of antibiotics. Instead, the use of auxotrophic bacterial strains (and function-replacement plasmids) is preferred.

## CHEMISTRY OF ANTIBIOTICS

The treatment of pain and disease is one of the most important goals of humankind. Since ancient times people have been using potions, natural products and even the dust of mummies for the treatment of health problems.

The healing effects of remedies were often ascribed to spirits and mythical entities, but some of the herbal preparations did possess curative properties.

In the 1800's scientists began to investigate potions to determine what chemicals were present that could cause the observed healing.

Thus, the early days of medicinal chemistry began with the study of naturally occurring materials that were effective in treating human disorders. The studies were tedious and required much sample purification and structure determination at a time when instrumental methods of analysis were unavailable. Also, screening methods for chemical efficacy against disease had to be developed so that humans were not used as trials.

Modern therapy by chemicals, chemotherapy, is attributed to Paul Ehrlich (Germany, Nobel Prize in 1908) who synthesized the first antibiotic, an arsenic compound patterned after an azo dye that he found to stain a microorganism selectively.

The compound first called compound 606 was introduced commercially in 1910 as a treatment of syphilis under the name of Sylvarsan.

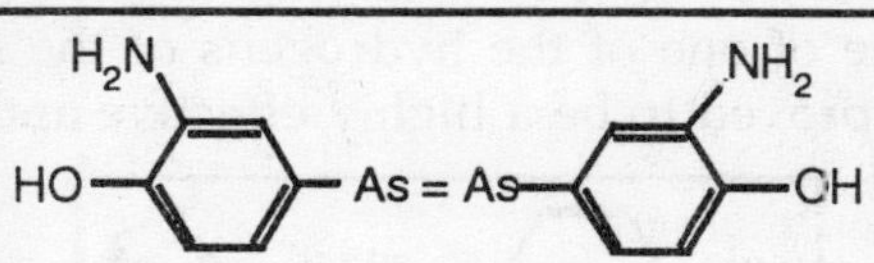


Arsphenamine
(Sylvarsan)

Many compounds were investigated over the next 50 years as antibacterial agents. Some structures are very complex and necessitated the development of new synthetic organic reactions in order to prove their structures.

An intense effort to develop medicinal agents against malaria was required because many soldiers were afflicted with the disease. Quinine, discovered active against malaria in 1990, was reasonably toxic, and other agents were required. Chloroquine was synthesized and found to be highly effective against malaria.

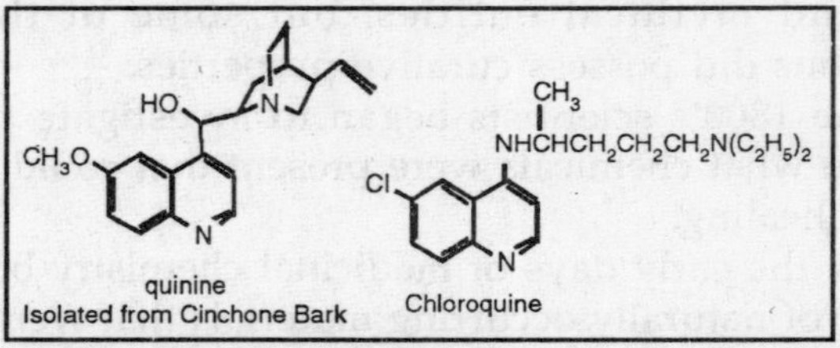


Careful studies of the antibacterial compound known as Prontisil, a dye that strongly stains proteins, showed that it was metabolized to sulfanilamide, a more effective antibiotic.

Prontosil is therefore termed a prodrug as it is not the substance responsible for the biological effect but it does produce the effective drug.

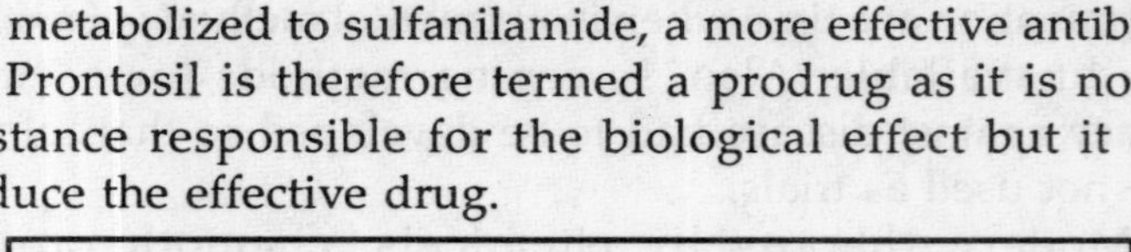


These studies led to the investigation of compounds containing the sulfonamide function as potential antibiotics, and led to a number of very effective antibiotic agents. Many of these compounds are sulfanilamides that have an organic group in place of one of the hydrogens of the sulfonamide. Sulfathiazole proved to be a highly effective antibiotic.

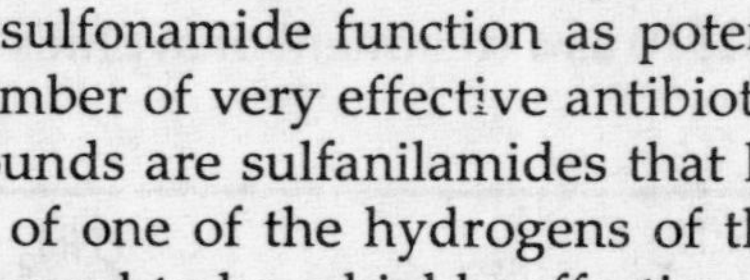

As the search for better antibiotics continued, a revolutionary drug was developed by H. W. Florey and E. Chain in 1938. Penicillin was produced by microorganisms of mold and was found to inhibit the growth of other microorganisms. Penicillin was so important in the treatment of bacterial infections that many research groups from all over the world combined their research efforts in the isolation, purification, testing and synthesis of penicillin drugs. The structurally related cephalosporin antibiotics were also discovered during this time.

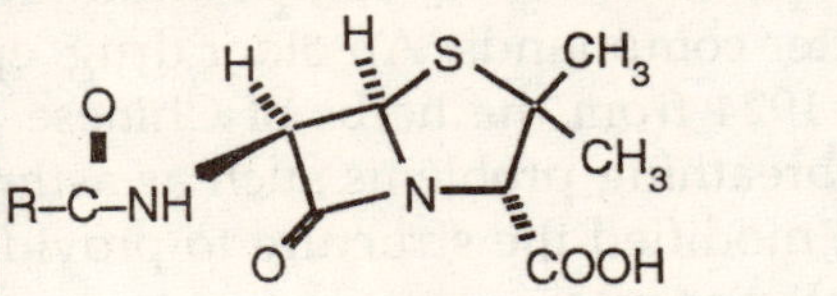

| | R |
|---|---|
| Penicillin F | $CH_3CH_2CH = CHCH_2$ |
| Penicillin G | $PhCH_2$— |
| Penicillin V | $PhCH_2$– |

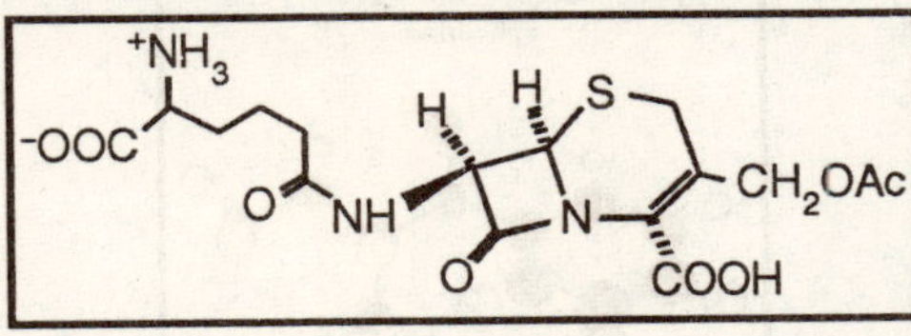

## METHODS OF DRUG DISCOVERY

The discovery of new drugs is exemplified in the above sections on antibiotics and analgesics. The procedure is much more refined now than nearly a hundred years ago, but the steps in discovering new drugs or lead compounds to drugs are still similar.

### Drug Screening

Perhaps the largest effort of the pharmaceutical industry is the search for new drugs. Many compounds from many sources, both natural and synthetic, are tested for effectiveness against many types of medical problems. Screening requires many involved tests in both test tubes and in live subjects. Analysts need to be very astute in their observations in order not to miss a new drug or to improperly evaluate an effective drug. Once a compound is found to be an effective medicinal agent, then it is the lead compound. New compounds are synthesized in the laboratory in order to find perhaps a better medicine or one with less toxicity. The process takes many years of intense work.

Some examples of compounds found in natural sources have been seen as the antibiotics or the analgesics. Scientists then follow up on the lead compounds and attempt to synthesize better compounds. An older drug, ephedrine, was discovered in 1924 from the herbs of Chinese medicine as a treatment for breathing problems such as asthma. Medicinal chemists have modified the structure to provide a wide base of bronchodilator agents.

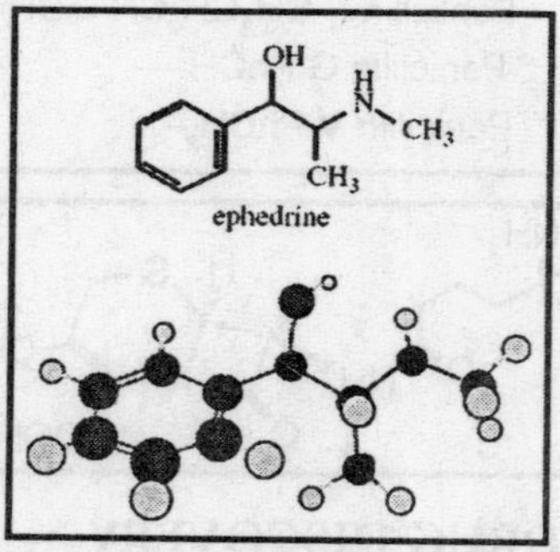


Taxol, is a very complicated substance found in the California yew tree bark. It is a very important new anti-cancer treatment, but it is in very short supply. Chemists are very active in the synthesis of taxol and related compounds in order to produce more effective and more available materials.

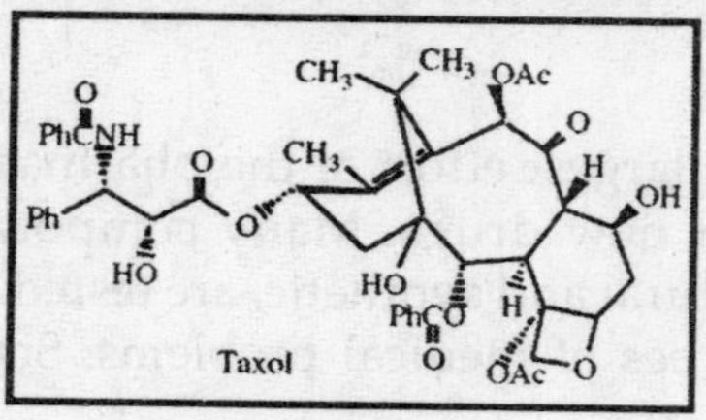

Other interesting drugs have been synthesized in the laboratory but their effectiveness as medicines was not discovered immediately.

AZT, an important agent against HIV, was first prepared many years ago but was later screened as an anti-HIV agent because the AIDS virus was discovered after AZT was prepared.

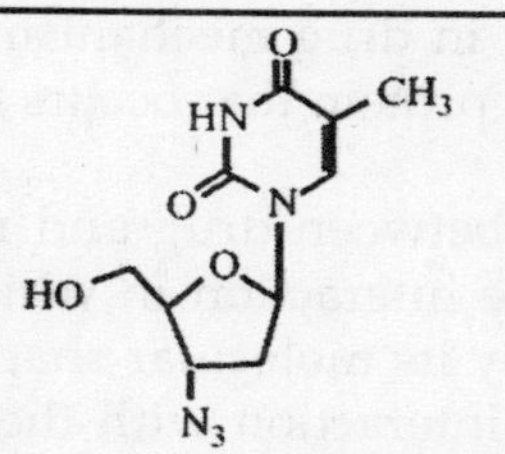

3"-adido-3'-deoxythymidine

AZT

Librium, an important tranquilizer and somewhat abused drug, was tested two years after its first laboratory synthesis because it was not originally thought to be an important structure. As a lead compound Librium has led to several other important tranquilizers.

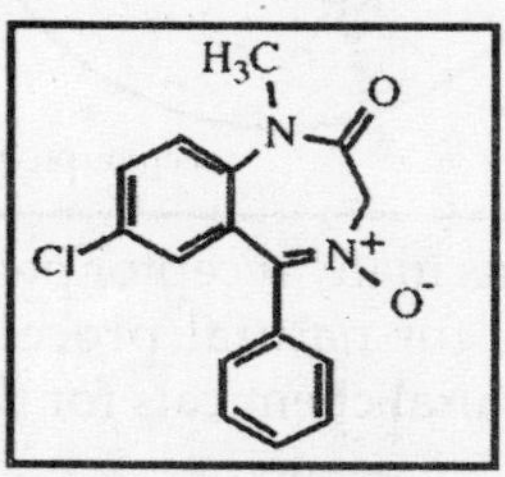

The examples shown above serve to illustrate the beginning of a process. Many other cases are known where drug discovery is based on unusual natural products, or materials based on herbal remedies, or from fortuitous accidents.

## DRUG MECHANISM

The mechanism of how a drug exerts its effect is a very significant finding in the determination of new and improved drugs. Early medicinal chemists had to rely on screening and drug modification for new drugs, but the inclusion of modern mechanistic theories into drug searches advances the field considerably.

However, the fortuitous discovery of a drug without much knowledge of how or why it works still plays an important role in medicinal chemistry.

A major finding in drug mechanism is that many drugs react with a receptor protein that occurs in cell walls or in the cytoplasm of cells.

The interaction between drug and receptor is similar to the enzyme-substrate interaction in which the drug must fit into a receptor cite by its molecular shape.

The drug in its interaction with the receptor may cause an enhanced biological response (agonist), a decreased biological response (antagonist) or be delivered to a site in the cell where the drug effects beneficial changes.

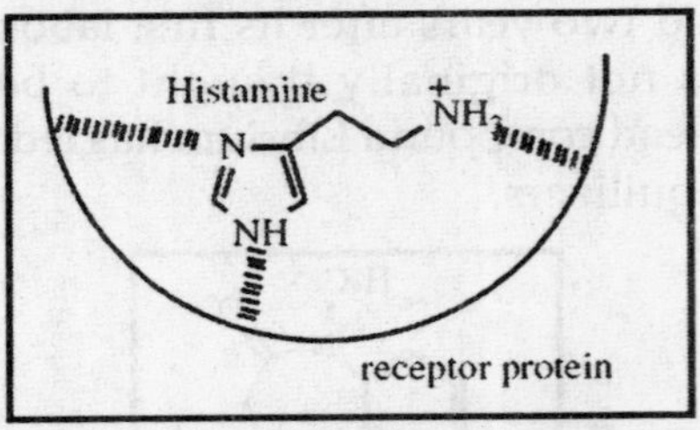


The body contains many receptor proteins that are present as receptor proteins for natural processes. The drug must compete with the natural chemicals for the protein in order to be effective.

The study of histamine and its receptor permitted rational design of new drugs. In this case, histamine was found to bind with a receptor protein-called the histamine-2 receptor - as shown below.

New drugs were deigned that would mimic histamine binding but would not permit histamine to bind. The effects of these types of drugs were to act as antihistamines.

The interaction of the antihistamine promine with the histamine receptor is shown below.

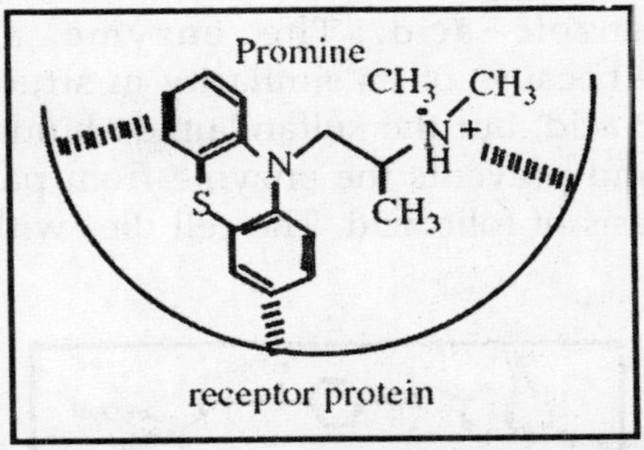


A novel approach to the treatment of breast cancer is the use of agents that bind with the estrogen receptor protein. Mammary cancers are known to have a buildup of estrogen receptor protein and estradiol, the primary female hormone. An estradiol analog with a radioactive fluorine atom in the 16a position competes very strongly for the estrogen receptor protein.

Thus the mammary cancer becomes labeled for diagnostic purposes and the radiation produced from the 18F can destroy the nearby cancer cells. The radioactive fluorine compound is called a radiopharmaceutical.

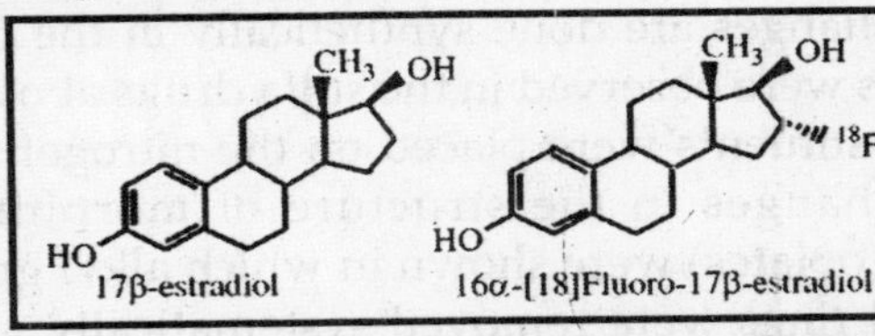


A very important type of drug is one that interacts with an enzyme. The enzyme is fooled into using the drug as a natural substrate, but the drug does not continue the function of the enzyme and its activity is inhibited. Such drugs are called mechanism-based suicide inhibitors.

The reaction mechanism is used to design the drug and the enzyme commits suicide when it accepts the drug. An example of this behaviour is found with many antibiotic drugs that inhibit the growth of bacterial cells. Bacterial cells must synthesize folic acid whereas humans obtain folic acid from food. An enzyme named dihydropteroate synthetase is responsible for the synthesis of folic acid in a process that uses paraaminobenzoic acid. The enzyme also accepts sulfanilamide because of its similarity in structure to para-aminobenzoic acid, but the sulfanilamide binds tightly with the enzyme and prevents the enzyme from participating in further synthesis of folic acid. The cell dies without the folic acid.

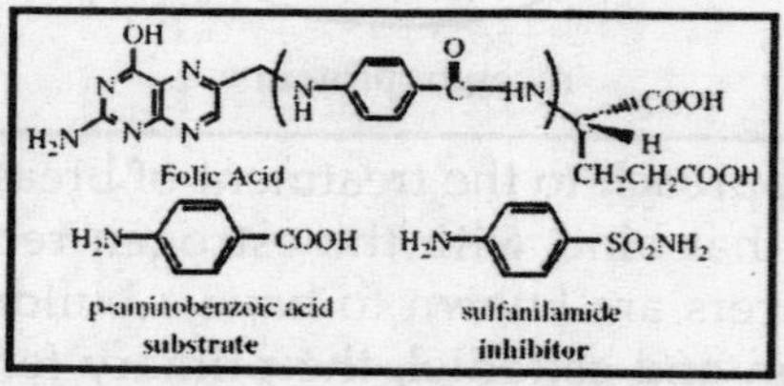


The mechanism of action of most drugs involves receptor binding and enzyme inhibition. The study of enzymes and the structure of active sites are thus major efforts in medicinal studies.

## DRUG ALTERATION

Once a lead compound with medicinal properties is discovered changes are done synthetically in the compound. Such changes were observed in the sulfa drugs above in which different substituents were placed on the nitrogen.

Many changes in the structure of morphine-related compounds (opiates) were shown in which alkyl groups were changed and rings were removed systematically.

The important finding is the lead compound, but very often the altered drug shows better properties or less toxicity. Another alteration of drugs is the incorporation of fluorine. Fluorine atoms allow the original structure to retain its molecular size because fluorine is a small atom.

Also, the fluorine is very electronegative and thus introduces polarity into the molecule. The change can sometimes be very beneficial in drug discovery.

Steroid compounds are often used as anti-inflammatory agents and many with incorporation of fluorine atoms are effective at lower doses, as is the case with fluorocortolone shown below.

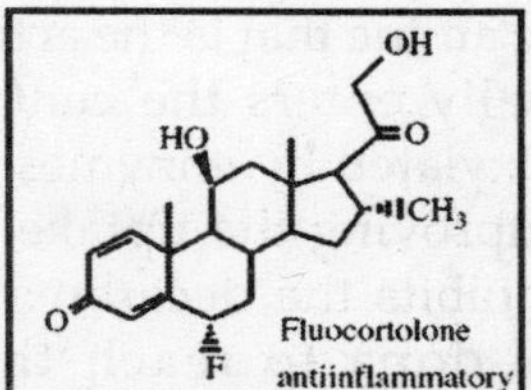


Fluocortolone
antiinflammatory

Synthetic incorporation of fluorine into other drug systems is also well known and very effective. Fluorazepam is an often prescribed relative of valium.

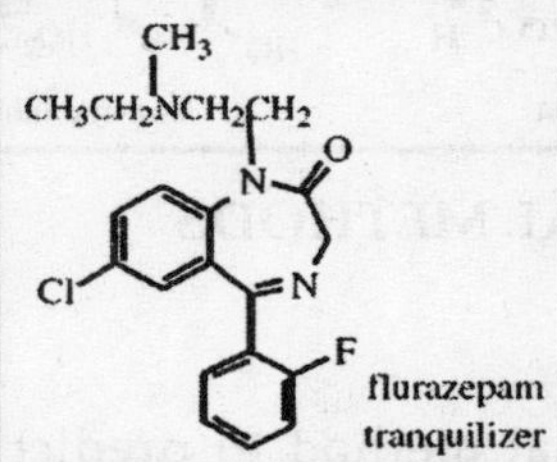


flurazepam
tranquilizer

Once a drug is discovered many experiments are conducted to determine the pharmokinetics of the drug. These studies show how the drug is delivered to the site of action, how the drug is distributed throughout the body and how the drug is metabolized.

The results of the studies sometimes provide clues as to how the drug could be altered to improve its pharmokinetic properties and effectiveness. Biodistribution studies of the drug acyclovir, used in the treatment of herpes simplex virus, show that it is only absorbed about 15% when taken orally. A better absorption is found when the carbonyl group is replaced by an amino group.

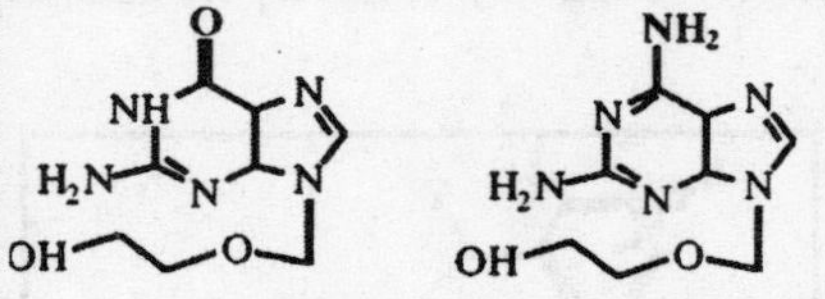


Acyclovir amino-acyclovir

L-Dopa is a well-know drug for the treatment of Parkinson's disease. It is actually a prodrug because it is decarboxylated to the amine that is the active drug. Only about 1 % of L-dopa actually enters the central nervous system because it is decarboxylated by enzymes in the liver.

A solution to improving the uptake of L-dopa is to add another drug that inhibits the decarboxylation enzyme thus permitting more L-dopa to reach the active site. The administered dose of Ldopa can be reduced more than 50 % when used in conjunction with the enzyme inhibitor.

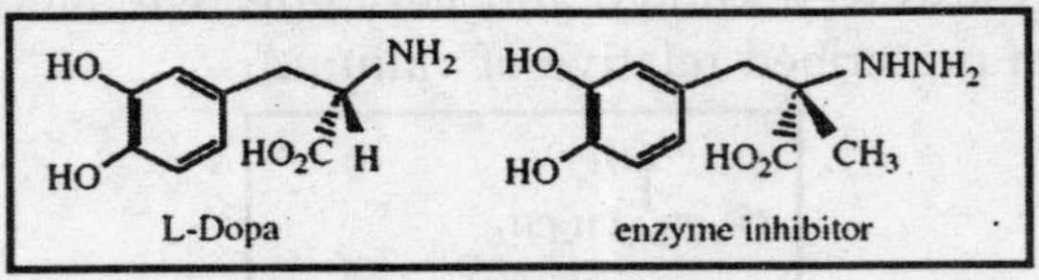


## COMPUTATIONAL METHODS

### Hansch Equation

A computational method to predict drug effectiveness based on physical properties instead of molecular structure was introduced by Hansch in 1960. In this method parameters on the hydrophobic (water dislike) character of the compound (P), the hydrophobic contributions of the substituents (p), electronic characteristics of the substituents (s, known as Hammett constants) and steric factors (Es, known as Taft constants) are correlated with drug effectiveness. The general Hansch equation is shown below.

$$\text{drug effectiveness} = k_1 \log P + k_2\, p + k_3\, s + k_4\, E_s + k_5$$

The k values indicate the significance of each term. When applied to a number phenethylamine compounds related to ephedrine, the drug effectiveness was found to depend only on substituent (X and Y) hydrophobic and electronic properties.

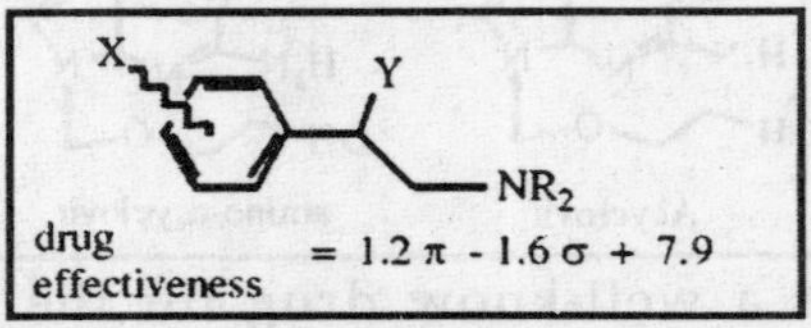


The equation says that compounds with highly

hydrophobic (positive p values) and electron donation (negative s values) will prove to have greater effectiveness.

The Hansch equation for the above compounds is relatively simple, but for some drugs a very complicated relationship is observed. The Hansch study of drugs requires that many compounds be evaluated and correlated with the various parameters, not a simple task.

## Molecular Modeling

Modern high-speed computers have the capability of carrying out many complicated calculations in a very short time. The structural parameters for a specific protein receptor (or enzyme) can be placed in a computer along with structural parameters for a drug molecule (real or hypothetical) and the computer will calculate and graph the fit of the drug with the protein active site.

The molecules may be manipulated in three dimensions to enhance the view and show the best fit of the "docking" of the molecules. Such molecular modeling can be used to predict the structure and effectiveness of new medicinal agents. Below is a model of captopril, a blood pressure medication.

This model is produced by drawing the structure with a ChemDraw programme, and placing it into a Chem 3D programme.

The structure is presented in colour and may be manipulated in 3D with the programme. Examination of the structure when one has the shape of the enzyme active site can give information about the desired location of substituents.

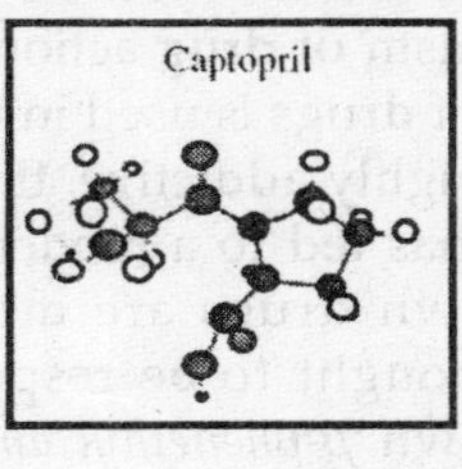


## Successful Drugs

Medicines have been developed to treat almost every

disease. The development of medicinal agents takes many years of intense work by many scientists skilled in different fields. A few of the commonly prescribed medications are shown below.

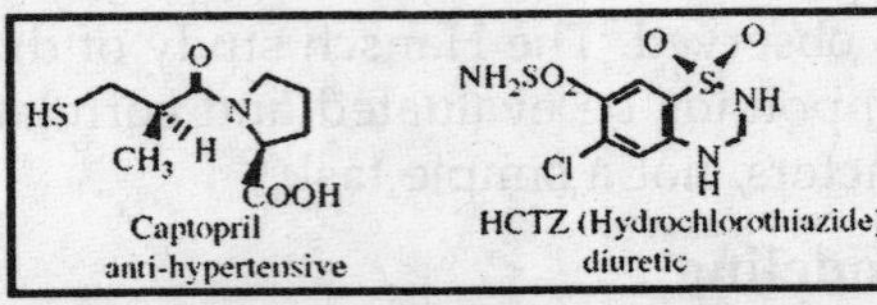


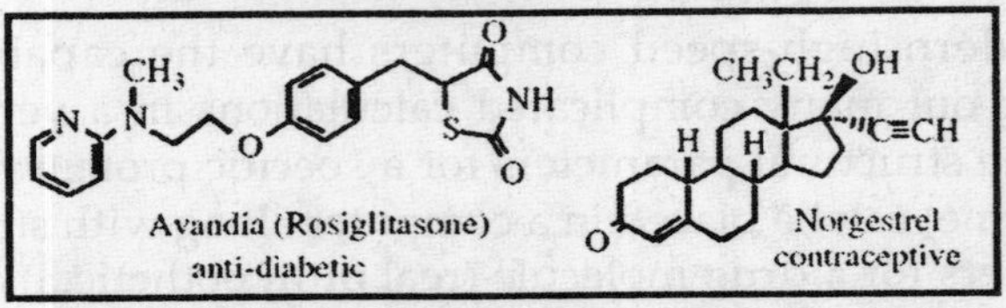


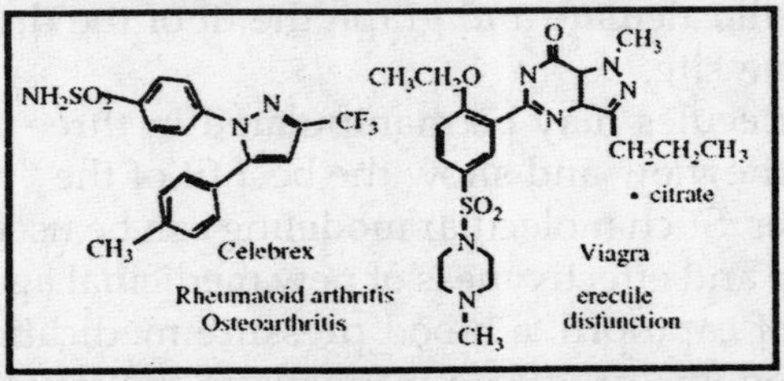


Although various treatments for diseases have been used for centuries, the early history of chemotherapy, chemical treatment of disease, started with *Paul Ehrlich in the 1900' and his discovery of antibiotic compounds.*

Many antibiotics with a wide variety of applications and structures are now known. Drugs known as *prodrugs* that release the true drug have become common through the studies of the mechanism of drug action.

The *opiate family* of drugs is used in the treatment of pain. Although, many are highly addictive, the systematic study of their mode of action has led to a modern approach for drug discovery. Now known drugs are modified according to structural features thought to be responsible for the drug activity. The wellknown *β-phenethyl amine structural unit of opiates* is identified in many structures with known chemotherapeutic properties. Drugs are often *discovered by extensive screening tests* of materials synthesized in the laboratory or obtained from natural sources.

Studies are then conducted to gain information on the *mechanism of the drug action.* Drug *interactions with enzymes* as substrates or inhibitors then lead to the structural features required in designing new drugs.

The drug structure is modified synthetically according to the drug mechanism in order to provide new drug molecules. *Computational methods* are used to show the correlation of drug structure with physical and biochemical properties of the drug, and to determine the efficacy of the drug.

The computations lead to drug modifications for changing the required properties. Computers are often used to *model drug chemistry.* Computer programs will allow the observation in *three-dimensions of a drug interaction with a protein, or permit the determination of the stereochemistry of the drug.*

# Chapter 5

# Phytotherapy

Phytotherapy is the study of the use of extracts from natural origin as medicines or health-promoting agents. Even though phytotherapy is usually regarded as "alternative medicine" in the Western countries, when critically carried out, is considered an essential component of modern pharmacognosy.

## POINTS TO CONSIDER IN PHYTOTHERAPY

### STANDARDIZATION

In herbal medicine, standardization refers to providing processed plant material that meets a specified concentration of a specific marker constituent. Active constituent concentrations may be misleading measures of potency if cofactors are not present. A further problem is that the important constituent is often unknown.

For instance St John's wort is often standardized to the antiviral constituent hypericin which is now known to be the "active ingredient" for antidepressant use. Other companies standardize to hyperforin or both, although there may be some 24 known possible constituents.

Only a minority of chemicals used as standardization markers are known to be active constituents. Standardization has not been standardized yet: different companies use different markers, or different levels of the same markers, or different methods of testing for marker compounds.

Herbalist and manufacturer David Winston points out

that whenever different compounds are chosen as "active ingredients" for different herbs, there is a chance that suppliers will get a substandard batch (low on the chemical markers) and mix it with a batch higher in the desired marker to compensate for the difference.

## Quality

*The quality of crude drugs or plant medicines depends upon a variety of factors*:

- Genetically strong seed,
- Use of correct species,
- Maturity of the plant at harvest,
- Soil and air quality,
- Climate,
- Organoleptic factors (i.e. sensory properties of a particular chemical, the taste, colour, odour and feel),
- Flavour and odor,
- Post-harvest processing and a variety of other factors.

These conditions have been noted in historical herbals such as Culpepper's Complete Herbal or The Shen Nong or Divine Farmer's Materia Medica. This was standard pharmacognosy curriculum for many years.

Storage after collection is a factor worthy of study; researchers in Nara, Japan have stored samples of ginseng root (Panax ginseng), licorice root (Glycyrrhiza glabra) and rhubarb root (Rheum emodi) that have been shown to retain their active properties for over 1,200 years.

In modern times the foregoing aspects are no less important, but have been neglected with the advent of laboratory testing, although it generally is true that only certain constituents are identified and measured.

Processes like HPLC (High performance liquid chromatography), GC (gas chromatography), UV/VIS (Ultraviolet/Visible spectrophotometry) or AA (Atomic Absorption spectroscopy) are used to identify species, measure bacteriological contamination, assess potency and eventually creating Certificates of Analysis for the material.

Quality should be overseen by either authorities ensuring

Good Manufacturing Practices or regulatory agencies by the US FDA. In the United States one frequently sees comments that herbal medicine is unregulated, but this is not correct since the FDA and GMP regulations are in place. In Germany, the Commission E has produced a book of German legal-medical regulations which includes quality standards.

## Safety

The safety and effectiveness of alternative medicines have not be been scientifically proven and remains largely unknown. A number of herbs are thought to be likely to cause adverse effects. Furthermore, "adulteration, inappropriate formulation, or lack of understanding of plant and drug interactions have led to adverse reactions that are sometimes life threatening or lethal."

Proper double-blind clinical trials are needed to determine the safety and efficacy of each plant before they can be recommended for medical use. Although many consumers believe that herbal medicines are safe because they are "natural", herbal medicines may interact with synthetic drugs causing toxicity to the patient, may have contamination that is a safety consideration, and herbal medicines, without proven efficacy, may be used to replace medicines that have a proven efficacy.

The political issues around the safety of crude drugs vary from considering natural remedies "safe" regardless of potential dangers to considering them a dangerous unknown.

Ephedra has been known to have numerous side effects, including severe skin reactions, irritability, nervousness, dizziness,trembling,headache,insomnia,profuse perspiration, dehydration,itchy scalp and skin, vomiting, hyperthermia, irregular heartbeat, seizures, heart attack, stroke, or death.

Poisonous plants which have limited medicinal effects are often not sold in material doses in the United States or are available only to trained practitioners, these include:

- Aconite
- Arnica
- Belladonna

- Bryonia
- Datura
- Gelsemium
- Henbane
- Male Fern
- Phytolacca
- Podophyllum and
- Veratrum

Furthermore, herbs such as Lobelia, Ephedra and Eonymus that cause nausea, sweating, and vomiting, have been traditionally prized for this action. Plants such as Comfrey and Petasites have specific toxicity due to hepatotoxic pyrrolizidine alkaloid content. There are other plant medicines which require caution or can interact with other medications, including St. John's wort and grapefruit.

## Recommended Standards for Random Clinical Trials

The Consolidated Standards of Reporting Trials (CONSORT) group came up with standards for random clinical trials (RTC) of herbs in 1996, revised in 2002. This statement comprises a 22-item checklist and flow diagram to guide authors, peer reviewers, editors, and readers on the essential information required in reports of two-group parallel RCTs of natural products. The CONSORT statement is endorsed by leading medical journals, editorial groups, professional societies, and funding bodies.

- The title and/or abstract should include the Latin binomial for the plant species from which the herbal medicine(s) originated, the part(s) of the plant used in the preparation, and the type of preparation (e.g., dried crude herb, ethanolic extract). The background should include a statement explaining the rationale for investigation of the specific herbal medicinal product and whether the indication for which it is being tested is new or is based on traditional use. Participant eligibility criteria in a trial testing a traditional indication (e.g., in traditional Chinese herbal medicine, a trial may test the effects of an herbal medicine intervention for liver chi (Qi) deficiency) should describe the theories and concepts underlying this indication.

- The description of the intervention must include the herbal medicinal product name, manufacturer, plant part used, type of preparation, source and authentication of the herbal material, pharmaceutical quality (e.g., herbal drug-to-extract ratio, type and concentration of the extraction solvent, quantity of known active constituents per unit dose), and dosage regimen and qualitative testing (purity). Also, reporting of the rationale for the control/placebo used in the trial is recommended. For studies involving herbal medicine practitioners as part of the intervention, details of practitioners (e.g., training, registration status) should be reported. Not all recommendations are relevant for all types of herbal medicine interventions. Therefore, we begin this section with the words "where applicable." For example, a report of an RCT of an herbal medicinal product comprising crude herbal material (e.g., leaves, stems, root) prepared as a tea or decoction does not require reporting of the "type and concentration of solvent used and the plant to plant extract ratio" In addition, herbal interventions made by the investigators specifically for the study will not have a finished product or extract name or manufacturer For such products, all methods used in preparing and formulating the product must be reported. Similarly, allegiance is only relevant for studies in which the practitioner is a part of the intervention. In other studies, the practitioner may serve a more neutral role and thus their characteristics need not be reported. With these exceptions, all information outlined in these recommendations are suggested to be reported for all herbal medicine interventions.

- Also, outcome measures should reflect the intervention and indications tested while considering their underlying theories and concepts. For the results section, it is recommended that in addition to other baseline data, RCTs of herbal medicine interventions report any concomitant medication, herbal medicinal product, or other CAM use. It is recommended that when interpreting the results there be consideration of the specific herbal product and dosage regimen tested. This includes an overview of evidence on this particular herbal medicinal product. When considering generalizability), it is suggested that authors report how the product used in the trial generalizes to products used in self-care and/or in clinical practice.

### *Studies Performed without Proper Identification of Assay of Plant Materials*

With the decline in pharmacognosy education in the United States, it has been common for herbal research to be done on plants that have not been botanically identified, which have not been assayed for strength and which do not allow for proper understanding of the herb named in the research. For instance, Eleutherococcus senticosus is frequently identified as "ginseng" although it is not part of the Panax genus and has significantly different medicinal characteristics. As Jonathan Treasure, NIMH, has written:

"Inaccurate spelling of herb names is not uncommon in medical literature as all herbalists can attest, but more frequently there is a complete failure to use proper scientific nomenclature for botanicals."

This is not a trivial issue, because without a validated description of a herb by its binomial name (and preferably the naming authority) the identity of the herb cannot be established."

## ACONITUM

*Aconitum*, known as aconite, monkshood, wolfsbane,

leopard's bane, women's bane, Devil's helmet or blue rocket, is a genus of flowering plant belonging to the buttercup family (Ranunculaceae). There are over 250 species of *Aconitum*.

**Fig.** Aconitum Variegatum

## Overview

These herbaceous perennial plants are chiefly natives of the mountainous parts of the northern hemisphere, growing in moisture retentive but well draining soils on mountain meadows. Their dark green leaves lack stipules. They are palmate or deeply palmately lobed with 5–7 segments.

Each segment again is 3-lobed with coarse sharp teeth. The leaves have a spiral or alternate arrangement. The lower leaves have long petioles. These are handsome plants, the tall, erect stem being crowned by racemes of large and eye-catching blue, purple, white, yellow or pink zygomorphic flowers with numerous stamens. They are distinguishable by having one of the five petaloid sepals (the posterior one), called the galea, in the form of a cylindrical helmet; hence the English name monkshood. There are 2–10 petals, in the form of nectaries.

The two upper petals are large. They are placed under the hood of the calyx and are supported on long stalks. They have a hollow spur at their apex, containing the nectar. The other petals are small and scale like or non forming. The 3–5 carpels are partially fused at the base. The fruit is a follicle, a follicle being a dry, unilocular, many-seeded, fruit formed from one carpel, and dehiscing by the ventral suture in order to release seeds.

### *Uses*

The most common plant in this genus, *Aconitum napellus* (the Common Monkshood) was considered to be of therapeutic and of toxicological importance. Its roots have occasionally been mistaken for horseradish.

It has a short underground stem, from which dark-colored tapering roots descend. The crown or upper portion of the root gives rise to new plants. When touched to one's lip, the juice of the aconite root produces a feeling of numbness and tingling. This plant is used as a food plant by some Lepidoptera species including Dot Moth, The Engrailed, Mouse Moth, Wormwood Pug, and Yellow-tail.

The roots of *Aconitum ferox* supply the Nepalese poison called *bikh, bish,* or *nabee*. It contains large quantities of the alkaloid pseudaconitine, which is a deadly poison. *Aconitum palmatum* yields another of the bikh poisons. The root of *Aconitum luridum,* of the Himalaya, is said to be as virulent as that of *A. ferox* or *A. napellus*.

Fig. Northern Blue Monkshood (*Aconitum Noveboracense*)

Several species of Aconitum have been used as arrow poisons. The Minaro in Ladakh use *A. napellus* on their arrows to hunt ibex, while the Ainu in Japan used a species of Aconitum to hunt bear. The Chinese also used Aconitum poisons both for hunting, and for warfare.

Many species of *Aconitum* are cultivated in gardens, having either blue or yellow flowers. *Aconitum lycoctonum* (Alpine wolfsbane), is a yellow-flowered species common in the Alps of Switzerland. As garden plants the aconites are very ornamental, hardy perennial plants. They thrive in the garden soils, and will grow in the shade of trees. They are easily propagated by divisions of the root or by seeds; care should be taken not to leave pieces of the root where livestock might be poisoned.

### *Traditional Uses*

Aconite has long been used in the traditional medicine of Asia (India, China). In Ayurveda the herb is used to increase *pitta* (bile) and to enhance penetration in small doses. However more frequently the herb is detoxified according to the samskaras process and studies, cited in the detoxification section below show that it no longer possesses active toxicity.

It is used in traditional Chinese medicine as a treatment for Yang deficiency, "coldness", general debilitation. The herb is considered hot and toxic. It is prepared in extremely small doses. More frequently ginger processed aconite, of lower toxicity, "fu zi" is used.

Aconite is one ingredient of Tribhuvankirti, an Ayurvedic preparation for treating a "cold in the head" and fever. Aconite was mixed with patrinia and coix, in a famous treatment for appendicitis described in a formula from the Jingui Yaolue Aconite was also described in Greek and Roman medicine by Theophrastus, Dioscorides, and Pliny the Elder, who most likely prescribed the Alpine species Aconitum lycoctonum.

The herb was cultivated widely in Europe, probably reaching England before the tenth century, where it was farmed with some difficulty, but came to be widely valued as an anodyne, diuretic, and diaphoretic.

In the nineteenth century much aconite was imported from China, Japan, Fiji, and Tonga, with a number of species used to manufacture alkaloids of varying potency but generally similar effect, most often used externally and rarely internally. Effects of different preparations were standardized by testing on guinea pigs. In Western medicine preparations of aconite were used until just after the middle of the 20th century, but it is no longer employed as it has been replaced by safer and more effective drugs and treatments. The 1911 British Pharmaceutical Codex regarded the medical uses and toxicity of aconite root or leaves to be virtually identical to that of purified aconitine.

Aconite first stimulates and later paralyses/numbs the nerves to the sensations of pain, touch, and temperature if applied to the skin or to a mucous membrane; the initial tingling therefore gives place to a long-continued anaesthetic action. Great caution was required, as abraded skin could absorb a dangerous dose of the drug, and merely tasting some of the concentrated preparations available could be fatal. The local anaesthesia of peripheral nerves can be attributed to at least eleven alkaloids with varying potency and stability.

Internal uses were also pursued, to slow the pulse, as a sedative in pericarditis and heart palpitations, and well diluted as a mild diaphoretic, or to reduce feverishness in treatment of colds, pneumonia, quinsy, laryngitis, croup, and asthma due to exposure. Taken internally, aconite acts very notably on the circulation, the respiration, and the nervous system.

The pulse is slowed, the number of beats per minute being actually reduced, under considerable doses, to forty, or even thirty, per minute. The blood-pressure synchronously falls, and the heart is arrested in diastole. Immediately before arrest, the heart may beat much faster than normally, though with extreme irregularity, and in animals the auricles may be observed occasionally to miss a beat, as in poisoning by veratrine and colchicum.

The action of aconitine on the circulation is due to an initial stimulation of the cardio-inhibitory centre in the medulla oblongata (at the root of the vagus nerves), and later to a directly toxic influence on the nerve-ganglia and muscular fibres of the heart itself. The fall in blood-pressure is not due to any direct influence on the vessels. The respiration becomes slower owing to a paralytic action on the respiratory centre and, in warm-blooded animals, death is due to this action, the respiration being arrested before the action of the heart.

Aconite further depresses the activity of all nerve-terminals, the sensory being affected before the motor. In small doses, it therefore tends to relieve pain, if this is present. The activity of the spinal cord is similarly depressed. The pupil is at first contracted, and afterwards dilated.

The cerebrum is totally unaffected by aconite, consciousness and the intelligence remaining normal to the last. The antipyretic action which considerable doses of aconite display is not specific but is the result of its influence on the circulation and respiration and of its slight diaphoretic action.

## *Toxicology*

Marked symptoms appear quickly following the ingestion of a poisonous dose of aconite. The initial signs are gastrointestinal including nausea, vomiting, and diarrhea. There is followed by a sensation of burning, tingling, and numbness in the mouth and face, and of burning in the abdomen. In severe poisonings pronounced motor weakness occurs and cutaneous sensations of tingling and numbness spread to the limbs.

Cardiovascular features include hypotension, bradycardia, sinus tachycardia, and ventricular arrhythmias. Other features may include sweating, dizziness, difficulty in breathing, headache, and confusion. The main causes of death are ventricular arrhythmias and asystole. The only post-mortem signs are those of asphyxia.

Treatment of poisoning is mainly supportive. All patients require close monitoring of blood pressure and cardiac rhythm. Gastrointestinal decontamination with activated charcoal can be used if given within 1 hour of ingestion.

The major physiological antidote is atropine, which is used to treat bradycardia. Other drugs used for ventricular arrhythmia include lidocaine, amiodarone, bretylium, flecainide, procainamide, and mexiletine. Cardiopulmonary bypass is used if symptoms are refractory to treatment with these drugs. Successful use of charcoal hemoperfusion has been claimed in patients with severe aconite poisoning.

Poisoning may also occur following picking the leaves without wearing gloves; the aconitine toxin is absorbed easily through the skin. From practical experience, the sap oozing from eleven picked leaves will cause cardiac symptoms for a couple of hours. In this event, there will be no gastrointestinal effects.

Tingling will start at the point of absorption and extend up the arm to the shoulder, after which the heart will start to be affected. The tingling will be followed by unpleasant numbness. Treatment is similar to poisoning caused by oral ingestion.

Aconitine is a potent neurotoxin that blocks tetrodotoxin-sensitive sodium channels. Pretreatment with barakol 10 mg/kg IV reduces the incidence of aconitine-induced ventricular fibrillation and ventricular tachycardia, as well as mortality. Five ìg/kg IV of tetrodotoxin has the same effect. The protective effects of barakol are probably due to the prevention of intracellular sodium ion accumulation.

Canadian actor Andre Noble died during a camping trip on July 30, 2004 after the accidental consumption of aconite from monkshood.

Aconite was reported by the *Sunday Mirror* to have been used as poison in the murder of Pakistan cricket coach Bob Woolmer during the 2007 Cricket World Cup. However there is now evidence that Bob Woolmer was not murdered but died of natural causes.

### *Detoxification*

Both Chinese medicine and Ayurveda have methods of processing aconite to reduce its toxicity.

In Chinese medicine, the traditional pao zhi or preparation of aconite is to steam it with ginger in a fairly elaborate procedure. Due to the variable levels of toxicity in any given sample of the dried herb, there are still issues with using it. Most but not all cases of aconite toxicity in Taiwan were due to the consumption of unprocessed aconite.

According to an article by the Indian scientists Thorat and Dahanukar, "Crude aconite is an extremely lethal substance. However, the science of Ayurveda looks upon aconite as a therapeutic entity. Crude aconite is always processed i.e. it undergoes 'samskaras' before being utilized in the Ayurvedic formulations. This study was undertaken in mice, to ascertain whether 'processed' aconite is less toxic as compared to the crude or unprocessed one.

It was seen that crude aconite was significantly toxic to mice (100% mortality at a dose of 2.6 mg/mouse) whereas the fully processed aconite was absolutely non-toxic (no mortality at a dose even 8 times as high as that of crude aconite). Further, all the steps in the processing were essential for complete detoxification"

## ACONITINE

Aconitine is a highly poisonous alkaloid derived from various aconite species. It is a neurotoxin that opens TTX-sensitive $Na^+$ channels in the heart and other tissues, and is used for creating models of cardiac arrhythmia. Aconitine was previously used as an antipyretic and analgesic, and still has some limited application in herbal medicine although the narrow therapeutic index makes calculating appropriate dosage difficult. Aconitine has the chemical formula $C_{34}H_{47}NO_{11}$, and is soluble in chloroform or benzene, slightly in alcohol or ether, and only very slightly in water.

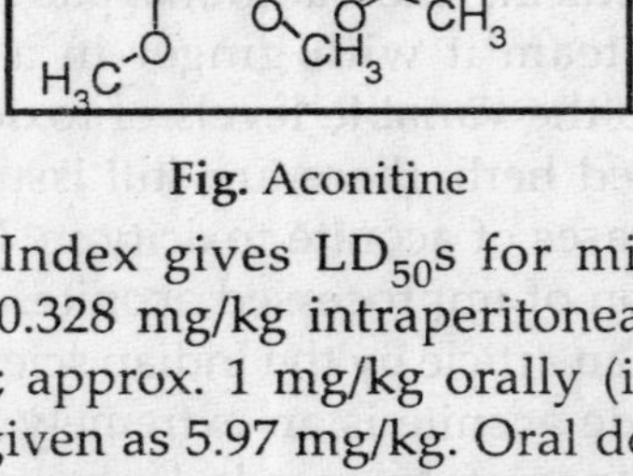


Fig. Aconitine

The Merck Index gives $LD_{50}$s for mice: 0.166 mg/kg (intravenously); 0.328 mg/kg intraperitoneally (injected into the body cavity); approx. 1 mg/kg orally (ingested). In rats, the oral $LD_{50}$ is given as 5.97 mg/kg. Oral doses as low as 1.5 – 6 mg aconitine were reported to be lethal in humans.

It is quickly absorbed via mucous membranes, but also via skin. Respiratory paralysis, in very high doses also cardiac arrest, leads to death. A few minutes after ingestion paresthesia starts, which includes tingling in the oral region.

This extends to the whole body, starting from the extremities. Anesthesia, sweating and cooling of the body, nausea and vomiting and other similar symptoms follow. Sometimes there is strong pain, accompanied by cramps, or diarrhea. There is no antidote, so only the symptoms can be treated, traditionally with compounds such as atropine, strychnine or barakol, although it is unclear whether any of these are effective. Some other toxins such as tetrodotoxin which bind to the same target site but have opposite effects, can reduce the effects of aconitine, but are so toxic themselves that death may result regardless. Serum or urine concentrations of the chemical may be measured to confirm diagnosis in hospitalized poisoning victims, while postmortem blood levels have been reported in at least 5 fatal cases.

## ARNICA

Arnica is a genus with about 30 perennial, herbaceous species, belonging to the sunflower family (Asteraceae). The genus name *Arnica* may be derived from the Greek *arna*, "lamb", in reference to the soft, hairy leaves.

This circumboreal and montane genus occurs mostly in the temperate regions of western North America, while two are native to Eurasia (*A. angustifolia* and *A. montana*).

*Arnica* used to be included in the tribe Senecioneae, because it has a pappus of fine bristles. This was soon questioned and Nordenstam placed it tentatively in tribe Heliantheae s.l. This arrangement also became uncertain because of the sesquiterpene lactone chemistry in certain species. Lately Arnica was placed in an unresolved clade together with Madiinae, Eupatorieae, Heliantheae s.s. and Pectidinae. Several species, such as *Arnica montana* and *Arnica chamissonis*, contain helenalin, which is a sesquiterpene lactone that is a major ingredient in anti-inflammatory preparations (mostly against bruises). *Arnica* species are used as food plants by the larvae of some Lepidoptera species including *Bucculatrix arnicella*.

## Characteristics

They have a deep-rooted, erect stem that is usually unbranched. Their downy, opposite leaves are borne towards the apex of the stem. The ovoid, leathery, basal leaves are arranged in a rosette.

Fig. A.Chamissonis

They show large yellow or orange flowers, 6-8 cm wide with 10-15 long ray florets and numerous disc florets. The phyllaries (a bract under the flowerhead) has long spreading hairs Each phyllary is associated with a ray floret. Species of *Arnica,* with an involucre (a circle of bracts arranged surrounding the flower head) arranged in two rows, have only their outer phyllaries associated with ray florets. The flowers have a slight aromatic smell. The seed-like fruit has a pappus of plumose, white or pale tan bristles. The entire plant has a strong and distinct pine-sage odor when the leaves of mature plants are rubbed or bruised.

## Arnica Montana

The species *Arnica montana,* native to Europe, has long been used medicinally, but this use has not been substantiated.

Fig. Frigid Arnica

### *Medicinal Uses*

Arnica montana has been used medicinally for centuries. The roots contain derivatives of thymol, which are used as fungicides and preservatives and may have some anti-inflammatory effect.

Arnica is currently used in liniment and ointment preparations used for strains, sprains, and bruises.

Commercial arnica preparations are frequently used by professional athletes. Arnica should not be taken internally due to its toxicity, with the spurious exception of homeopathic preparations that are diluted at 24X or more, since only water remains. The thymol derivatives concentrated in the plants roots have been clinically shown to be effective vasodilators of subcutaneous blood capillaries.

Arnica preparations used topically have been demonstrated to act as an anti-inflammatory and assist normal healing processes by facilitating transport of blood and fluid accumulations through a dilating action of subcutaneous blood capillaries. In one double-blind trial, Arnica montana was found to be equally effective as the more expensive diclofenac for accelerating wound healing after foot surgery, but was less effective than the same drug for pain relief.

However, Diclofenac does not promote wound healing as it is an anti-inflammatory drug and hence this comparison is not useful. A study of wound-healing after surgery to treat varicose veins found a trend towards a beneficial effect of reduction of pain and hematoma following surgery.

### Homeopathy

Homeopathic preparations of Arnica are widely marketed and used, and enjoy popularity. In the UK the Medicines and Healthcare products Regulatory Agency has registered the product for sprains and bruising under the'National Rules for Homoeopathic Products'.

These rules allow claims of efficacy for these conditions to be made on the packaging in the absence of similar evidence to that required for conventional medicines under the Medicines Act 1968 and 1971. One small trial was claimed to suggest that the homeopathic use of Arnica to be no more effective than a placebo. In some quarters, the fact that homeopathic Arnica has been the subject of published clinical trials at all has drawn criticism grounded on the allegation that the basic premise of the high dilutions used in homeopathy would be inherently flawed.

With respect to the range of homeopathic Arnica creams available on the market it should be noted that these are generally formulated using the mother tincture rather than a dilution, and they therefore do in fact contain measurable quantities of the medicinally active substance.

***Toxicity***

Arnica contains the toxin helenalin, which can be poisonous if large amounts of the plant are eaten, and contact with the plant can also cause skin irritation. If enough of the material is ingested, the toxin helenalin produces severe gastroenteritis, and internal bleeding of the digestive tract.

## ATROPA BELLADONNA

Atropa belladonna, commonly known as belladonna or deadly nightshade, is a perennial herbaceous plant in the family Solanaceae, native to Europe, North Africa, and Western Asia. The foliage and berries are extremely toxic, containing tropane alkaloids.

These toxins include scopolamine and hyoscyamine which cause a bizarre delirium and hallucinations. The drug atropine is derived from the plant.

It has a long history of use as a medicine, cosmetic, and poison. Before the Middle Ages, it was used as an anesthetic for surgery, and it was used as a poison by early men, ancient Romans, including the wives of two Emperors, and by Macbeth of Scotland before he became a Scottish King.

The genus name"atropa" comes from Atropos, one of the three Fates in Greek mythology (the one who cuts the thread of life), and the name"atropa bella donna" is derived from an admonition in Italian and Greek meaning"do not betray a beautiful lady".

## Description

**Fig.** Atropa Belladonna

Atropa belladonna is a branching herbaceous perennial, often growing as a subshrub, from a fleshy rootstock. Plants grow to 1.5 metres (4.9 ft) tall with 18 centimetres (7.1 in) long ovate leaves. The bell-shaped flowers are dull purple with green tinges and faintly scented.

The fruits are berries, which are green ripening to a shiny black, and approximately 1 centimetre (0.39 in) in diameter. The berries are sweet and are consumed by animals that disperse the seeds in their droppings, even though the seeds contain toxic alkaloids. There is a pale yellow flowering form called Atropa belladonna var. lutea with pale yellow fruit.

Atropa belladona is rarely used in gardens, but when grown it is usually for its large upright habit and showy berries. It is naturalized in parts of North America, where it is often found in shady, moist locations with limestone-rich soils. It is considered a weed species in parts of the world, where it colonizes areas with disturbed soils.

Germination of the small seeds is often difficult, due to hard seed coats that cause seed dormancy. Germination takes several weeks under alternating temperature conditions but can be sped up with the use of gibberellic acid. The seedlings need sterile soil to prevent damping off and resent root disturbance during transplanting.

## Naming and Taxonomy

The first botanical description was by Linnaeus in *Species Plantarum* in 1753. It is in the nightshade family (*Solanaceae*), which it shares with potatoes, tomatoes, eggplants, jimsonweed, tobacco, wolfberry, and chili peppers. The common names for this species include belladonna, deadly nightshade, divale, dwale, banewort, devil's cherries, naughty man's cherries, black cherry, devil's herb, great morel, and dwayberry.

The name Atropa is thought to be derived from that of the Greek goddess Atropos, one of the three Greek fates or destinies who would determine the course of a man's life by the weaving of threads that symbolized their birth, the events in their life and finally their death; with Atropos cutting these threads to mark the latter. The name "belladonna" comes from the Italian language, meaning "beautiful lady"; originating either from its usage as cosmetic for the face, or, more probably, from its usage to increase the pupil size in ladies.

**Toxicity**

**Fig.** Flowers of *Belladonna*

Belladonna is one of the most toxic plants found in the Western hemisphere. All parts of the plant contain tropane alkaloids. The berries pose the greatest danger to children because they look attractive and have a somewhat sweet taste.

The consumption of two to five berries by children and ten to twenty berries by adults can be lethal. The root of the plant is generally the most toxic part, though this can vary from one specimen to another. Ingestion of a single leaf of the plant can be fatal to an adult.

The active agents in Belladonna, atropine, hyoscine (scopolamine), and hyoscyamine, have anticholinergic properties. Atropa belladonna has been mistaken for blueberries and ingestion of six berries resulted in acute anticholinergic syndrome.

The symptoms of belladonna poisoning include dilated pupils, sensitivity to light, blurred vision, tachycardia, loss of balance, staggering, headache, rash, flushing, dry mouth and throat, slurred speech, urinary retention, constipation, confusion, hallucinations, delirium, and convulsions.

The plant's deadly symptoms are caused by atropine's disruption of the parasympathetic nervous system's ability to regulate non-volitional/subconscious activities such as sweating, breathing, and heart rate. The antidote for belladonna poisoning is physostigmine or pilocarpine, the same as for atropine.

*Atropa belladonna* is also toxic to many domestic animals, causing narcosis and paralysis. However, cattle and rabbits seem to eat the plant without suffering harmful effects. Its anticholinergic properties will cause in humans the disruption of cognitive capacities like memory and learning.

## Uses

### *Cosmetics*

The common name *belladonna* originates from its historic use by women - *Bella Donna* is Italian for *beautiful lady*. Drops prepared from the belladonna plant were used to dilate women's pupils, an effect considered attractive. Today it is known that the atropine in belladonna acts as an antimuscarinic, blocking receptors in the muscles of the eye that constrict pupil size.

Belladonna is currently rarely used cosmetically, as it carries the adverse effects of causing minor visual distortions, inability to focus on near objects, and increased heart rate. Prolonged usage was reputed to cause blindness.

### *Medicine*

There is currently insufficient scientific evidence to recommend the use of *A. belladonna* in its natural form for any condition, although some of its components, in particular *l*-atropine which was purified from belladona in the 1830s, have accepted medical uses. Donnatal is a prescription pharmaceutical, approved in the United States by the FDA, that combines natural belladonna alkaloids in a specific, fixed ratio with phenobarbital to provide peripheral anticholinergic/antispasmodic action and mild sedation.

According to its labeling, it is possibly effective for use as adjunctive therapy in the treatment of irritable bowel syndrome (irritable colon, spastic colon, mucous colitis) and acute enterocolitis.

### Traditional and Alternative Medicine

**Fig.** Berries of Belladonna

*A. belladonna* has been used in traditional treatments for centuries for an assortment of conditions including headache, menstrual symptoms, peptic ulcer disease, histaminic reaction, inflammation, and motion sickness, with at least one 19th century eclectic medicine journal explaining how to prepare a Belladona tincture for direct administration to patients.

Homeopathic remedies prepared from the belladonna plant have been sold as treatments for various conditions, although there is no scientific evidence to support the efficacy of this use. Clinically and in research trials, the most common preparation is diluted to the 30C level in homeopathic notation.

This level of dilution contains no molecules of the original plant, although preparations with lesser dilutions which statistically contain trace amounts of the plant are advertised for sale.

### Recreational Drug

*Atropa belladonna*, along with related plants such as jimson weed (*Datura stramonium*), have occasionally been used as a recreational drug because of the vivid hallucinations and delirium that it produces. These hallucinations are most commonly described as very unpleasant, however, and recreational use is considered extremely dangerous because of the high risk of unintentional fatal overdose. In addition, the central nervous system effects of atropine include memory disruption, which may lead to severe confusion.

## *Poison*

It was used by early men in poisonous arrows. In Ancient Rome, it was used as a poison by Agrippina the Younger, wife of Emperor Claudius, and Livia, who is rumored to have used it to kill her husband Emperor Augustus.

Macbeth of Scotland, when he was still one of the lieutenants of King Duncan I of Scotland, used it during a truce to poison the troops of the invading Harold Harefoot, King of England, to the point that the English troops were unable to stand their ground and had to retreat to their ships.

## Folklore

In the past, it was believed that witches used a mixture of belladonna, opium poppy, and other plants, typically poisonous (such as monkshood and poison hemlock) in flying ointment they applied to help them fly to gatherings with other witches.

**Fig.** Leaves of Belladonna

Carlo Ginzburg and others have argued that flying ointments were preparations meant to encourage hallucinatory dreaming; a possible explanation for the inclusion of belladonna and opium poppy in flying ointments concerns the known antagonism between tropane alkaloids of belladonna (specifically scopolamine) and opiate alkaloids in the opium poppy, *Papaver somniferum* (specifically morphine), which produces a dream-like waking state.

This antagonism was known in folk medicine, discussed in eclectic (botanical) medicine formularies, and posited as the explanation of how flying ointments might have actually worked in contemporary writing on witchcraft.

The antagonism between opiates and tropanes is the original basis of the Twilight Sleep that was provided to Queen Victoria to deaden pain as well as consciousness during childbirth, and which was later modified so that isolated alkaloids were used instead of plant materials. The belladonna herb was also notable for its unpredictable effects from toxicity.

## BRYONY

Bryony is the common name for any of twelve species in the genus Bryonia. These are perennial, tendril-climbing, dioecious herbs with palmately lobed leaves and flowers in axillary clusters. The fruit is a smooth, globular berry.

**Fig.** Bryonia alba (White Briony)

The English species *Bryonia alba* is known as white bryony and grows in hedgerows as far north as Yorkshire. There are eight varieties established in Europe.

Some species find use in herbal medicine. *Bryonia* is used as a food plant by the larvae of some Lepidoptera species including Cabbage Moth.

## Other

**Fig.** A Close-up View of the Male Flowers of White Bryony.

Variants of the plant name, such as Briony, Bryonie, and Bryony are used, in some cultures, as names for women or girls. It was quite popular in the 18th century. The name is most popular in and around Scottish regions where the plant is mainly seen and grown. This results in many Scottish versions of the name.

## DATURA

*Datura* is a genus of nine species of vespertine flowering plants belonging to the family Solanaceae. Its precise and natural distribution is uncertain, owing to its extensive cultivation and naturalization throughout the temperate and tropical regions of the globe.

Its distribution within the Americas, however, is most likely restricted to the United States and Mexico, where the highest species diversity occurs.

**Fig.** Datura Stramonium

Some South American plants formerly thought of as

*Daturas* are now treated as belonging to the distinct genus *Brugmansia* {this genus differs in being woody, making shrubs or small trees, and in having pendulous flowers}. Other related genera include *Hyoscyamus* and *Atropa.*

## Description

*Datura* are herbaceous, leafy annuals and short-lived perennials which can reach up to 2 meters in height. The leaves are alternate, 10–20 cm long and 5–18 cm broad, with a lobed or toothed margin.

The flowers are erect or spreading (not pendulous like those of the closely allied Brugmansia), trumpet-shaped, 5–20 cm long and 4–12 cm broad at the mouth; colors vary from white to yellow, pink, and pale purple. The fruit is a spiny capsule 4–10 cm long and 2–6 cm broad, splitting open when ripe to release the numerous seeds. The seeds disperse freely over pastures, fields and even wasteland locations.

*Datura* belongs to the classic "witches' weeds," along with deadly nightshade, henbane, and mandrake. Most parts of the plants contain toxic hallucinogens, and *Datura* has a long history of use for causing delirious states and death. It was well known as an essential ingredient of love potions and witches' brews.

Common names include Thorn Apple (from the spiny fruit), Pricklyburr (similarly), Jimson Weed, Moonflower, Hell's Bells, Devil's Weed, Devil's Cucumber, and Devil's Trumpet, (from their large trumpet-shaped flowers). Nathaniel Hawthorne refers to one type in The Scarlet Letter as Apple-Peru.

The word *datura* comes from the Hindi *Dhatura* (thorn apple); record of this name dates back to 1662 (OED). In Tamil it is called "oomathai". In Oriya it is called "Dudura".

*Datura* species are food plants for the larvae of some Lepidoptera (butterfly and moth) species including *Hypercompe indecisa.*

### *Species and Cultivars*

It is difficult to classify a datura as to its species, and it often happens that descriptions of new species are accepted prematurely. Later it is found that these "new species" are simply varieties that have evolved due to conditions at a specific location. They usually disappear in a few years. Contributing to the confusion are the facts that various species such as *D. wrightii* and *D. inoxia* are very similar in appearance, and that the variation within a species can be extreme.

For example, *Datura* have the interesting property of being able to change size of plant, size of leaf, and size of flowers, all depending on location.

The same species, when growing in a half-shady damp location can develop into a magnificent flowering bush half as tall as a person, but when growing in a very dry location will only grow into a thin little plant just higher than his ankles, with tiny flowers and a few miniature leaves.

*Today, experts classify only nine species of Datura*:

- *Datura ceratocaula*
- *Datura discolor*: Desert Thorn-apple
- *Datura ferox*: Long Spined Thorn-apple
- *Datura inoxia* or *Datura innoxia*: Thorn-apple, downy thorn-apple, Indian-apple, moonflower, sacred datura, toloatzin, or toloache
- *Datura leichhardtii* (syn. *D. pruinosa*): Leichhardt's Datura
- *Datura metel*
- *Datura quercifolia*: Oak-leaf Thorn-apple
- *Datura stramonium* (syn. *D. inermis*): Jimsonweed, Thorn-apple
- *Datura wrightii*: Sacred datura, Sacred Thorn-apple

American Brugmansia & Datura Society, Inc. (ABADS), is designated in the 2004 edition of the International Code of Nomenclature for Cultivated Plants as the official International Cultivar Registration Authority for *Datura*. This role was delegated to ABADS by the International Society for Horticultural Science in 2002.

### *Cultivation*

Datura are usually planted annually from the seed

produced in the spiny pods, but with care, plants can be overwintered. Most species are suited to being planted outside or in containers. As a rule, they need warm, sunny places and soil that will keep their roots dry. When grown outdoors in good locations, the plants tend to reseed themselves and may become invasive. In containers, they should have porous, aerated potting soil with adequate drainage. The plants are susceptible to fungi in the root area, so organic enrichers such as compost and manure should be avoided.

**Fig.** Fruit

### *Toxicity*

All *Datura* plants contain tropane alkaloids such as scopolamine, hyoscyamine, and atropine, primarily in their seeds and flowers. Because of the presence of these substances, *Datura* has been used for centuries in some cultures as a poison and hallucinogen.

There can be a 5:1 toxin variation across plants, and a given plant's toxicity depends on its age, where it is growing, and the local weather conditions. This variation makes *Datura* exceptionally hazardous as a drug. In traditional cultures, a great deal of experience with, and detailed knowledge of, *Datura* was critical in order to minimize harm.

**Fig.** *D. Inoxia* with Ripe, Split-open Fruit

Many tragic incidents result from modern recreational users ingesting *Datura*. For example, in the 1990s and 2000s, the United States media contained stories of adolescents and young adults dying or becoming seriously ill from intentionally ingesting *Datura*.

There are also several reports in the medical literature of deaths from *Datura stramonium* and *Datura ferox* intoxication. Children are especially vulnerable to atropine poisoning, and their prognosis is likely to be fatal.

In some parts of Europe and India, *Datura* has been a popular poison for suicide and murder. From 1950–1965, the State Chemical Laboratories in Agra, India investigated 2,778 deaths that were caused by ingesting *Datura*.

### *Effects of Ingestion*

Due to the potent combination of anticholinergic substances it contains, *Datura* intoxication typically produces effects similar to that of an anticholinergic delirium: a complete inability to differentiate reality from fantasy (delirium, as contrasted to hallucination); hyperthermia; tachycardia; bizarre, and possibly violent behaviour; and severe mydriasis with resultant painful photophobia that can last several days. Pronounced amnesia is another commonly reported effect.

According to the drug information site Erowid, no other substance has received as many "Train Wreck" (i.e., severely negative experience) reports as has *Datura*, noting that "the overwhelming majority of those who describe to us their use of *Datura* (and to a lesser extent, Belladonna, Brugmansia and Brunfelsia) find their experiences extremely mentally and physically unpleasant and not infrequently physically dangerous."

### *Treatment*

Due to their agitated behaviour and confused mental state, victims of *Datura* poisoning are typically hospitalized. Gastric lavage (stomach pumping) and the administration of activated charcoal can be used to reduce the stomach's absorption of the ingested material.

The drug physostigmine is used to reverse the effect of the poisons. Benzodiazepines can be given to curb the patient's agitation, and supportive care with oxygen, hydration, and symptomatic treatment is often provided. Observation of the patient is indicated until the symptoms resolve, usually from 24–36 hours after ingestion of the *Datura*.

## Gelsemium

*Gelsemium* is a genus of flowering plants belonging to family Gelsemiaceae. The genus contains three species of shrubs to straggling or twining climbers.

Two species are native to North America, and one to China and Southeast Asia. Carolus Linnaeus first classified *G. sempervirens* as *Bignonia sempervirens* in 1753; Antoine Laurent de Jussieu renamed the genus in 1789. *Gelsemium* is a Latinized form of the Italian word for jasmine, *gelsomino*. All three species of this genus are poisonous. *Gelsemium* has been shown to contain methoxyindoles.

## Hyoscyamus Niger

Henbane (*Hyoscyamus niger*), also known as stinking nightshade, is a plant of the family Solanaceae that originated in Eurasia, though it is now globally distributed.

## Toxicity and Historical Usage

It was historically used in combination with other plants, such as mandrake, deadly nightshade, and datura as an anaesthetic potion, as well as for its psychoactive properties in "magic brews."

These psychoactive properties include visual hallucinations and a sensation of flight. Its usage was originally in continental Europe, Asia and the Arabic world, though it did spread to England sometime during the Middle Ages. The use of Henbane by the ancient Greeks was documented by Pliny. The plant, recorded as *Herba Apollinaris*, was used to yield oracles by the priestesses of Apollo.

Henbane can be toxic, even fatal, to animals in low doses. Its name dates at least to 1265. The origins of the word are unclear but "hen" probably originally meant death rather than referring to chickens.

Hyoscyamine, scopolamine, and other tropane alkaloids have been found in the foliage and seeds of the plant. Common effects of henbane ingestion in humans include hallucinations, dilated pupils, restlessness, and flushed skin. Less common symptoms such as tachycardia, convulsions, vomiting, hypertension, hyperpyrexia and ataxia have all been noted. Not all animals are susceptible; the larvae of some Lepidoptera species including Cabbage Moth eat henbane.

It was sometimes one of the ingredients in grut, traditionally used in beers as a flavouring, until replaced by hops in the 11th to 16th centuries (for example, the Bavarian Purity Law of 1516 outlawed ingredients other than barley, hops, and water).

**Toxicity and Historical Usage**

It was historically used in combination with other plants, such as mandrake, deadly nightshade, and datura as an anaesthetic potion, as well as for its psychoactive properties in "magic brews." These psychoactive properties include visual hallucinations and a sensation of flight. Its usage was originally in continental Europe, Asia and the Arabic world, though it did spread to England sometime during the Middle Ages. The use of Henbane by the ancient Greeks was documented by Pliny. The plant, recorded as *Herba Apollinaris*, was used to yield oracles by the priestesses of Apollo.

Henbane can be toxic, even fatal, to animals in low doses. Its name dates at least to 1265. The origins of the word are unclear but "hen" probably originally meant death rather than referring to chickens.. Hyoscyamine, scopolamine, and other tropane alkaloids have been found in the foliage and seeds of the plant.

Common effects of henbane ingestion in humans include hallucinations, dilated pupils, restlessness, and flushed skin. Less common symptoms such as tachycardia, convulsions, vomiting, hypertension, hyperpyrexia and ataxia have all been noted. Not all animals are susceptible; the larvae of some

Lepidoptera species including Cabbage Moth eat henbane. It was sometimes one of the ingredients in grut, traditionally used in beers as a flavouring, until replaced by hops in the 11th to 16th centuries (for example, the Bavarian Purity Law of 1516 outlawed ingredients other than barley, hops, and water).

**Fig.** Henbane in Flower

In 1910, an American homeopathic doctor living in London, Hawley Harvey Crippen, allegedly used scopolamine, an alkaloid extracted from henbane, to poison his wife. Henbane is thought to have been the "hebenon" poured into the ear of Hamlet's father (although other candidates for hebenon exist).

### Misidentification

In 2008 celebrity chef Antony Worrall Thompson recommended Henbane as a "tasty addition to salads" in the August 2008 issue of *Healthy and Organic Living* magazine. He subsequently said that he had made an error, confusing the herb with Fat Hen, a member of the spinach family. He apologised, and the magazine sent subscribers an urgent message stating that Henbane "is a very toxic plant and should never be eaten."

## DRYOPTERIS FILIX-MAS

*Dryopteris filix-mas* (Common Male Fern or Male Fern) is one of the most common ferns of the temperate Northern Hemisphere, occurring throughout much of Europe, Asia, and North America. It favours damp shaded areas and is common in the understory of woodlands, but is also found in shady places on hedge-banks, rocks, and screes. It is much less abundant in North America than in Europe.

**Fig.** Dryopteris Filix-mas

The half-evergreen leaves have an upright habit and reach a maximum length of 1.5 m, with a single crown on each rootstock. The bipinnate leaves consist of 20-35 pinnae on each side of the rachis.

The leaves taper at both ends, with the basal pinnae about half the length of the middle pinnae. The pinules are rather blunt and equally lobed all around. The stalks are covered with orange-brown scales. On the abaxial surface of the mature blade 5 to 6 sori develop in two rows. When the spores ripen in August to November, the indusium starts to shrivel, leading to the release of the spores. This species hybridises easily with *Dryopteris affinis* (Scaly Male Fern) and *Dryopteris oreades* (Mountain Male Fern).

## Cultivation and Uses

The root was used, until recent times, as an anthelmintic to expel tapeworms. It is sometimes referred to in ancient literature as Worm Fern. It is also grown as an ornamental fern in gardens.

## Pokeweed

The pokeweeds, also known as poke, pokebush, pokeberry, pokeroot, polk salad, polk salat, polk sallet, inkberry or ombú, comprise the genus *Phytolacca*, perennial plants native to North America, South America, East Asia and New Zealand.

Pokeweed contains *phytolaccatoxin* and *phytolaccigenin*, which are poisonous to mammals. However, the berries are eaten by birds, which are not affected by the toxin because the small seeds with very hard outer shells remain intact in the digestive system and are eliminated whole.

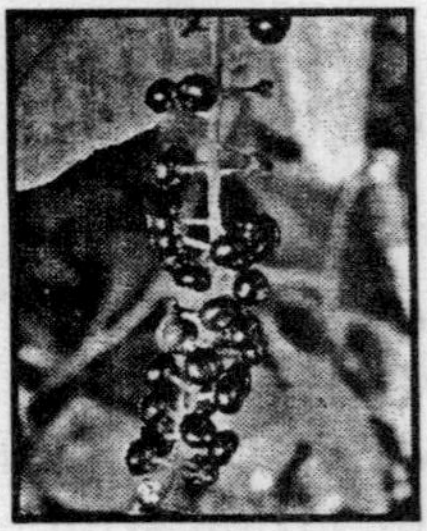

**Fig.** Pokeweed

Pokeweeds are herbs growing from 1 to 10 ft. tall, although specimens as tall as 14 ft. have been observed. They have single alternate leaves, pointed at the end, with crinkled edges. The stems are often pink or red. The flowers are greenish-white, in long clusters at the ends of the stems. They develop into dark purple berries.

*Phytolacca dioica*, the ombú, grows as a tree on the pampas of South America and is one of the few providers of shade on the open grassland. It is a symbol of Argentina and gaucho culture.

## Uses

All parts of pokeweed are toxic including the raw aboveground leaves sprouting in the early spring. The poisonous principles are found in highest concentrations in the rootstock, less in the mature leaves and stems, and least in the fruits.

Young leaves, if collected before acquiring a red colour, are edible if boiled for 5 minutes, rinsed, and reboiled. Berries are toxic when raw but cooked juice is edible (the seeds remain toxic after cooking).

Young pokeweed leaves can be boiled three times to reduce the toxin, discarding the water after each boiling. The result is known as *poke salit*, or *poke salad*, and is occasionally available commercially. Many authorities advise against eating pokeweed even after thrice boiling, as traces of the toxin may still remain. It should never be eaten uncooked.

For many decades, poke salad has been a staple of southern U.S. cuisine, despite campaigns by doctors who believed pokeweed remained toxic even after being boiled. The lingering cultural significance of Poke salad can be found in the 1969 hit song "Polk Salad Annie," written and performed by Tony Joe White, and famously covered by Elvis Presley, as well as other bands including the El Orbits of Houston, Texas.

Pokeberry juice is added to other juices for jelly by those who believe it can relieve the pain of arthritis. There are poke salad festivals held annually in Blanchard, Louisiana; Gainesboro, TN; Harlan, KY; and, Arab, Alabama.

**Fig.** A Garden Cultivar of *P. Americana* with Large Fruit

Since pioneer times, pokeweed has been used as a folk remedy to treat many ailments. It can be applied topically or taken internally. Topical treatments have been used for acne and other ailments. Internal treatments include tonsilitis, swollen glands and weight loss.

Grated pokeroot was used by Native Americans as a poultice to treat inflammations and rashes of the breast. Independent researchers are investigating phytolacca's use in treating AIDS and cancer patients. Especially to those who have not been properly trained in its use, pokeweed should be considered dangerous and possibly deadly.

Ingestion of poisonous parts of the plant may cause severe stomach cramping, nausea with persistent diarrhea and vomiting, slow and difficult breathing, weakness, spasms, hypotension, severe convulsions, and death.

However, consuming fewer than 10 uncooked berries is generally harmless to adults. Several investigators have reported deaths in children following the ingestion of uncooked berries or pokeberry juice. Severe poisonings have been reported in adults who ingested mature pokeweed leaves and following the ingestion of tea brewed from one-half teaspoonful of powdered pokeroot.

Pokeweed berries yield a red ink or dye, which was once used by aboriginal Americans to decorate their horses. The United States Declaration of Independence was written in fermented pokeberry juice (hence the common name 'inkberry').

Many letters written home during the American Civil War were written in pokeberry ink; the writing in these surviving letters appears brown. The red juice has also been used to symbolize blood, as in the anti-slavery protest of Benjamin Lay. A rich brown dye can be made by soaking fabrics in fermenting berries in a hollowed-out pumpkin.

Some pokeweeds are also grown as ornamental plants, mainly for their attractive berries; a number of cultivars have been selected for larger fruit panicles. Pokeweeds are used as food plants by the larvae of some Lepidoptera species including Giant Leopard Moth.

## Toxic Principle

Toxic constituents have been identified including the alkaloid phytolaccine (and the alkaloid phytolaccotoxin), as well as a glycoprotein.

### *Clinical Signs*

- *In humans:* The eating of limited quantities of poke, perhaps of the shoots, may cause retching or vomiting after two hours or more. These signs may be followed by dyspnea, perspiration, spasms, severe purging, prostration, tremors, watery diarrhea and vomiting (sometimes bloody) and, sometimes, convulsions. In severe poisonings, symptoms are weakness, excessive yawning, slowed breathing, fast heartbeat, dizziness, and possibly seizures, coma and death.

- *In horses:* Colic, diarrhea, respiratory failure.
- *In swine:* Unsteadiness, inability to rise, retching. Jerking movements of the legs. Below-normal temperature.
- *In cattle:* Same general signs plus a decrease in milk production.

## PODOPHYLLUM

*Podophyllum* is a genus of six species of herbaceous perennial plants in the family Berberidaceae, native to eastern Asia (five species) and eastern North America (one species, Mayapple *P. peltatum*). They are woodland plants, typically growing in colonies derived from a single root.

**Fig.** Podophyllum Peltatum in Flower

The stems grow to 30–40 cm tall, with palmately lobed umbrella-like leaves up to 20–40 cm diameter with 3–9 shallowly to deeply cut lobes.

The plants produce several stems from a creeping underground rhizome; some stems bear a single leaf and do not produce any flower or fruit, while flowering stems produce a pair or more leaves with 1–8 flowers in the axil between the apical leaves.

The flowers are white, yellow or red, 2–6 cm diameter with 6–9 petals, and mature into a green, yellow or red fleshy fruit 2–5 cm long.

**Fig.** Podophyllum Hexandrum Flowers & Leaves

All the parts of the plant, excepting the fruit, are poisonous. Even the fruit, though not dangerously poisonous, can cause unpleasant indigestion. The substance they contain (podophyllotoxin or podophyllin) is used as a purgative and as a cytostatic. Posalfilin is a drug containing podophyllin and salicylic acid that is used to treat the plantar wart. They are also grown as ornamental plants for their attractive foliage and flowers.

## VERATRUM

*Veratrum* is a genus of coarse, highly poisonous perennial herbs of the Melanthiaceae family. In English they are usually known as the False hellebores. Members of *Veratrum* are known both in western herbalism and traditional Chinese medicine as toxic herbs to be used with great caution.

It is one of the medicinals ("Li lu") cited in Chinese herbal texts as incompatible with many other common herbs because of its potentiating effects. Especially, many root (and root-shaped) herbs, particularly ginseng, san qi, and hai seng, will create and or exacerbate a toxic effect.

**Fig.** Young Veratrum Lobelianum

*Veratrum* species are used as food plants by the larvae of some Lepidoptera species including Setaceous Hebrew Character.

Birth defects in livestock grazing on *Veratrum californicum* (native to the western United States) led to the study of cyclopamine and jervine which are important in animal developmental biology including cancer treatment.

## Distribution

*Veratrum* is found in many areas of the temperate Northern Hemisphere. Widely distributed in montane habitats throughout North America.

*Veratrum* species prefer full sunlight and deep, wet soils, and are common in wet mountain meadows, swamps, and near streambanks.

*Veratrum* species occur from Alaska south into the mountains of California, and are widely distributed throughout the Rocky Mountains.

*Veratrum* is very abundant in Eastern North America from Quebec southward through the Appalachians into North Carolina. Thirteen species are found in China.

## Toxicity

*Veratrum* species contain highly toxic steroidal alkaloids (e.g. veratridine), that activate sodium ion channels and cause rapid cardiac failure and death if ingested. All parts of the plant are poisonous, with the root and rhizomes being the most poisonous parts of the plant. Following ingestion symptoms typically occur between 30 minutes and 4 hours after ingestion.

Symptoms include nausea and vomiting, abdominal pain, numbness, headache, sweating, muscle weakness, bradycardia, hypotension, cardiac arrhythmia, and seizures.

Treatment for poisoning includes gastrointestinal decontamination with activated charcoal followed by supportive care including antiemetics for persistent nausea and vomiting, along with atropine for treatment of bradycardia and fluid replacement and vasopressors for the treatment of hypotension.

## Uses

Native Americans used the juice pressed from the roots of this plant to poison arrows before combat. The dried powdered root of this plant was also used as an insecticide. Western American Indian tribes have a long history of the use of this plant as an effective treatment for cancerous tumors, and combined minute amounts of the winter-harvested root of this plant with *Salvia dorii* to potentiate its effects and reduce the toxicity of the herb. The plants teratogenic properties and ability to induce severe birth defects were well known to Native Americans.

Fig. Leaves of Veratrum Lobelianum

*Veratrum* species produce highly toxic steroidal alkaloids only when the plants are in active growth. During the winter months, when the plant enters its dormant stage, it degrades and metabolizes most of its toxic alkaloids.

Herbalists and Native Americans who used this plant for medicinal purposes harvested the roots during the winter months when the levels of toxic constituents were at their lowest. The roots of *V. nigrum* and *V. schindleri* have been used in Chinese herbalism (where plants of this genus are known as "li lu". Li lu is used internally as a powerful emetic of last resort, and topically to kill external parasites, treat tinea and scabies, and stop itching.

Some herbalists refuse to prescribe li lu internally, citing the extreme difficulty in preparing a safe and effective dosage, and that death has occurred at a dosage of 0.6 grams.During the 1930s *Veratrum* extracts were investigated in the treatment of high blood pressure in humans. Patients treated often suffered side effects due to the narrow therapeutic index of these products.

Due to their toxicity and the availability of other less toxic drugs, use of *Veratrum* as a treatment for high blood pressure in humans was discontinued. *Veratrum* species are an important source of life-saving medications used in modern medical preparations which lower blood pressure, slow the heartbeat, and are used for cancer treatment.

## Chapter 6

# The Vitamins

Vitamin, any of the organic (carbon-containing) compounds that the body requires in small amounts to maintain health and function properly. Children additionally need vitamins to grow. The body gets most of its vitamins from the foods we eat.

A healthy diet with plenty of fruits and vegetables should provide nearly all of the vitamins a person needs. Scientists have classified 13 compounds as vitamins. They have given most of these vitamins letter or letter plus number names, such as A, B12, and D. Most vitamins are produced by plants. Some, such as vitamin D, are produced only by animals. A few vitamins are made by the body itself. For example, bacteria in the digestive tract help produce vitamin K, and the skin uses sunlight to produce vitamin D.

Vitamins are also manufactured for sale as supplements for people who need additional vitamins to meet their body's requirements. For example, doctors often prescribe vitamin supplements for pregnant and nursing women to provide the additional nutrients needed by a rapidly growing fetus or infant. Older adults may not meet their vitamin requirements through food because the body's ability to absorb vitamins is impaired with age.

Expressed in milligrams (mg) or international units (IU) for adults and children of normal health, these recommendations provide useful guidelines for daily intake. Such guidelines are useful not only for professionals in nutrition but also for the growing number of families and individuals who eat irregular meals and rely on prepared foods, most of which are now required to carry nutritional labeling.

## VITAMINS ARE VITAL

The word vitamine, later shortened to vitamin, was coined by Polish-American chemist Casimir Funk in the early 20th century. Funk was searching for the then-unknown substance in foods that prevents such diseases as beriberi, rickets, and scurvy. After experiments on pigeons, Funk guessed that an amine-a compound containing nitrogen and hydrogen-in foods was responsible. He called this substance a vital (necessary for life) amine, or vitamine. Scientists later discovered that not all vitamins were amines, however.

Vitamins help the body carry out essential biochemical processes. Vitamins generally combine with proteins to create enzymes that promote chemical reactions. These enzymes play an important role in metabolism-the reactions that break down the fats, carbohydrates, and proteins in food so that the body can use them for energy and cell repair.

The enzymes also promote reactions involved in the formation of bone, hormones, blood cells, nervous-system chemicals, and genetic material. Without vitamins, many of these reactions would slow down or cease. The different vitamins are not chemically related, and most differ in their actions in the body.

Deficiency of particular vitamins can lead to various diseases. Too little vitamin C, for example, can cause rickets, a disease in which the bones fail to develop properly. Bowlegs or"knock knees" are signs of rickets. Rickets and the other vitamin-deficiency diseases that interested Casimir Funk have largely disappeared in the developed world as the result of fortified foods and improved nutrition. But these diseases still occur in the developing world, especially where malnutrition is common.

Interest in vitamins grew during the 1990s, especially in those vitamins that act as antioxidants-vitamins A, C, and E. Antioxidants neutralize molecules known free radicals that cause cell damage. Free radicals have been linked to a number of disorders, including Alzheimer's disease, arteriosclerosis, cancer, diabetes, and Parkinson disease. Researchers theorized that increased doses of antioxidants might also prevent and even cure such diseases. These claims have so far not panned out, however, as scientific studies have failed to demonstrate the preventive abilities of antioxidants. Research on antioxidants and other vitamins continues.

## WATER-SOLUBLE VITAMINS

Water-soluble vitamins include eight well-recognized members of the vitamin B complex: thiamine, riboflavin, pyridoxine, pantothenic acid, niacin, biotin, folic acid and vitamin B12; the water-soluble essential nutritional factors: choline, inositol, ascorbic acid; and vitamins with less-defined activity for fish: p-aminobenzoic acid, lipoic acid and citrin.

**Table. Water-Soluble Vitamin Test Diet H-440**

| *Complete test diet (g)* | | *Vitamin mix* | *(mg)* | *Mineral mix* | *(mg)* |
|---|---|---|---|---|---|
| Vitamin-free casein | 38 | Thiamine HCl | 5 | USP XII No. 2 | plus |
| Gelatin | 12 | Riboflavin | 20 | $AlCl_3$ | 15 |
| Corn oil | 6 | Pyridoxine HCl | 5 | $ZnSO_4$ | 300 |
| Cod liver oil | 3 | Choline chloride | 500 | CuCl | 10 |
| White dextrin | 28 | Nicotinic acid | 75 | $MnSO_4$ | 80 |
| α-Cellulose mixture | 9 | Calcium pantothenate | 50 | KI | 15 |
| α-Cellulose | 8 | Inositol | 200 | $CaCl_2$ | 100 |
| Vitamins | | Biotin | 0.5 | per 100 g of salt mixture | |
| | | Folic acid | 1.5 | | |
| Mineral mix | 4 | L-Ascorbic acid | 100 | | |
| Water | 200 | Vitamin B12 | 0.01 | | |
| Total diet as fed | 300 | Menadione (K) | 4 | | |
| | | -Tocopherol acetate (E) | 40 | | |

The first eight, though required only in small amounts in the diet, play major roles in growth, physiology and metabolism. Choline, inositol and ascorbic acid are required in appreciable quantities in the diet and sometimes are not referred to as vitamins but as major dietary nutrients. A typical vitamin test diet for fish control over the water-soluble vitamins

## THIAMINE

Experimental avian polyneuritis, a condition resembling beriberi, was produced by Eijkman in Java in 1886 and the anti-beriberi factor was crystallized and named"vitamine". The term"thiamine" was introduced when the chemical nature of the factor was established. Thiamine was isolated from rice polishings in 1926 and synthesized in 1936.

Thiamine hydrochloride is a water-soluble, colourless, monoclinic, crystalline compound. It is comparatively stable to dry heat but is rapidly broken down in neutral or alkaline solutions and is split by sulphites into constituent pyrimidine and thiazole moieties. It has a characteristic yeast-like odour. The pyrimide ring is relatively stable, but the thiazole ring is easily opened by hydrolysis.

Several derivatives are stable to heat and appear to be more completely soluble in weak alkaline solutions than thiamine itself and still show biological activity in animals. These derivatives include thiamine propyl disulphide, benzoylthiamine disulphide, dibenzoylthiamine, and benzoylthiamine monophosphate. Both thiamine hydrochloride and thiamine mononitrate have been successfully used as the active vitamin in test diets for fish nutrition studies.

### Positive Functions

Thiamine functions in all cells as the coenzyme cocarboxylase, thiamine pyrophosphate, which participates in the oxidative decarboxylation of pyruvic acid to acetate for entry into the tricarboxylic acid (TCA) cycle.

## THIAMINE PYROPHOSPHATE

Thiamine pyrophosphate is also a coenzyme of the transketolase system by which direct oxidation of glucose occurs in the cytoplasm of cells via the pentose phosphate pathway. Erythrocyte (RBC) levels of metabolites of this system have been used to indicate thiamine status in experimental animals, including salmon and trout.

Thiamine is essential for good appetite, normal digestion, growth and fertility. It is needed for normal functioning of the nervous tissue and the requirement is determined by the caloric density of the diet.

## Deficiency Syndrome

Deficiency signs in salmonids include impaired carbohydrate metabolism, nervous disorders, poor appetite, poor growth, and increased sensitivity to shock. A trunk-winding symptom in eels has been reported, together with haemorrhage at the base of the fins.

Skin congestion and subcutaneous haemorrhage occurs in carp fed thiamine-deficient diets. Typical symptoms observed in salmonids, carp and catfish. Thiamine deficiency has also been reported in marine flatfish started on clam neck diets stored long enough for thiaminase present to hydrolyze the thiamine in the ration. Typical nervous paralysis occurred with rapid mortality from physical shock.

**Table: Vitamin Deficiency Syndromes**

| *Vitamin* | *Symptoms in salmon, trout, carp, catfish* |
|---|---|
| Thiamine | Poor appetite, muscle atrophy, convulsions, instability and loss of equilibrium, oedema, poor growth |
| Riboflavin | Corneal vascularization, cloudy lens, haemorrhagic eyes - photophobia, dim vision, incoordination, abnormal pigmentation of iris, striated constrictions of abdominal wall, dark colouration, poor appetite, anaemia, poor growth |
| Pyridoxine | Nervous disorders, epileptiform fits, hyperirritability, ataxia, anaemia, loss of appetite, oedema of peritoneal cavity, colourless serous fluid, rapid postmortem |

| Vitamin | Symptoms in salmon, trout, carp, catfish |
|---|---|
| | rigor mortis, rapid and gasping breathing, flexing of opercles |
| Pantothenic acid | Clubbed gills, prostration, loss of appetite, necrosis and scarring, cellular atrophy, gill exudate, sluggishness, poor growth |
| Inositol | Poor growth, distended stomach, increased gastric emptying time, skin lesions |
| Biotin | Loss of appetite, lesions in colon, colouration, muscle atrophy, spastic convulsions, fragmentation of erythrocytes, skin lesions, poor growth |
| Folic acid | Poor growth, lethargy, fragility of caudal fin, dark colouration, macrocytic anaemia |
| Choline | Poor growth, poor food conversion, haemorrhagic kidney and intestine |
| Nicotinic acid | Loss of appetite, lesions in colon, jerky or difficult motion, weakness, oedema of stomach and colon, muscle spasms while resting, poor growth |
| *Vitamin* | *Symptoms in salmon, trout, carp, catfish* |
| Vitamin B12 | Poor appetite, low haemoglobin, fragmention of erythrocytes, macrocytic anaemia |
| Ascorbic acid | Scoliosis, lordosis, impaired collagen formation, altered cartilage, eye lesions, haemorrhagic skin, liver, kidney, intestine, and muscle |
| p-Aminobenzoic acid | No abnormal indication in growthappetite, mortality |

## Requirements

In determining dietary thiamine requirements of fish, some considerations must be placed upon the composition of dietary ingredients in the ration.

Fat content of the diet may affect not only caloric intake but also the thiamine requirement because cocarboxylase participates in the oxidation of that through a-ketoglutarate. Therefore, fish on a high fat diet and low thiamine intake might take longer to develop deficiencies and will give an erroneous requirement.

**Sources and Protection**

Common sources for thiamine are dried peas, beans, cereal bran, and dried yeast. Fresh glandular tissue is also a good source for thiamine and other members of the vitamin B water-soluble complex, but is seldom used in modern commercial fish diets.

Thiamine can be easily lost by holding diet ingredients too long in storage or by preparing the diet under slightly alkaline conditions or in the presence of sulphide. Wet or frozen diets pose a problem because moisture content increases the chance of enzymatic (thiaminase) hydrolysis and subsequent destruction of thiamine. Obviously, wet or moist diet, preparations containing any fresh fish or shellfish tissue must be used immediately.

**Antimetabolites and Inactivation**

Acetylcholine is an antagonist to thiamine and pyrithiamine. Oxythiamine and normal butylthiamine are specific antimetabolites. Several thiaminases occur which destroy thiamine. These rupture the thiazole ring at the sulphur bond making the residue inactive. Freshwater fish tissues have high thiaminase activity as do tissues from clams, shrimp and mussels. Thiaminases have also been found in beans and mustard seed and in several micro-organisms.

Thiaminase activity is low in most saltwater fish tissues, however, and the enzyme is inactivated by heating or prolonged pasteurization. Thiamine present in fresh Torula yeast is relatively unavailable to fish, but the yeast becomes an excellent thiamine source after rupturing the cells by steam treatment or by dehydration.

**Clinical Assessment**

Clinical assessment of thiamine status have been made

by measuring erythrocyte transketolase activity. Typical saturated levels for thiamine activity in sea salmon range from 15 to 20 g of thiamine/g of wet liver tissue. Fingerling chinook or coho salmon reared in 10 or 15°C water on test diets containing the listed amount or more of thiamine hydrochloride: assayed at 8-10 g of thiamine/g of wet liver tissue. These liver storage levels and normal erythrocyte transketolase activity in the absence of any deficiency sign will indicate an adequate thiamine intake for that fish population.

## RIBOFLAVIN

Following the recognition that the original water-soluble B consisted of more than one factor, a new growth-promoting factor consisting of yellow-green pigments was isolated in 1879. This new factor was designated G by some and 83 by others. The second water-soluble vitamin discovered was given its specific chemical name riboflavin. Lactoflavin, hepatoflavin, and ovoflavin were also shown to be identical with the pure riboflavin. Riboflavin occurs in the free form only in the eye, whey and urine.

**Table: Vitamin Requirements for Growth**

| *Vitamin (mg/kg dry diet)* | *Rainbow trout* | *Brook trout* | *Brown trout* | *Atlantic salmon* | *Chinook salmon* | *Coho salmon* |
|---|---|---|---|---|---|---|
| Thiamine | 10-12 | 10-12 | 10-12 | 10-15 | 10-15 | 10-15 |
| Riboflavin | 20-30 | 20-30 | 20-30 | 5-10 | 20-25 | 20-25 |
| Pyridoxine | 10-15 | 10-15 | 10-15 | 10-15 | 15-20 | 15-20 |
| Pantothenate | 40-50 | 40-50 | 40-50 | * | 40-50 | 40-50 |
| Niacin | 120-150 | 120-150 | 120-150 | * | 150-200 | 150-200 |
| Folacin | 6-10 | 6-10 | 6-10 | 5-10 | 6-10 | 6-10 |
| Cyanocobalamin | * | * | * | * | 0.015-0.02 | 0.015-0.02 |
| myo-Inositol | 200-300 | * | * | * | 300-400 | 300-400 |
| Choline | * | * | * | * | 600-800 | 600-800 |
| Biotin | 1-1.5 | 1-1.5 | 1.5-2 | - | 1-1.5 | 1-1.5 |
| Ascorbate | 100-150 | * | * | * | 100-150 | 50-80 |
| Vitamin A | 2 000-2 500 I.U. | * | * | - | * | * |
| Vitamin E | * | * | * | - | 40-50 | * |
| Vitamin K | * | * | * | - | * | * |

* Denotes a requirement, the level of which has not been established

**Table: Vitamin Requirements for Growth**

| Vitamin (mg/kg dry diet) | Carp | Channel catfish | Eel | Sea bream | Turbot | Yellowtail |
|---|---|---|---|---|---|---|
| Thiamine | 2-3 | 1-3 | 2-5 | * | 2-4 | * |
| Riboflavin | 7-10 | * | * | * | * | - |
| Pyridoxine | 5-10 | * | * | 2-5 | * | * |
| Pantothenate | 30-40 | 25-30 | * | * | * | * |
| Niacin | 30-50 | * | - | * | - | - |
| Folacin | - | * | * | - | * | - |
| Cyanocobalamin | - | * | - | * | - | - |
| myo-Inositol | 200-300 | * | - | 300-500 | - | - |
| Choline | 500-600 | * | - | * | * | - |
| Biotin | 1-15 | * | * | - | * | * |
| Ascorbate | 30-50 | 30-50 | - | * | - | * |
| Vitamin A | 1 000-2 000 I.U. | * | - | - | - | * |
| Vitamin E | 80-100 | * | - | - | - | * |
| Vitamin K | * | * | - | - | - | - |

* Denotes a requirement, the level of which has not been established

## RIBOFLAVIN

Riboflavin is a yellow-brown crystalline pigment. The vitamin is very slightly soluble in water but soluble in alkali. It is insoluble in most organic solvents. Riboflavin is stable to oxidizing agents in strong mineral acids and in neutral aqueous solution. It is also stable to dry heat but is irreversibly decomposed on irradiation with ultraviolet rays or visible light, breaking down to lumiflavin. Riboflavin phosphate is the chemically active group of Warburg's'yellow' enzyme.

## POSITIVE FUNCTIONS

Riboflavin functions in the tissues in the form of flavin adenine dinucleotide (FAD) or as flavin mononucleotide (FMN). The flavo-proteins function as enzymes of tissue respiration and are involved in hydrogen transport to catalyze the oxidation of reduced pyridine nucleo-tides (NADH and NADPH).

Thus, they function as coenzymes for many oxidases and redunctases such as cytochrome e reductase, D- and L-amino acid oxidases, xanthine and aldehyde oxidase, succinic dehydrogenase, glucose oxidase and fumaric dehydrogenase. Riboflavin is also involved with pyridoxine in the conversion of tryptophan to nicotinic acid and is most important in the respiration of poorly vascularized tissues such as the cornea of the eye. Riboflavin is involved in the retinal pigment during light adaptation and lack of it causes impaired vision and photophobia in experimental animals, including fish.

## DEFICIENCY SYNDROME

Tissue riboflavin is exhausted in young salmonids after 10 to 12 weeks on riboflavin-deficient diets in 10-15 °C water systems. Poor appetite and poor diet efficiency are the first signs, followed by photophobia, mono or bilateral cataract's, corneal vascularization, eye haemorrhage, incoordination, and general anaemia.

Dark pigmentation, coupled with striated constrictions of abdominal wall in salmon have been noted. Skin atrophy has been reported for some fish species and abnormal pigmentation of both skin and iris has been noted. Replacement of riboflavin in the diet reduced the symptoms except when cataracts have developed.

This irreversible condition will continue in monolateral cataracts throughout the life of the fish, whereas bilateral cataracts largely result in eventual starvation and death of the afflicted animal. The first specific signs have consistently appeared in and about the eyes of salmonids, carps and catfish.

## REQUIREMENTS

The requirements of fish for riboflavin under experimental conditions in 10-15°C water supplies Values for the trout are slightly lower than those reported for salmon. The requirements may vary depending upon the balance of other dietary ingredients, caloric density and environmental conditions under which the fish is raised. The values established under these standard test conditions should serve as tentative-levels which will satisfy biological demands for normal growth, health, and physiological function. Most of these studies have been made on very young fish, often initially feeding fry, with the logical assumption that their vitamin needs would be more than that of larger fish having advanced metabolic enzyme systems capable of synthesizing at least some of these vitamins to partially meet the requirements.

## SOURCES AND PROTECTION

Riboflavin is widely distributed in plants and in animal glandular tissues. Milk, liver, kidney, heart, yeast, germinated grains, peanuts, soybeans and eggs are rich sources. Keeping feeds from sunlight or intense artificial light is necessary to minimize loss of the vitamin by conversion to lumiflavin.

## ANTIMTABOLITES AND INACTIVATION

When the ribose group in the molecule is replaced by other groups, analogues are formed which either have reduced activity or become antimetabolites. Galactoflavin is an antagonist to riboflavin and inhibits growth of rats when the diet contains this compound.

Flavin monosulphate inhibits D-amino acid oxidase and appears to act as a competitor and inhibitor for growth of Lactobacillus casei. The hydroxyethyl analogue is an antagonist for riboflavin function in both rats and bacteria and also shows antifungal activity.

## CLINICAL ASSESSMENT

Liver tissue of actively feeding sea salmon contains 6-8 g of riboflavin/g of wet tissue. In a freshwater environment, young fish fed test diets in 15 ºC water systems showed liver storage of 3.5-4.0 ωg/g. Riboflavin content of blood plasma does not change significantly in riboflavin deficiency in experimental animals. However, the erythrocyte riboflavin content has been reported at around 10 g/100 ml blood for man on low riboflavin intake and approximately twice that level on high intake. Urinary excretion of riboflavin has been used clinically to indicate dietary status, with 200ωg/24 it suggesting adequate intake and less than 100ωg indicating low intake. Excretion of 50ωg or less daily is strong indication of extended dietary deficiency. Several studies show that excretion of less than 200ωg of riboflavin/g of creatinine would be indicative of deficiency.

## PYRIDOXINE

A new factor which could cure dermatitis in rats was reported by Györgi in 1935 and was named vitamin B6. The name pyridoxine is also attributed to Györgi. The active material was isolated in 1939 and pyridoxine was subsequently synthesized. First quantitative requirements for fish were described in 1944. Pyridoxine deficiency has since been reported in trout and in salmon.

### Pyrodoxine Hydrochloride

Compounds which have vitamin B6 activity include: pyridoxine, pyridoxal and pyridoxamine. Pyridoxine hydrochloride is readily soluble in water and is, heat stable in either acid or alkaline solution. It acts as a coenzyme in a number of enzyme systems. Pyridoxine is sensitive to ultraviolet light in neutral or alkaline solutions.

Pyridoxamine and pyridoxal in dilute solutions are labile compounds which are rapidly destroyed on exposure to air, heat, or light. Therefore, most vitamin supplementation is in the form of pyridoxine hydrochloride and analysis for pyridoxine activity by microbiological assay of diet ingredients probably measures pyridoxal phosphate and other intermediates as well.

### Positive Functions

Pyridoxal phosphate is the coenzyme, codecarboxylase, involved in the decarboxylation of amino acids. It is also the co-factor of the 22 different transaminases present in animal tissues. As codecarboxylase, pyridoxal phosphate has been shown to participate in the decarboxylation of 5-

hydroxytryptophan to produce 5-hydroxytryptamine or serotonin. As a co-factor of the enzyme desulphydrase converts cysteine to pyruvic acid.

Pyridoxal phosphate is the co-factor for the synthesis of - amino-levulinate, the latter a precursor of haeme. Many neuro hormones require pyridoxal phosphate as a coenzyme in their synthesis. Pyridoxine is also involved in fat metabolism, especially of the essential fatty acids. It is involved in the synthesis of messenger RNA which determines amino acids sequence in polypeptide synthesis. Pyridoxine plays a most important role in protein metabolism and, as a result, carnivorous fish have stringent requirements for the vitamin in the diet and stores are rapidly exhausted.

**Deficiency Syndrome**

Signs of pyridoxine deficiency in fish Since salmonids, ictalurids, and very young cyprinids are carnivorous, with protein requirements for young animals between 40-50 per cent of the ration, pyridoxine stores are rapidly exhausted when fish are held on pyridoxine-deficient rations. Acute deficiency signs occur in salmon after 14-21 days on a high protein diet of pyridoxine and the entire population dies within 28 days in 12-15 C water.

Deficiency is followed by general nervous disorders, and alteration in control of melanophore contraction. Postmortem rigor mortis occurs very rapidly. Rapid and gasping breathing with flexing of the opercules is a common observation and oedema in the peritoneal cavity with colourless serous fluid occurs in fish on some experimental treatments. Salmon, trout, carp and yellowtail exhibit premortem rigor a few hours before death. Recovery at late stage deficiency is very unlikely unless fish are injected with pyridoxal phosphate.

Handling the animals generally induces more damage than vitamin administration will correct. Recovery among fish still feeding is equally rapid and dramatic upon administration of pyridoxine hydrochloride in the diet. Deficiency signs disappear within a day or two. Erythrocyte and plasma transaminase activities reflect the deficiency state.

## Requirements

Pyridoxine requirements for trout, salmon, carp, and yellowtail Supplementing commercial fish diets with pyridoxine is desirable because of the important role the vitamin plays in protein metabolism.

## Sources and Protection

Good sources of pyridoxine are yeast, whole cereals, egg yolk, liver and glandular tissues. Pyridoxine compounds in phosphorylated form present in agricultural products are fairly stable but are sensitive to ultraviolet radiation. Some pyridoxal phosphate will be lost on exposure to air. Free forms or pyridoxal and pyridoxamine are rapidly destroyed by air, light and heat when moist.

## Antimetabolites and Inactivation

Antagonists may compete for reaction sites of the apoenzyme or may react with pyridoxal phosphate to form inactive compounds. Deoxypyridoxine is a potent pyridoxine antagonist because of competition for apoenzyme sites but is a useful agent to accelerate pyridoxine deficiency in experimental animals. This same compound inhibits tyrosine decarboxylase. Methoxypyridoxine is another antagonist. Oxopyrimidine (2-methyl-4-amino-5-hydroxymethyl-pyrimidine) produces liver damage and inhibits glutamate decarboxylase.

## Clinical Assessment

Plasma and erythrocyte transaminase activity in most instances reflects pyridoxine status of fish although high tryptophan load in the diet tends to increase the pyridoxine requirement.

Liver storage measured by microbiological assay showed 5-6 V-g of pyridoxine activity/g in fresh sea salmon liver; whereas, fingerling salmon fed a 50 per cent protein diet in freshwater had 2-3 mg/g of wet tissue. Assay of diet for pyridoxine by microbiological methods gives a truer representation of total pyridoxine activity including intermediates.

## Pantothenic Acid

A chick dermatitis was cured by Elvehjem and Köehn in 1935 using a factor containing -alanine. The term pantothenic acid was given earlier by Williams to a yeast growth factor which was later recognized as the anti-dermatitis factor. Pantothenic acid was synthesized by Stiller in 1940. Phillips observed clubbed gills in trout fed pantothenic acid-deficient diets in 1945. Rucker detected the same condition in salmon fed low pantothenic acid diets. Pantothenic acid may be considered as dihydroxydimethylbutyric acid bonded to -alanine.

The free acid is a yellow, viscous oil and therefore the compound generally used in fish diet preparation is the calcium salt. This salt is a white crystalline powder readily soluble in water, mild acid, and is almost insoluble in organic solvents. It is stable to oxidizing and reducing agents and to autoclaving, but is labile to dry heat, hot alkali, or hot acid. Pantothenol has almost as much activity as pantothenic acid for growth of chicks.

Pantothenic acid acetate, benzoate, and diphosphate esters are biologically active for animals but not for lactic acid bacteria. The optical isomer L-pantothenic acid, appears physiologically inert. Some organisms may utilize a portion of the molecule. Bacteria appeared to require only the dihydroxydimethyl-butyric acid, and some yeasts utilize only g-alanine. Animals, however, need the entire pantothenic acid molecule or its reduced alcohol form.

## Positive Functions

Pantothenic acid is part of acetyl coenzyme A which occurs in many enzymatic processes involving 2-carbon compounds. It has been shown to be required by all animal species studied and by many micro-organisms.

The acetyl coenzyme A system is involved in the acetylation of aromatic amines and choline; condensation reactions for synthesis of acetate, fatty acids, and citrate; the oxidation of pyruvate and acetaldehyde; and is essential for the development of the central nervous system.

The 2-carbon fragment called'active acetate', or acetyl coenzyme A, is an essential intermediate in metabolism. It is involved in acylation of acetate, succinate, benzoate, propionate and butyrate. Pantothenic acid is involved in adrenal function and for the production of cholesterol. Coenzyme A is also involved in many other steps of intermediate metabolism of carbohydrates, fats and proteins.

**Deficiency Syndromes**

Deficiency signs for pantothenic acid Under standard test conditions with deficient diet fed in 10-15°C water systems, salmon and trout exhaust pantothenic acid stores within 8-12 weeks.

Fish stop feeding and close examination of gill filament show proliferation of epithelial surface plus swelling and clubbing together of the filaments and lamellae. The opercules become distended and the surface of the gills is often covered with an exudate. Fish become prostrate or sluggish. Necrosis, scarring and cellular atrophy of the tender gill elements occur and anaemia develops after prolonged deficiency.

The same type of symptom has been observed in salmon, trout, eel, carp and catfish. After replacement of pantothenic acid in the diet, recovery is rapid for those fish still feeding and gross deficiency symptoms disappear after about four weeks on the recovery diet although evidence of necrosis and scarring remains.

**Sources and Protection**

Good sources for pantothenic acid are cereal bran, yeast, liver, kidney, heart, spleen and lung. Fish flesh is a relatively rich source, although the content is only about 20 per cent of pantothenic acid found in animal glandular tissue. Royal jelly probably contains the greatest amount as it contains over 500ωg of pantothenol/g dry weight.

The calcium or sodium salt of pantothenic acid is relatively stable and can be incorporated into either moist or dry fish diets. Some loss is incurred during autoclaving and excessive heat should therefore be minimized during diet preparations.

Since the free acid is labile to heat and also to acid and alkali, some loss can be expected during moist diet preparation or during storage.

Certain cereal brans may have pantothenic acid bound in a form unavailable to fish because of the low digestibility coefficient and should not be relied upon as the sole pantothenic acid source in the diet.

### Antimetabolites and Inactivation

Since pantothenic acid affects the respiration of many types of cells, compounds like 6-mercaptopurine, 2,6-diaminopurine, and 8-azaguanine, which inhibit growth of tumors are antagonistic toward pantothenic acid.

Pantoyltaurine is an antimetabolite of pantothenic acid and has been used to accelerate deficiency syndromes in experimental animals. Methyl- -pantothenic acid was reported to interfere with the formation of acetyl coenzyme A and accelerates deficiency syndromes in animals.

This compound inhibits sulfanilamide acetylation in pigeon liver homogenates but did not prevent citric acid formation. Pantothenic acid can be used to overcome these inhibitory effects, including the reversal of mitosis blockage by 7-mecaptopurine in animals. High levels of calcium pantothenate in the diet also has a transient effect on the migratory urge of salmon.

### Clinical Assessment

Assay of pantothenic acid content in the diet may be misleading unless care is exercised in proper hydrolysis of the raw materials being assayed since pantothenic acid is only slowly liberated by normal hydrolytic procedures. Complete hydrolysis with enzyme preparations will liberate all of pantothenic acid from biologically active material of glandular tissues, fish flesh, yeast, and bran.

Salmon feeding actively in the oceans showed liver pantothenic acid content of 18-20/g of fresh tissue. Young chinook and coho salmon fingerlings reared in fresh water at 12-15°C showed maximum liver storage at about 14-16ωg of pantothenic acid/g of fresh liver tissue. Load tests and acetylation reactions of sulfanilamide have been used in man and other experimental animals but have not yet been extended for assessment of pantothenic acid status in fish.

## NIACIN

Nicotinic acid was synthesized in 1873 but was left on the shelf as an organic compound unrelated to the severe pellagra afflictions occurring throughout the world at that time. Sixty years later the compound was shown to be present in coenzymes I and II and two years thereafter Elvehjem cured'black tongue' in dogs with the vitamin.

### Nicotinic Acid

Niacin is the preferred nomenclature. Nicotinic acid amide or niacinamide is the common form in which the vitamin is physiologically active. Niacin is a white, crystalline solid, soluble in water and alcohol.

It is stable in the dry state and may be autoclaved for short periods without destruction. It is also stable to heat in mineral acids and alkali. Niacin is both a carboxylic acid and an amine and forms quaternary ammonium compounds because of its basic nature. Acidic characteristics include salt formation with alkali. Niacin can be esterified easily, then converted to amides.

Niacinamide is a crystalline powder soluble in water and ethanol and the dry material is stable up to about 60°C. In aqueous solutions it is stable for a short period when autoclaved. It is the form in which the vitamin is normally found in niacinamide adenine dinucleotide (NAD) and in niacinamide adenine dinucleotide phosphate (NADP).

## POSITIVE FUNCTIONS

The major function of niacin in NAD and NADP is hydrogen transport in intermediary metabolism. Most of these enzyme systems function by alternating between the oxidized and reduced state of the coenzymes NAD-NADH and NADP-NADPH. Oxidation-reduction reactions may be anaerobic as when pyruvate acts as the hydrogen acceptor and lactate is formed, or the reactions may be coupled to electron transport systems with oxygen as the ultimate hydrogen acceptor; such aerobic reactions occur in respiration. Both NAD and NADP are involved in the synthesis of high energy phosphate bonds which furnish energy for certain steps in glycolysis, in pyruvate metabolism, amino acid and protein metabolism, and in photosynthesis.

An interrelationship between thiamine and niacin exists since both vitamins are coenzymes in intermediary metabolism whereby food is oxidized to furnish energy for physiological functions, to maintain homeostasis, and för body temperature maintenance in homeotherms.

## DEFICIENCY SYNDROME

Stores of niacin are more slowly exhausted under experimental conditions than are some of the other vitamins resulting in less defined and more slowly developing symptoms. Niacin deficiencies in fish were experimentally induced in the late forties and early fifties by using basal diets which had a low niacin content. Loss of appetite and poor food conversion were the first signs noted.

Then the fish turned dark and went off feed, followed by the appearance of lesions in the colon, erratic motion, oedema of the stomach and colon and muscle spasms while fish were apparently resting. A predisposition to sunburn in fish confined in the open in shallow ponds or raceways Common carp showed a congestion of the skin with subcutaneous hemorrhages. Common symptoms of niacin deficiency in most fish studied were muscular weakness and spasms, coupled with poor growth and poor food conversion.

### Requirements

In homeotherms on a balanced test ration the niacin requirement is generally estimated to be about ten times that of the thiamine requirement. These rations generally contain considerable carbohydrate material to furnish energy to maintain body temperature.

In fish the requirement appears to be twenty to thirty

times that of the thiamine needs determined for the same test conditions and test rations.

This difference may be due to low carbohydrate content of young fish diets and the higher protein content of these rations. Conversion of tryptophan to niacin occurs in the mammalian liver and possibly also in the liver of fish. This conversion may account for the slow development of the niacin-deficiency syndrome in fish.

However, after 10-14 weeks on diets devoid of niacin, deficiency symptoms did occur in several species of fish. The symptoms were reduced by replacement of niacin in the ration even when high protein diets containing an excess of tryptophan were fed. Too much niacin inhibits growth.

**Sources and Protection**

Niacin is found in most animal and plant tissues. Rich sources are yeast, liver, kidney, heart, legumes, and green vegetables. Wheat contains more niacin than corn and the vitamin is also found in milk and egg products.

The vitamin is very stable since it is generally found in coenzyme form in raw materials. Niacin added to the diet as a supplement remains relatively unaltered during diet manufacture, processing, and storage.

**Antimetabolites and Inactivation**

Pyridine-3-sulphonic acid and 3-acetylpyridine are compounds structurally related to niacin and are antimetabolites for this vitamin in animals and in micro-organisms. Additional niacin can overcome the anti-metabolic effect. Deficiency symptoms in rats may be induced by 6-amino niacinamide. The symptoms are reversed by addition of ten times more niacinamide than the antimetabolite. Thioacetamide has been reported to be a niacin antagonist in fish.

**Clinical Assessment**

Salmon feeding actively in the oceans showed liver niacin content of 70-80ωg of niacin/g of fresh tissue. About half of this amount is present in fingerling salmon raised in fresh water at 12-15°C and fed test rations containing 40-50 per cent protein and niacin supplements 500-750 mg/kg dry diet. Urinary metabolities of niacin have been measured in other animals on standard niacin load in test rations containing a standard tryptophan load.

The technique is well developed to measure the N1-methyl derivative in mammalian urine. These data have not been reported for fish but metabolism chambers are available for collecting branchial and urinary wastes from large fish intubated with different diet material.

## BIOTIN

Certain foods, notably liver and kidney, were found to be protective against a form of dermatitis resulting from the consumption of egg white by rats, in the early thirties. It was soon learned that a specific component of egg albumin, avidin, rendered dietary biotin unavailable, hence producing the symptoms.

Biotin was variously called coenzyme R and'vitamin H'. It was isolated by Du Vigneaud in 1941 and synthesized by workers of Merck and Company in 1943. Biotin was once thought to be part of factor H for fish. Blue slime patch disease due to biotin deficiency was reported in trout.

### Biotin

Biotin is a monocarboxylic acid slightly soluble in water and alcohol and insoluble in organic solvents. Salts of the acid are soluble in water. Aqueous solutions or the dry material are stable at 100° C and to light.

The vitamin is destroyed by acids and alkalis and by oxidizing agents such as peroxides or permanganate. Biocytin is a bound form of biotin isolated from yeast, plant, and animal tissues. Other bound forms of the vitamin can generally be liberated by peptic digestion. Oxybiotin has partial vitamin activity but oxybiotin sulphonic acid and other analogues are antimetabolites inhibiting the growth of bacteria.

Avidin, a protein found in raw egg white, binds biotin and makes it unavailable to fish and other animals. Heating to denature the protein makes the bound biotin available again to the fish.

Biocytin or -biotinyl lysine (the epsilon amino group of lysine and the carboxyl of biotin being combined in a peptide bond) is hydrolyzed by the enzyme biotinase making the protein-bound biotin available.

## POSITIVE FUNCTIONS

Biotin is required in several specific carboxylation and decarboxylation reactions, including the carboxylation of pyruvic acid to form oxaloacetic acid. It is part of the coenzyme of several carboxylating enzymes fixing $CO_2$ such as propionyl coenzyme A involved in the conversion of propionic acid to succinic acid in methylmalonyl coenzyme A.

Biotin is also involved in the conversion of acetyl $CO_2$ to malonyl coenzyme A in the formation of long chain fatty acids. It has possible involvement in citrulline synthesis and may have effects on purine and pyrimidine synthesis. It is involved in the conversion of unsaturated fatty acids to the stable cis form in the synthesis of biologically active fatty acids.

## DEFICIENCY SYNDROME

Some signs of biotin deficiency in salmonids are skin disorders, muscle atrophy, lesions in the colon, loss of appetite, and spastic convulsions. Haematology discloses fragmentation of erythrocytes. Poor growth is a common symptom and has been reported for salmonids, common carp, goldfish (Carassius auratus) and eel.

Blue slime patch disease in brook trout deficient in biotin appears typical for this species. Fish reared in 10 -15° C water exhaust biotin stores in 8-12 weeks and the first signs are anorexia, poor food conversion, and general listlessness before the more acute deficiency symptoms become detectable.

### Sources and Protection

Rich sources of biotin are liver, kidney, yeast, milk products, and egg yolks. Nut meats contain good supplies of biotin. The diet should be protected from strong oxidizing agents or conditions which promote oxidation of ingredients. Raw egg white should not be incorporated into moist fish diets. Cooking will inactivate the avidin.

**Antimetabolites and Inactivation**

Many biotin homologues with different side chain lengths inhibit the growth of bacteria. Oxybiotin, in which sulphur is replaced by oxygen, has about the same biological activity as the natural biotin. On the other hand, oxybiotin sulphonic acid inhibits biotin activity.

**Clinical Assessment**

Measurement or urinary excretion of biotin in animals does not prove a good clinical method since biotin is synthesized by several organisms in the gut. In fish, this technique needs to be explored and may well be valuable as a clinical tool since the gastrointestinal tract of many freshwater fish contains only small quantities of bacteria. Biotin is one of the most expensive vitamins to add to fish rations. Salmon feeding actively in the oceans had liver biotin concentrations of 10-12 mg of wet liver tissue

The concentrations in the liver of young salmon fingerlings in fresh water fed test diets containing an excess of biotin were between 6-8 mg of the vitamin/g of tissue. Fish with these levels of biotin in the liver should probably be in sound biotin nutritional status.

## FOLIC ACID (FOLACIN)

A factor effective in curing metaloblastic anaemia in monkeys was found in yeast and liver concentrates and was designated vitamin M in 1935. In 1939 an anti-anaemic factor was found in liver and called vitamin BC. These were later shown to be the same substance with folic acid as the active ingredient. Folic acid was synthesized in 1946 and was soon used in fish diets for preventing purified diet anaemia.

**Folic Acid**

Folic acid crystallizes into yellow spear-shaped leaflets

which are soluble in water and dilute alcohol. It can be precipitated with heavy metal salts. It is stable to heat in neutral or alkaline solution, but unstable in acid solution. It deteriorates when exposed to sunlight, or during prolonged storage. Several analogues have biological activity including pteroic acid, rhizopterin, folinic acid, xanthopterin and several formyltetrahydropteroyl-glutamic acid derivatives. These have closely allied ring structures and many have been isolated as derivatives in various animals or microbiological preparations. One simple form, xanthopterin, present in the pigments of insects, is shown below and is of special interest because of early work with this compound as the anti-anaemic factor H for fish.

### Positive Functions

Folic acid is required for normal blood cell formation and is involved as a coenzyme in one-carbon transfer mechanisms. In the presence of ascorbic acid, folic acid is transformed into the active (5-formyl-5, 6,7,8) tetrahydrofolic acid. Folic acid is involved in many one-carbon metabolism systems such as serine and glycine interconversion, methionine-homocysteine synthesis, histidine synthesis, and pyrimidine synthesis.

Several coenzyme forms of the active vitamin have been isolated. Folic acid is involved in the conversion of megaloblastic bone marrow to normoblastic type. It has a role in blood glucose regulation and improves cell membrane function and hatchability of eggs.

### Deficiency Syndrome

Macrocytic normochromic anaemia occurs in several experimental animals, including fish fed diets devoid of the folic acid. Increasing numbers of senile cells are observed as the deficiency progresses until only a few old and degenerating cells are found in the blood of deficient fish.

Anterior kidney imprints disclose only adult cells and no preforms present. Other signs observed have been poor growth, anorexia, general anaemia, lethargy, fragile fins, dark skin pigmentation, and infarction of spleen.

## SOURCES AND PROTECTION

Yeast, green vegetables, liver, kidney, glandular tissue, fish tissue, and fish viscera are good sources of folic acid. Insects contain xanthopterin which has folic acid activity. At one time the yellow pigment of xanthopterin was identified as the fish anti-anaemic factor H, but subsequent experiments showed only partial activity and that folic acid itself was a much more potent antimacrocytic anaemia factor.

Insects may contribute significantly to the folic acid requirements of wild fish, but in scientific fish husbandry artificial diets are more reliable sources.

Activity is lost during extended storage and when material is exposed to sunlight. Therefore, dry feeds should be carefully protected during manufacture and moist diet rations should be carefully preserved. Both types of fish diets should be fed soon after manufacture to assure minimal loss of folic acid activity.

## ANTIMETABOLITES AND INACTIVATION

One antagonist of folacin is 4-aminopteroylglutamic acid or aminopterin. This material, when incorporated in the diet of guinea pigs and rats, induces anaemia and leucopenia and has been used to treat leukemia in man.

Amethopterin (4-amino-N10-methylpteroylglutamic acid) can also be used to induce deficiency by inhibiting purine, pyrimidine, and nucleic acid protection; viz., inhibition of nucleic acid synthesis results in macroytic anaemia.

## CLINICAL ASSESSMENT

Haematology is used as a simple clinical tool to assess haemopoiesis in fish. Anterior kidney imprints easily disclose normal distribution of immature cells and preforms undergoing reticulosis.

Salmon actively feeding in the ocean and young salmon fingerlings raised in fresh water and fed diets rich in folacin show liver storage of 3-4ωg of folic acid/g of wet tissue. Microbiological assay is preferred for assessment of total folic acid in dietary raw materials because the total biological activity it measures includes all the various coenzyme forms and folic acid analogues.

Assessment of the dietary intake of folic acid is important for intensive cold water fish husbandry. In pond culture, aquatic and terrestrial insects, algae, etc., may also be available and folic acid in the supplementary feed may not be as critical. Since folic acid is labile in storage, excess amounts are generally added to manufactured feed in anticipation of storage losses.

However, prudent fish husbandry dictates rapid use of manufactured rations with minimum storage. Routine periodic haematology of fish assures proper nutritional status for maximum production and sound health.

The author has noted in several series of experiments that when fish diseases occur through inadvertent contamination of the water supply, those groups of fish partially or completely deficient in folic acid were among the first to show acute disease symptoms. Therefore, folic acid must also play an important role in resistance to disease.

## VITAMIN B12

The antipernicious anaemia factor found to be contained in liver was isolated and crystallized in the mid forties. This substance, named vitamin B12 by its discoverers, was later to be recognized as essential for growth of chicken fed diets entirely of plant origin and was designated animal protein factor (APF).

When anaemic salmon were injected with crystalline B12 in combination with folic acid and xanthopterin positive haemopoiesis occurred within a few days, and the salmon showed rapid recovery from the anaemia. Vitamin B12 or cynacobalamin has the following approximate chemical structure.

### Cyanocobalamin

The molecule has a planar group and a nucleotide group lying nearly at right angles to one another. This cobalt-containing vitamin has a net charge of one at the central cobalt atom to which is attached a replaceable cyano group. Vitamin B12 is stable to mild heat in neutral solution, but is rapidly destroyed by heating in dilute acid or alkali. Crude concentrates are more unstable and rapidly lose activity.

The compound is similar to the porphyrins in its spatial configuration with a central cobalt atom linked to four reduced pyrrole rings in the haeme series. Replacing the cyanide ion with a variety of anions produce derivatives which have comparable biological activities; viz., hydroxocobalamin, nitritocobalamin, chlorocobalamin and sulphatocobalamin.

## Positive Functions

Cyanocobalamin is involved with folic acid in haemopoiesis. It is required by many micro-organisms and is a growth factor for many animals. The animal protein factor present in fish and animal by-products was not recognized until crystalline vitamin B12 was injected into anaemic chinook salmon fingerlings in 1949 and positive haemopoiesis was observed. A coenzyme incorporating vitamin B12 is involved in the reversible isomerization of methyl-malonyl coenzyme A to succinyl coenzyme A and in the isomerization of methylaspartate to glutomate. Cyanocobalamin is involved in the coenzyme for the methylation of homocystine to form methionine.

It is also involved in several other one-carbon reactions and in the synthesis of labile methyl compounds. One vitamin B12 containing coenzyme acts in methylation of the purine ring during thymine synthesis. Vitamin B12 is also involved in cholesterol metabolism, in purine and pyrimidine biosynthesis, and in the metabolism of glycols.

## Deficiency Syndrome

Deficiency signs in young pigs, chicks, and rats show abnormal blood elements, poor growth, and pernicious anaemia. An intrinsic factor is necessary for good absorption of the vitamin from the gut.

This factor is a low molecular weight mucoprotein which normally occurs in gastric juice, and especially in hog gut mucosa. Pernicious anaemia in chinook and coho salmon is characterized by fragmented, erythrocytes with many aberrant forms present.

Haemoglobin levels are inconsistent and erythrocyte counts have a range extending from frank anaemia to a near normal blood pattern. Cyanocobalamin stores in fish tissues are slowly exhausted and only after 12-16 weeks on test do the symptoms appear in deficient salmon populations. Poor appetite, poor growth, poor food conversion, and some dark pigmentation can be observed before frank anaemia is detected.

**Sources and Protection**

Rich sources of vitamin B12 are found in fish meal, fish viscera, liver, kidney, glandular tissues, and slaughter house wastes. Since vitamin B12 is labile on storage, and in mild acid solution is easily destroyed by heating, care must be exercised in diet preparation containing flesh or meat scraps.

**Antimetabolites and Inactivation.**

The vitamin B12 coenzymes are very unstable under light, which rapidly decomposes the coenzymes. Photo-sensitivity is increased in dilute acid solutions.

**Clinical Assessment**

Generalized anaemia with fragmentation of erythrocytes and extremely variable haemoglobin levels and erythrocyte counts indicate possible B12 deficiency. Prompt response in individual fish is obtained by injecting B12 alone or in combination with folic acid in the ratio of 1 part vitamin B12 to 100 parts folic acid. Careful interpretation of haemotological data will enable one to distinguish one form of anaemia from the other.

## ASCORBIC ACID

The isolation of ascorbic acid was due to Szent-Györgyi of Hungary and C.G. King of the U.S.A. Vitamin C synthesis was accomplished in 1933 after the chemical structure of ascorbic acid was established by British and Swiss workers. McCay and Tunison reported scoliosis in brook trout fed formalin-preserved meat in 1934 and McLaren observe haemorrhages in trout fed rations low in ascorbic acid. It was not until the sixties that a critical need for L-ascorbic acid by trout and salmon was demonstrated. L-ascorbic acid is a white, odourless, crystalline compound, soluble in water but insoluble in fat solvents.

It is readily oxidized to dehydroascorbic acid, the less biologically potent form. Ascorbic acid is very stable in acid solution because of the preservation of the lactone ring, but in alkaline solution hydrolysis occurs rapidly and vitamin activity is lost. It is very heat labile and prone to atmospheric oxidation, especially in the presence of copper, iron, or several other metallic catalysts. The reduced form is the most biologically active but several derivatives or salts are obtainable which have varying degrees of ascorbate activity.

**Positive Functions**

L-ascorbic acid acts as a biological reducing agent in hydrogen transport. It is involved in many enzyme systems for hydroxylation; i.e., hydroxylation of tryptophan, tyrosine, or proline. It is involved in the detoxification of aromatic drugs and also acts in the production of adrenal steroids.

Ascorbic acid is necessary for the formation of hydroxy proline which is a constituent of collagen, a component of intercellular material in bones and soft tissues. Ascorbic acid plays a synergistic role with vitamin E as intracellular antioxidants and free radical traps. The conversion of folic acid to folinic acid requires vitamin C. Ascorbic acid is involved in the formation of chondroitin sulphate and intercellular ground substance.

Labelled ascorbic acid fed to fish previously deficient in the vitamin was shown to be rapidly mobilized and fixed in areas of rapid collagen synthesis and became concentrated in the thick collagen of the skin and in cartilagenous bones, as well as in the glands of the anterior kidney. Ascorbic acid is also involved in erythrocyte maturation.

## Deficiency Syndrome

Scurvy with impaired collagen formation, perifollicular haemorrhages, loose teeth and poor bone formation, anaemia, and oedema have been reported in other animals. Deficiency signs in fish are generally related to impaired collagen formation. Fish soon show hyperplasia of jaw and snout. The same symptoms have been observed in trout, salmon, yellowtail, carp, guppies and char.

Histologically, hypertrophy of the adrenal tissues and haemorrhage at the bases of fins have been observed in coho salmon. Deficiency signs cease to develop and new growth becomes normal upon replacement of ascorbic acid in the ration. Anaemia eventually develops in extremely deficient fish and scoliosis and lordosis do not repair but are walled off by new growth around the afflicted areas of the spine when ascorbic acid is once again added to the ration.

## Requirements

In the rainbow trout, reasonable blood and anterior kidney storage levels were obtained with an intake of about 100 mg of vitamin C/kg of dry ration in 10°, 12°, or 15° C water systems. When wound repair experiments were initiated, however, or when fish were exposed to other stress then the requirements doubled or tripled.

When severe abdominal or intramuscular wounds were inflicted, young fish needed at least 500 mg of active ascorbate for tissue repair comparable with control fish receiving 1 g or more of ascorbate in the diet/kg of dry diet. Coho salmon appear to need about half of these requirements for adequate tissue levels and for maximum severe wound repair rates.

The requirement for ascorbic acid is related to stress, growth rate and size of the animal, as well as to the other nutrients present in the diet. A compromise value of about 200 mg of ascorbic acid/kg diet for trout and salmon raised in freshwater systems between 10-15°C would ensure reasonable tissue storage levels and furnish some excess for mild stress conditions and for ascorbic acid loss from the diet through oxidation.

Large common carp can synthesize some ascorbate and the requirement for this species may be dependent on fish size and the environment in which they are reared.

**Table. Growth and Tissue Ascorbate**

| Vitamin C diet treatment | Trout | | | Salmon | | |
|---|---|---|---|---|---|---|
| | *Average weight at 24 weeks* | *Ascorbate concentrate* [1/] | | *Average weight at 24 weeks* | *Ascorbate concentrate* [1/] | |
| | | *blood* | *kidney* | | *blood* | *kidney* |
| *mg/100 g* | *g* | *g/g* | *g/g* | *g* | *g/g* | *s/s* |
| 0 | 2.4 | [2/] | [2/] | 5.0 | 22.3±2.2 | 89 |
| 5 | 9.6 | 34.4±2.9 | 125 | 6.0 | 30.5±1.2 | 132 |
| 10 | 10.6 | 34.6±1.3 | 137 | 5.7 | 35.8±1.6 | 265 |
| 20 | 10.1 | 38.8±3.3 | 132 | 6.1 | 34.2±2.3 | 183 |
| 40 | 10.2 | 46.8±6.2 | 162 | 6.3 | 33.7±2.0 | 225 |
| 100 | 10.8 | 51.0±4.6 | 247 | 6.0 | 37.8±2.3 | 321 |

1/ Average of five samples for blood (± S.D.) and two for head kidney tissue

2/ No fish available for assay

## Sources and Protection

Ascorbic acid is widely distributed in nature with citrus fruits, cabbage, liver, and kidney tissue good sources for the vitamin. Fresh insects and fish tissues contain reasonable amounts of the vitamin. Synthetic ascorbic acid is also readily available. Fish food should be protected from oxidizing agents and kept sealed or frozen until used to prevent loss of the vitamin.

## Antimetabolites and Inactivation

D-ascorbic acid, the optical isomer of the active form, has no vitamin activity and competes for sites of several enzyme reactions mediated by L-ascorbic acid. 6-deoxy-L-ascorbic acid, dehydroascorbic acid and L-glucoascorbic acid have very little activity.

## Clinical Assessment

Ascorbic acid status for experimental animals is normally

attempted by tissue ascorbate analysis. Most of the assays previously used measure total ascorbate and not biologically active L-ascorbic acid. Consequently these are fraught with errors and misconception of true vitamin C status.

In fish tissues, blood and liver do not adequately reflect the ascorbic acid intake and status, whereas assay of the anterior kidney which contains adrenal tissue provides a fairly representative picture of tissue storage of the vitamin. Stress rapidly reduces the ascorbic acid content of this tissue with concurrent production of adrenal steroids. Conversely, dietary repletion is reflected by up to four or five-fold storage levels from the deficient state. Examination of fragile support cartilage in the gill filaments under low magnification will detect early hypovitaminosis before clinically acute symptoms become noticeable.

However, the best tissue for routine clinical analysis to assess vitamin C status in trout and salmon appears to be the anterior kidney with samples selected from the junction of the two forward wings. Tissues are blotted free of blood with filter paper, and then assayed for total ascorbate by one of the improved quick methods to determine total ascorbate.

## Inositol

Muscle'sugar' was discovered by Scherer in 1850 and was characterized as inositol in 1887. Inositol was shown to be an alopecia (a form of hairlessness) preventing factor for mice in 1940. Poor growth and poor food passage in inositol-deficient fish was observed in salmon and carp.

## Inositol

Seven optically inactive and two optically active isomers of hexahydroxycyclohexane can exist. One of the optically active forms, myo-inositol, is a white crystalline powder soluble in water and insoluble in alcohol and ether. The material can be synthesized, but is easily isolated from biological material in free or combined forms.

The mixed calcium-magnesium salt of the hexophosphate is phytin. Isomers have little biological activity but will compete in chemical reactions. Inositol is a highly stable compound.

## POSITIVE FUNCTIONS

Myo-inositol is a structural component in living tissues. It has lipotropic action by preventing accumulation of cholesterol in one type of fatty liver disease and is involved with choline in maintaining normal lipid/metabolism.

It is a growth-promoting substance for micro-organisms and prevents an alopecia in mice. It is a reserve carbohydrate in muscle as well as a major component of phosphoglycerides in animal tissues.

## DEFICIENCY SYNDROME

Poor growth, increased gastric emptying time, oedema, dark colour, and distended stomachs are symptoms observed in salmon, trout, carp and catfish held for long periods on inositol-deficient test rations.

A'spectacle-eye' condition for rats has not been observed under the experimental conditions used in fish studies. The major deficiency sign is inefficiency in digestion and food utilization and concomitant poor growth leading to a population of fish with distended abdomens.

## SOURCES AND PROTECTION

Myo-inositol occurs ubiquitously in large amounts wherever biological tissue is found. Wheat germ, dried peas, and beans are rich sources.

Brain, heart, and glandular tissues are very good sources of biologically active inositol. Citrus fruit pulp and dried yeast also contain inositol. The compound is stable.

## ANTIMETABOLITES AND INACTIVATION

Seven optically inactive and one optically active but biologically inactive stereo isomers occur. Since inositol is synthesized in the biologically active form by many microorganisms in the gut, only large quantities of chemically synthesized inactive isomers added to diets would interfere with the metabolism of inositol for growth and normal physiological function.

Biologically inactive stereoisomers of myo-inositol do not compete for critical sites in metabolism. Methyl derivatives and mono-, di- and triphosphoric acid esters occur naturally. Salts of the hexaphosphate or phytin make the bound inositol practically unavailable to the animal.

## CLINICAL ASSESSMENT

Assessment in fish has been based on lack of deficiency signs coupled with the most efficient food conversion. Salmon feeding actively in oceans show 1-1.5 mg of inositol/g of fresh liver tissue and young fingerlings raised in freshwater at 10-15°C had 600-700ωg/g of liver tissue. An alternate, better assessment may be based on a standard muscle section or whole carcass analysis for free or for bound inositol. Projection of inositol intake from normal fish diet ingredients should indicate an excess of this particular vitamin.

## CHOLINE

Methylation as a basic metabolic process was postulated by Hoffmeister. Methyl transfer was shown in vivo by Thompson and the interrelationships between choline, methionine, and homo-cystine were shown by du Vigneaud in 1939-42. Trout fed low choline rations developed haemorrhagic kidneys and salmon showed an aversion to food in choline-deficient diet.

### Choline

Choline is a very strong organic base and forms many derivatives widely distributed in animal and vegetable tissue. One derivative, acetylcholine, is involved in the transmission of nerve impulses across synapses. Choline is very hygroscopic, very soluble in water, and is stable to heat in acid, but decomposes in alkaline solutions.

### Positive Functions

Choline acts as a methyl donor in trans-methylation

reactions. It is a lipotropic and antihaemorrhagic factor preventing the development of fatty livers.

It is involved in the synthesis of phospholipids and in fat transport. Acetylcholine transmits the excitory state across the ganglionic synapses and neuromuscular junctions. Choline is essential for growth and good food conversion in fish.

**Deficiency Syndrome**

Deficiency signs include poor growth and poor food conversion accompanied by impaired fat metabolism. Haemorrhagic kidneys and intestines have been reported in trout and increased gastric emptying time has been observed in salmon.

**Sources and Protection**

Rich sources of choline are wheat germ, beans, brain, and heart tissue. Choline hydrochloride, the commercially available form, may inactivate -tocopherol and vitamin K when in direct contact with these vitamins and care should be exercised in selecting properly protected (gelatin coated) fat soluble vitamins in fish diet preparation.

**Clinical Assessment**

Choline status of fish can be estimated from the assay of choline content of the dietary ingredients with the absence of deficiency signs. Maximum liver storage may not be the best criteria to determine choline nutritional status but has been used to assess the tentative requirement listed for the two species of salmon.

## p-AMINOBENZOIC ACID

Para-aminobenzoic acid is a white crystalline powder which is water soluble and heat and light stable in aqueous and mild alkaline solution. It is a growth promoting vitamin for micro-organisms which require the vitamin for folic acid synthesis. Large intake has been shown to counteract the antimetabolite effect of sulphonamides in bacterial culture. No positive function or deficiency signs have been observed in fish.

## LIPOIC ACID

Lipoic acid is both fat soluble and water soluble. Its active form is the amide derivative known as lipoamide. Lipoic acid functions as a coenzyme in a -ketoacid decarboxylation. It was discovered independently in several laboratories during the period 1945-50 and shown to be an essential component of multienzyme, the pyruvate dehydrogenase complex. Pyruvate is converted to'active acetaldehyde' which in turn is picked up by lipoamide.

Subsequent oxidation of the aldehyde results in the reduction of lipoamide to a disulphydryl form. The multi-enzyme unit also includes thiamine pyrophosphate, coenzyme A, and flavin adenine dinucleotide. Glandular tissues are good sources of lipoic acid. No requirements have been determined for fish.

# FAT-SOLUBLE VITAMINS

Fat-soluble vitamins A, D, E, and K differ from the water-soluble vitamins in their accumulative action. Little evidence has been recorded for hypervitaminosis with the water-soluble vitamins since these compounds are rapidly metabolized and excreted when intake exceeds liver or tissue storage capacity, but hypervitaminosis is a common occurrence in fish and other animals when large quantities of any one of the fat-soluble vitamins are ingested.

Toxicity symptoms involving vitamins A and D are indistinguishable from deficiency symptoms for the same vitamins. On the other hand, symptoms of excess vitamins E and K intake are more discrete. Fish rations may often be enriched with fish oils to increase caloric density of the ration resulting in excessive intake of the fat-soluble vitamins.

## VITAMIN A

A fat-soluble factor that promoted growth in rats by Hopkins and by Osborne and Mendel at the beginning of this century. McCollum and Simmonds cured xerophthalmia, a disease of the eye, with this material. The chemical structure of vitamin A and its relationship to -carotene was shown by

Von Euler in 1928. Active vitamin A was synthesized in the mid-thirties.

The relationship of the vitamin A alcohols to naturally occurring -carotene Retinene, the aldehyde form of vitamin A, has been isolated from the retina of dark adapted eyes and is involved in vision in dim light. Retinoic acid, which is the oxidized form of vitamin A alcohol, has been shown to have some vitamin A activity. Vitamin A1 is found in saltwater fish, whereas vitamin A is more abundant in freshwater fish. Interconversion of the two forms in living fish tissue has been demonstrated.

Fish oils contain vitamin A as free alcohols or esters. Vitamin A alcohol occurs as a light coloured viscous oil which is heat labile and subject to air oxidation. Beta-carotene occurs as an orange, crystalline compound which is more stable to heat and oxidation. Vitamin A is water insoluble but is soluble in fat and organic solvent.

## POSITIVE FUNCTIONS

Vitamin A is essential in maintaining epithelial cells, preventing atrophy and keratinization of epithelial tissues. It is combined with a protein in visual purple and is important in night vision. Vitamin A also prevents xerophthalmia in rats and young children. Vitamin A promotes growth of new cells and aids in maintaining resistance to infection.

## THE SYNDROME OF DEFICIENCY OR EXCESS

Hypovitaminosis A is characterized by poor growth, poor vision, keratinization of epithelial tissue, xerophthalmia, night blindness, haemorrhage in the anterior chamber of the eye, haemorrhage of the base of the fins, and abnormal bone formation. Nerve degeneration has been reported in pigs, chickens, rats, rabbits, and ducks, but only occasionally observed in fish after long periods of deficiency.

Hypervitaminosis A fish and in other animals and involved enlargement of liver and spleen, abnormal growth, skin lesions, epithelial keratinization, hyperplasia. of head cartilage, and abnormal bone formation resulting in ankylosis and fusion of vertebrae. Hypervitaminosis A is reflected in very high liver oil vitamin A content and elevated serum alkaline phosphatase. Removal of excess vitamin A from the diet promotes rapid recovery.

## SOURCES AND PROTECTION

Cod liver oil is the best known source of vitamin A although black sea bass, swordfish, or ling cod oils contain much more of the vitamin. Whale liver oil contains kitol which has little or no biological activity until heated above 200° C when one molecule of biologically active vitamin A is generated per molecule of whale kitol.

This biologically inactive kitol may be deposited in the whale to avoid hypervitaminosis A during excessive vitamin A intake. The possibility of hypervitaminosis A occurs when tuna, shark, or ling cod viscera are used in preparation of moist fish diets. Synthetic vitamin A preparations, such as vitamin A palmitate, are available and are often used to supplement rations low in fish meal, fish viscera, or carotenes.

Some fish species seem able to utilize b-carotene as a vitamin A source, whereas others are unable to split the g-carotene molecule and vitamin A must be added to the diet.

## CLINICAL ASSESSMENT

Vitamin A status can best be assessed by the absence of deficiency signs and by assay of liver oil for vitamin A content. Assay for the vitamin in blood or plasma has not been found to be useful.

## VITAMIN D

Rickets was induced with test diets by Hopkins, and Mellanby cured the disease in dogs by adding cod liver oil to the ration. Ultraviolet light exposure was shown to have an anti-rachitic effect, and provitamin D activity had been ascribed to ergosterol. Crystalline vitamin D was isolated by Angus and activated 7-dehydrocholesterol was isolated by Windaus.

Vitamin $D_2$ or ergocalciferol, is one of several biologically active forms of vitamin D. Vitamin $D_3$ or activated

7-dehydrocholesterol has the chemical formula $C_{27}H_{44}O$ and contains a more simplified, unsaturated 8-carbon side chain. Vitamin $D_3$, also known as cholecalciferol, is formed in most animal tissue by the rupture of one of the ring bonds of 7-dehydrocholesterol by ultraviolet radiation.

Cholecalciferol is a white, crystalline compound soluble in fat and organic solvents and is stable to heat and oxidation in mild alkali or acid solution.

## POSITIVE FUNCTIONS

Vitamin D is essential for maintaining calcium and inorganic phosphate homeostasis. It is involved in alkaline phosphatase activity, promotes intestinal absorption of calcium, and influences the action of parathyroid hormone on bone. Fish may sequester calcium from water through the gill membrane; thus the major function of vitamin D for other animals may not be necessary to satisfy calcium requirements for fish.

## SYNDROME OF DEFICIENCY OR EXCESS

Rickets and abnormal bone formation for animals has not been observed in fish fed low vitamin D diets. However little work has been done under carefully controlled conditions with young growing fish and only alteration in alkaline phosphatase activity has been reported on different vitamin D diet intake.

Hypervitaminosis D, however, has been reported. Brook trout fed large doses of vitamin D showed impaired growth, lethargy, and dark colouration. High intake of vitamin D mobilizes phosphorus and calcium from the bone and tissues and may result in fragile bones, poor growth, and poor appetite related to the nausea in man afflicted with hypervitaminosis D. This area needs to be explored because of the potential for hypervitaminosis D in fish fed diets containing various fish viscera which might contain large amounts of the vitamin D. Tuna liver oil may contain, for example, 100 to 1 000 times as much active vitamin D as cod liver oil.

## SOURCES AND PROTECTION

Vitamin D requirements of many animals can be met by

ultraviolet irradiation of the skin where cholesterol derivatives are converted to calciferol. Since the vitamin is fat soluble and accumulates in lipid stores, fish liver oil is a rich source of the material.

Content varies tremendously in liver oil, however, with values of about 25 I.U./g present in shark liver oil and over 200 000 I.U./g in albacore tuna liver oil. Cod liver oil contains from 100-500 I.U./g and animal liver contains some vitamin D. One international unit (I.U.) is equal to 0.025 mg of crystalline vitamin D.

## CLINICAL ASSESSMENT

Absorption maxima in the ultraviolet region can be used to detect provitamins D in the non-saponifiable fraction of oils. Concentrated preparations of vitamin D can be assayed by the Carr-Price antimony trichloride reaction when assay is necessary to determine biologically active materials in liver oil of fish on different treatments.

The chick assay may not apply to fish liver storage levels because the biologically active form for fish has not been determined. Therefore, clinical assessment for hypervitaminosis A must rely on crude methods for determination of vitamin D in liver oil samples by the Carr-Price reaction or by measuring absorption in the UV spectrum.

## VITAMIN E

The existence of an antisterility vitamin was postulated by Evans and Bishop. This factor was named'vitamin E' by Sure. The active tocopherol was isolated, characterized, and synthesized by Karrer. Vitamin E is composed of a class of compounds known as tocopherols. One of the most important tocopherols is -tocopherol.

Eight naturally occurring tocopherol derivatives have been isolated and all belong to the D series. Synthetic -tocopherol is a racemic DL- -tocoperhol mixture. The derivatives of tocol or of tocotrienol are named, alpha, beta, gamma, delta, epsilon, eta, zeta1 and zeta2-tocopherol.

The pure tocopherols are fat-soluble oils which are capable

of esterification to form crystalline compounds. The tocopherols are stable to heat and acids in the absence of oxygen, but are rapidly oxidized in the presence of nascent oxygen, peroxides, or other oxidizing agents.

The tocopherols are sensitive to ultraviolet light and are excellent antioxidants in the free form. The esters are more stable and are commonly used as dietary supplements-anticipating hydrolysis in the gut and absorption of the free alcohol to act as an active intra- and intercellular antioxidant. Ethyl derivatives on the aromatic ring are also active.

Oxidation products of a-tocopherol can be reduced with hydrosulphite to -tocopherylhydroquinone or, in the presence of ascorbic acid, to -tocopherol.

**Table: The Tocopherols**

| | |
|---|---|
| Tocopherol (alpha) | 5,7,8-trimethyltocol |
| Tocopherol (beta) | 5,8-dimethyltocol |
| Tocopherol (gamma) | 7,8-dimethyltocol |
| Tocopherol ($zeta_2$) | 5,7-dimethyltocol |
| Tocopherol (eta) | 7-methyltocol |
| Tocopherol (delta) | 8-methyltocol |
| Tocopherol (epsilon) | 5,8-dimethyltocotrienol |
| Tocopherol ($zeta_1$) | 5,7,8-trimethyltocotrienol |

## POSITIVE FUNCTIONS

The tocopherols act as extra and intracellular antioxidants to maintain homeostasis of labile metabolites in the cell and tissue plasma. As physiological antioxidants, these usually protect oxidizable vitamins and labile unsaturated fatty acids. Vitamin E prevents encephalomalacia in chicks, erythrocyte haemolysis in several animals and steatitis in mink, pigs, and farm animals.

The tocopherols also prevent exudative diathesis in chicks, white muscle disease in lambs and calves, and dietary liver necrosis in rats. They act with selenium and with vitamin C for normal reproductive activity and are involved in prevention of nutritional muscular dystrophy in the chick, the yellowtail and carp.

The tocopherols act as free radical traps to stop the chain reaction during peroxide formation and stabilize unsaturated carbon bonds of polyunsaturated fatty acids and other long-chain labile compounds.

Vitamin E is involved in the maintenance of normal blood capillary permeability and the integrity of heart muscle. It was first shown to be involved in prevention of sterility and foetal resorption in rats. It may likewise affect embryo membrane permeability and hatch-ability of fish eggs.

## SYNDROME OF DEFICIENCY OR EXCESS

One of the first signs is erythrocyte fragility closely followed by anaemia, ascites, xerophthalmia, poor growth, poor food conversion, epicarditis, and ceroid deposits in spleen and liver. Muscle dystrophy and xerophthalmia have been in yellowtail and carp.

Non-specific forms of degenerative conditions have been described in several species of fish fed large quantities of polyunsaturated fatty acids with inadequate tocopherol in the ration. Hypervitaminosis E results in poor growth, toxic liver reaction, and death.

## SOURCES AND PROTECTION

Vegetable oils are rich sources of tocopherols. Synthetic - tocopherol in esterfied acetate or phosphate form is commonly used as a diet supplement. These esters are much more stable than the free form which is rapidly lost by air oxidation or in the presence of labile compounds like the polyunsaturated fish oils.

Addition of antioxidants such as BHT (butylated hydroxyanisole) and BHT (butylated hydroxytoluene) protects fats and other labile compounds in the ration from oxidation, but these antioxidants have no vitamin E activity.

## CLINICAL ASSESSMENT

The erythrocyte fragility test indicates the physiological state of fish. Absence of histologically detectable ceroid in liver and spleen from representative samples in the population is a good clue on the presence of adequate amounts of physiological antioxidants in the fish.

A barbituric acid test for oxidation of components has not been applied to fish tissues as a clinical tool for assessment of nutrition state except when liver oils become saturated with very labile polyunsaturated fatty acids such as when feeding squid or saury oils.

These assays are good indicators of the state of oxidation of the finished ration, but the absence of deficiency signs and normal erythrocyte fragility are better clinical tests. Analysis for tocopherol is difficult and time-consuming and only applicable under critical research experiment situation.

## VITAMIN K

The name vitamin K (for'koagulation') was proposed by Dam. Dam isolated the vitamin from alfalfa and from fish meal in 1939. It was synthesized later that year. The K vitamins $K_2$ contain 6,7, or 9 isoprene units in the side chain which varies from 30-45 carbon atoms. Many isosteres of vitamin K have been identified in animal tissues, plant tissues, and micro-organisms. Although fairly stable compounds, they are destroyed upon oxidation and exposure to ultraviolet radition. Menadione is very reactive and is subject in aqueous media to chemical interaction.

## POSITIVE FUNCTIONS

Vitamin K is involved in the hepatic synthesis of blood clotting proteins - prothrombin and proconvertin. Substituted forms of vitamin K are strongly bacteriostatic and may serve as an alternate defence mechanism for bacterial infections.

Vitamin K is structurally related to flavo compounds which function as electron carriers in the electron transport system. The primary role of vitamin K is to maintain a fast normal blood clotting rate which is so important to fish living in a water environment.

## SYNDROME OF DEFICIENCY OR EXCESS

Prothrombin time in salmon fed diets devoid of vitamin

K was increased three to five times and, during prolonged deficiency states, anaemia and haemorrhagic areas appeared in the gills, eyes, and vascular tissues.

Increased blood clotting time has also been reported for other fish reared on diets with low vitamin K content. Interrelationships with other vitamins have not been documented in fish where the primary deficiency signs are slow blood clotting and haemorrhage, severe anaemia, or death in wounded fish. Haemorrhagic areas often appear in fragile tissues such as the gills.

## SOURCES AND PROTECTION

Vitamin K sources are green, leafy vegetables. Alfalfa leaves are among the best sources of vitamin K. Low levels are found in soybeans and animal liver. Synthetic menadione is also available.

Although vitamin K in ground alfalfa is fairly stable, synthetic material should be protected from exposure to ultraviolet light and to excessive oxidizing or reducing conditions. The use of rapidly cured dehydrated alfalfa is essential to minimize formation of the physiological antagonist, dicumarol.

The diet should be kept dry, prepared with minimum exposure to air oxidation, and fed as soon as practicable after manufacture to minimize vitamin K loss.

## ANTIMETABOLITES AND INACTIVATION

Dicumarol was isolated from spoiled sweet clover hay and shown to prevent the normal function of vitamin K in maintenance of normal blood clotting times. Early work was with cattle and hogs but was soon extended to rats, other experimental animals, and man.

Dicumarol is an anticoagulant and has been used to prevent thrombosis in animals and man. It is not an antimetabolite competing for vitamin K sites but plays another role in preventing normal blood clotting.

Vitamin K counte-racts the dicumarol effect quantitatively. Another anticoa-gulant, warfarin, is a common rat poison which has five to ten times the anticoagulant activity of dicumarol. The effects of warfarin can also be reversed by administration of vitamin K.

## CLINICAL ASSESSMENT

Vitamin K status of fish is determined by measuring blood clotting time. Chemical methods for determining menadione content of active metabolite after storage are available but have not been applied to measure vitamin K activity in the liver or tissues of young, growing fish.

## Chapter 7

# Caffeine

Caffeine is a bitter, white crystalline xanthine alkaloid that is a psychoactive stimulant drug. Caffeine was discovered by a German chemist, Friedrich Ferdinand Runge, in 1819. He coined the term *kaffein*, a chemical compound in coffee, which in English became *caffeine*.

Caffeine is found in varying quantities in the beans, leaves, and fruit of some plants, where it acts as a natural pesticide that paralyzes and kills certain insects feeding on the plants. It is most commonly consumed by humans in infusions extracted from the cherries of the coffee plant and the leaves of the tea bush, as well as from various foods and drinks containing products derived from the kola nut.

Other sources include yerba mate, guarana berries, and the Yaupon Holly.In humans, caffeine is a central nervous system (CNS) stimulant, having the effect of temporarily warding off drowsiness and restoring alertness. Beverages containing caffeine, such as coffee, tea, soft drinks, and energy drinks enjoy great popularity.

Caffeine is the world's most widely consumed psychoactive substance, but unlike many other psychoactive substances it is legal and unregulated in nearly all jurisdictions. In North America, 90% of adults consume caffeine daily. The U.S. Food and Drug Administration lists caffeine as a "multiple purpose generally recognized as safe food substance".

Caffeine has diuretic properties, at least when administered in sufficient doses to subjects who do not have a tolerance for it. Regular users, however, develop a strong tolerance to this effect, and studies have generally failed to support the common notion that ordinary consumption of caffeinated beverages contributes significantly to dehydration.

## OCCURRENCE

Caffeine is found in many plant species, where it acts as a natural pesticide, with high caffeine levels being reported in seedlings that are still developing foliages, but are lacking mechanical protection; caffeine paralyzes and kills certain insects feeding upon the plant. High caffeine levels have also been found in the surrounding soil of coffee bean seedlings. It is therefore understood that caffeine has a natural function as both a natural pesticide and as an inhibitor of seed germination of other nearby coffee seedlings thus giving it a better chance of survival.

**Fig.** Roasted Coffee Beans, a Common Source of Caffeine.

Common sources of caffeine are coffee, tea, and to a lesser extent cocoa bean. Less commonly used sources of caffeine include the yerba maté and guarana plants, which are sometimes used in the preparation of teas and energy drinks.

Two of caffeine's alternative names, *mateine* and *guaranine,* are derived from the names of these plants. Some yerba mate enthusiasts assert that mateine is a stereoisomer of caffeine, which would make it a different substance altogether.

This is not true because caffeine is an achiral molecule, and therefore has no enantiomers; nor does it have other stereoisomers. The disparity in experience and effects between the various natural caffeine sources could be due to the fact that plant sources of caffeine also contain widely varying mixtures of other xanthine alkaloids, including the cardiac stimulants theophylline and theobromine and other substances such as polyphenols which can form insoluble complexes with caffeine. One of the world's primary sources of caffeine is the coffee "bean" (which is the seed of the coffee plant), from which coffee is brewed.

Caffeine content in coffee varies widely depending on the type of coffee bean and the method of preparation used; even beans within a given bush can show variations in concentration. In general, one serving of coffee ranges from 40 milligrams, for a single shot (30 milliliters) of *arabica*-variety espresso, to about 100 milligrams for a cup (120 milliliters) of drip coffee.

Generally, dark-roast coffee has less caffeine than lighter roasts because the roasting process reduces the bean's caffeine content. *Arabica* coffee normally contains less caffeine than the *robusta* variety. Coffee also contains trace amounts of theophylline, but no theobromine.

Tea is another common source of caffeine. Although tea contains more caffeine than coffee, a typical serving contains much less, as tea is normally brewed much weaker. Besides strength of the brew, growing conditions, processing techniques and other variables also affect caffeine content. Certain types of tea may contain somewhat more caffeine than other teas. Tea contains small amounts of theobromine and slightly higher levels of theophylline than coffee. Preparation and many other factors have a significant impact on tea, and colour is a very poor indicator of caffeine content. Teas like the pale Japanese green tea gyokuro, for example, contain far more caffeine than much darker teas like lapsang souchong, which has very little.

**Table. Caffeine Content of Select Common Food and Drugs.**

| Product | Serving Size | Caffeine per Serving (mg) | Caffeine per Liter (mg) |
|---|---|---|---|
| Caffeine tablet (regular strength) | 1 Tablet | 100 | — |
| Caffeine tablet (extra strength) | 1 Tablet | 200 | — |
| Excedrin tablet | 1 Tablet | 65 | — |

| | | | |
|---|---|---|---|
| Hershey's Special Dark (45% cacao content) | 1 bar (43 g; 1.5 oz) | 31 | — |
| Hershey's Milk Chocolate (11% cacao content) | 1 bar (43 g; 1.5 oz) | 10 | — |
| Percolated Coffee | 207 mL (7 U.S. fl oz) | 80–135 | 386–652 |
| Drip coffee | 207 mL (7 U.S. fl oz) | 115–175 | 555–845 |
| Coffee, Decaffeinated | 207 mL (7 U.S. fl oz) | 5-15 | 24-72 |
| Coffee, espresso | 44–60 mL (1.5-2 U.S. fl oz) | 100 | 1691–2254 |
| Black tea | 177 mL (6 U.S. fl oz) | 50 | 282 |
| Green tea | 177 mL (6 U.S. fl oz) | 30 | 169 |
| Coca-Cola Classic | 355 mL (12 U.S. fl oz) | 34 | 96 |
| Mountain Dew | 355 mL (12 U.S. fl oz) | 54.5 | 154 |
| Jolt Cola | 695 mL (23.5 U.S. fl oz) | 280 | 402 |
| Red Bull | 250 mL (8.2 U.S. fl oz) | 80 | 320 |

Caffeine is also a common ingredient of soft drinks such as cola, originally prepared from kola nuts. Soft drinks typically contain about 10 to 50 milligrams of caffeine per serving. By contrast, energy drinks such as Red Bull can start at 80 milligrams of caffeine per serving.

The caffeine in these drinks either originates from the ingredients used or is an additive derived from the product of decaffeination or from chemical synthesis. Guarana, a prime ingredient of energy drinks, contains large amounts of caffeine with small amounts of theobromine and theophylline in a naturally occurring slow-release excipient.Chocolate derived from cocoa bean contains a small amount of caffeine. The weak stimulant effect of chocolate may be due to a combination of theobromine and theophylline as well as caffeine.

A typical 28-gram serving of a milk chocolate bar has about as much caffeine as a cup of *decaffeinated* coffee. In recent years various manufacturers have begun putting caffeine into shower products such as shampoo and soap, claiming that caffeine can be absorbed through the skin.

However, the effectiveness of such products has not been proven, and they are likely to have little stimulatory effect on the central nervous system because caffeine is not readily absorbed through the skin. Various manufacturers market caffeine tablets, claiming that using caffeine of pharmaceutical quality improves mental alertness.

These effects have been borne out by research that shows that caffeine use (whether in tablet form or not) results in decreased fatigue and increased attentiveness. These tablets are commonly used by students studying for their exams and by people who work or drive for long hours.

Caffeine is also used pharmacologically to treat apnoea in premature newborns and as such is one of the 10 drugs most commonly given in neonatal intensive care, though questions are now raised based on experimental animal research whether it might have subtle harmful side-effects.

Humans have consumed caffeine since the Stone Age. Early peoples found that chewing the seeds, bark, or leaves of certain plants had the effects of easing fatigue, stimulating awareness, and elevating one's mood. Only much later was it found that the effect of caffeine was increased by steeping such plants in hot water. Many cultures have legends that attribute the discovery of such plants to people living many thousands of years ago.

According to one popular Chinese legend, the Emperor of China Shennong, reputed to have reigned in about 3000 BC, accidentally discovered that when some leaves fell into boiling water, a fragrant and restorative drink resulted. Shennong is also mentioned in Lu Yu's *Cha Jing*, a famous early work on the subject of tea. The history of coffee has been recorded as far back as the ninth century. During that time, coffee beans were available only in their native habitat, Ethiopia. A popular legend traces its discovery to a goatherder named Kaldi, who apparently observed goats that became elated and sleepless at night after grazing on coffee shrubs and, upon trying the berries that the goats had been eating, experienced the same vitality.

The earliest literary mention of coffee may be a reference to Bunchum in the works of the 9th century Persian physician al-Razi. In 1587, Malaye Jaziri compiled a work tracing the history and legal controversies of coffee, entitled "Undat al safwa fi hill al-qahwa".

In this work, Jaziri recorded that one Sheikh, Jamal-al-Din al-Dhabhani, mufti of Aden, was the first to adopt the use of coffee in 1454, and that in the 15th century the Sufis of Yemen routinely used coffee to stay awake during prayers. Towards the close of the 16th century, the use of coffee was recorded by a European resident in Egypt, and about this time it came into general use in the Near East.

The appreciation of coffee as a beverage in Europe, where it was first known as "Arabian wine," dates from the 17th century. A legend states that after the Ottoman Turks retreated from the walls of Vienna after losing a battle for the city, many sacks of coffee beans were found among their baggage. Europeans didn't know what to do with all the coffee beans, being unfamiliar with them.

So Franz George Kolschitzky, a Pole who had actually worked for the Turks, offered to take them. He subsequently taught the Viennese how to make coffee, and the first coffee house in the Western world was opened in Vienna, thus starting a long tradition of coffee appreciation. In Britain, the first coffee houses were opened in London in 1652, at St Michael's Alley, Cornhill. They soon became popular throughout Western Europe, and played a significant role in social relations in the 17th and 18th centuries.

The kola nut, like the coffee berry and tea leaf, appears to have ancient origins. It is chewed in many West African cultures, individually or in a social setting, to restore vitality and ease hunger pangs. In 1911, kola became the focus of one of the earliest documented health scares when the US government seized 40 barrels and 20 kegs of Coca-Cola syrup in Chattanooga, Tennessee, alleging that the caffeine in its drink was "injurious to health".

On March 13, 1911, the government initiated *United States v. Forty Barrels and Twenty Kegs of Coca-Cola,* hoping to force Coca-Cola to remove caffeine from its formula by making claims, such as that the excessive use of Coca-Cola at one girls' school led to "wild nocturnal freaks, violations of college rules and female proprieties, and even immoralities."

Although the judge ruled in favour of Coca-Cola, two bills were introduced to the U.S. House of Representatives in 1912 to amend the Pure Food and Drug Act, adding caffeine to the list of "habit-forming" and "deleterious" substances which must be listed on a product's label.

The earliest evidence of cocoa bean use comes from residue found in an ancient Mayan pot dated to 600 BC. In the New World, chocolate was consumed in a bitter and spicy drink called *xocoatl,* often seasoned with vanilla, chile pepper, and achiote.

Xocoatl was believed to fight fatigue, a belief that is probably attributable to the theobromine and caffeine content. Chocolate was an important luxury good throughout pre-Columbian Mesoamerica, and cocoa beans were often used as currency. Xocoatl was introduced to Europe by the Spaniards and became a popular beverage by 1700.

They also introduced the cacao tree into the West Indies and the Philippines. It was used in alchemical processes, where it was known as Black Bean. The leaves and stems of the Yaupon Holly (*Ilex vomitoria*) were used by Native Americans to brew a tea called Asi or the "black drink"· Archaeologists have found evidence of this use stretch back far into antiquity, possibly dating to Late Archaic times.

**Pharmacology**

Global consumption of caffeine has been estimated at 120,000 tonnes per year, making it the world's most popular psychoactive substance. This number equates to one serving of a caffeine beverage for every person, per day.

Caffeine is a central nervous system and metabolic stimulant, and is used both recreationally and medically to reduce physical fatigue and restore mental alertness when unusual weakness or drowsiness occurs. Caffeine and other methylxanthine derivatives are also used on newborns to treat apnea and correct irregular heartbeats.

Caffeine stimulates the central nervous system first at the higher levels, resulting in increased alertness and wakefulness, faster and clearer flow of thought, increased focus, and better general body coordination, and later at the spinal cord level at higher doses. Once inside the body, it has a complex chemistry, and acts through several mechanisms as described below.

### *Metabolism and Half-life*

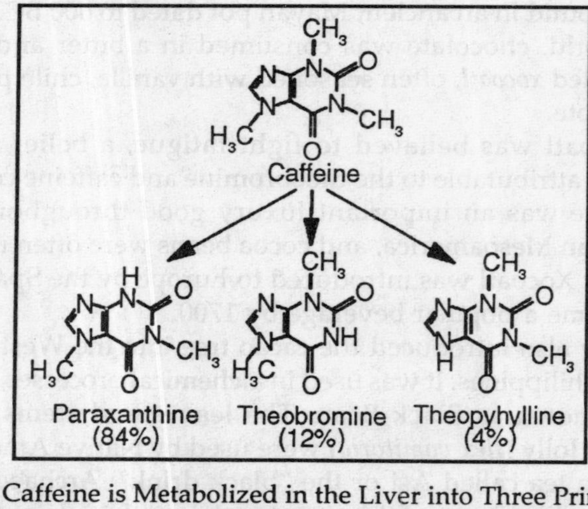


**Fig.** Caffeine is Metabolized in the Liver into Three Primary Metabolites: Paraxanthine (84%), Theobromine (12%), and Theophylline (4%)

Caffeine from coffee or other beverages is absorbed by the stomach and small intestine within 45 minutes of ingestion and then distributed throughout all tissues of the body. It is eliminated by first-order kinetics.

Caffeine can also be ingested rectally, evidenced by the formulation of suppositories of ergotamine tartrate and caffeine (for the relief of migraine) and chlorobutanol and caffeine (for the treatment of hyperemesis).

The half-life of caffeine — the time required for the body to eliminate one-half of the total amount of caffeine — varies widely among individuals according to such factors as age, liver function, pregnancy, some concurrent medications, and the level of enzymes in the liver needed for caffeine metabolism.

In healthy adults, caffeine's half-life is approximately 4.9 hours. In women taking oral contraceptives this is increased to 5–10 hours, and in pregnant women the half-life is roughly 9–11 hours.

Caffeine can accumulate in individuals with severe liver disease, increasing its half-life up to 96 hours. In infants and young children, the half-life may be longer than in adults; half-life in a newborn baby may be as long as 30 hours.

Other factors such as smoking can shorten caffeine's half-life. Fluvoxamine reduced the clearance of caffeine by 91.3%, and prolonged its elimination half-life by 11.4-fold (from 4.9 hours to 56 hours).

Caffeine is metabolized in the liver by the cytochrome P450 oxidase enzyme system (specifically, the 1A2 isozyme) into three metabolic dimethylxanthines, which each have their own effects on the body:

- *Paraxanthine* (84%): Has the effect of increasing lipolysis, leading to elevated glycerol and free fatty acid levels in the blood plasma.
- *Theobromine* (12%): Dilates blood vessels and increases urine volume. Theobromine is also the principal alkaloid in the cocoa bean, and therefore chocolate.
- *Theophylline* (4%): Relaxes smooth muscles of the bronchi, and is used to treat asthma. The therapeutic dose of theophylline, however, is many times greater than the levels attained from caffeine metabolism.

Each of these metabolites is further metabolized and then excreted in the urine.

## *Mechanism of Action*

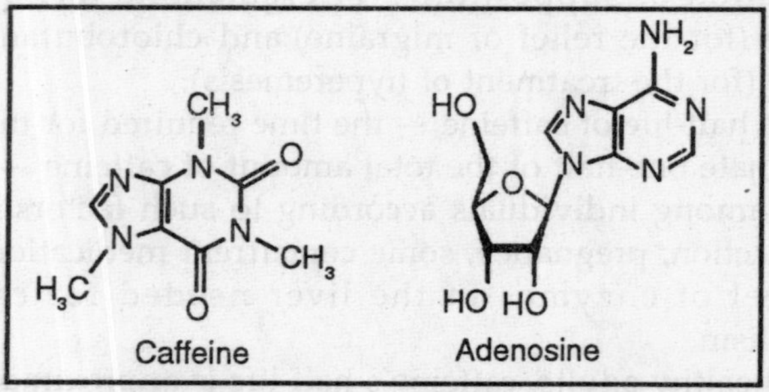


**Fig.** Caffeine's Principal Mode of Action is as an Antagonist of Adenosine Receptors in the Brain.

Caffeine readily crosses the blood–brain barrier that separates the bloodstream from the interior of the brain. Once in the brain, the principal mode of action is as a nonselective antagonist of adenosine receptors.

The caffeine molecule is structurally similar to adenosine, and binds to adenosine receptors on the surface of cells without activating them (an "antagonist" mechanism of action). Therefore, caffeine acts as a competitive inhibitor.

Adenosine is found in every part of the body, because it plays a role in the fundamental ATP-related energy metabolism, but it has special functions in the brain. There is a great deal of evidence that concentrations of brain adenosine are increased by various types of metabolic stress including anoxia and ischemia.

The evidence also indicates that brain adenosine acts to protect the brain by suppressing neural activity and also by increasing blood flow through A2A and A2B receptors located on vascular smooth muscle.

By counteracting adenosine, caffeine reduces resting cerebral blood flow between 22% and 30%. Caffeine also has a generally disinhibitory effect on neural activity. It has not been shown, however, how these effects cause increases in arousal and alertness.

Adenosine is released in the brain through a complex mechanism. There is evidence that adenosine functions as a synaptically released neurotransmitter in some cases, but stress-related adenosine increases appear to be produced mainly by extracellular metabolism of ATP.

It is not likely that adenosine is the primary neurotransmitter for any group of neurons, but rather that it is released together with other transmitters by a number of neuron types.

Unlike most neurotransmitters, adenosine does not seem to be packaged into vesicles that are released in a voltage-controlled manner, but the possibility of such a mechanism has not been completely ruled out. Several classes of adenosine receptors have been described, with different anatomical distributions. $A_1$ receptors are widely distributed, and act to inhibit calcium uptake.

$A_{2A}$ receptors are heavily concentrated in the basal ganglia, an area that plays a critical role in behaviour control, but can be found in other parts of the brain as well, in lower densities. There is evidence that $A_{2A}$ receptors interact with the dopamine system, which is involved in reward and arousal. ($A_{2A}$ receptors can also be found on arterial walls and blood cell membranes.) Beyond its general neuroprotective effects, there are reasons to believe that adenosine may be more specifically involved in control of the sleep-wake cycle.

Robert McCarley and his colleagues have argued that accumulation of adenosine may be a primary cause of the sensation of sleepiness that follows prolonged mental activity, and that the effects may be mediated both by inhibition of wake-promoting neurons via $A_1$ receptors, and activation of sleep-promoting neurons via indirect effects on $A_{2A}$ receptors.

More recent studies have provided additional evidence for the importance of $A_{2A}$, but not $A_1$, receptors. Some of the secondary effects of caffeine are probably caused by actions unrelated to adenosine. Like other methylated xanthines, caffeine is both a

- Competitive nonselective phosphodiesterase inhibitor which raises intracellular cAMP, activates PKA, inhibits TNF-alpha and leukotriene synthesis, and reduces inflammation and innate immunity

- Nonselective adenosine receptor antagonist.

Phosphodiesterase inhibitors inhibit cAMP-phosphodiesterase (cAMP-PDE) enzymes, which convert cyclic AMP (cAMP) in cells to its noncyclic form, thus allowing cAMP to build up in cells.

Cyclic AMP participates in activation of protein kinase A (PKA) to begin the phosphorylation of specific enzymes used in glucose synthesis. By blocking its removal caffeine intensifies and prolongs the effects of epinephrine and epinephrine-like drugs such as amphetamine, methampheta-mine, or methylphenidate.

Increased concentrations of cAMP in parietal cells causes an increased activation of protein kinase A (PKA) which in turn increases activation of H+/K+ ATPase, resulting finally in increased gastric acid secretion by the cell. Cyclic AMP also increases the activity of the funny current, which directly increases heart rate. Caffeine is also a structural analogue of strychnine and like it (though much less potent) a competitive antagonist at ionotropic glycine receptors.

Metabolites of caffeine also contribute to caffeine's effects. Paraxanthine is responsible for an increase in the lipolysis process, which releases glycerol and fatty acids into the blood to be used as a source of fuel by the muscles. Theobromine is a vasodilator that increases the amount of oxygen and nutrient flow to the brain and muscles. Theophylline acts as a smooth muscle relaxant that chiefly affects bronchioles and acts as a chronotrope and inotrope that increases heart rate and efficiency.

### *Effects When Taken in Moderation*

The precise amount of caffeine necessary to produce effects varies from person to person depending on body size and degree of tolerance to caffeine. It takes less than an hour for caffeine to begin affecting the body and a mild dose wears off in three to four hours.

Consumption of caffeine does not eliminate the need for sleep, it only temporarily reduces the sensation of being tired throughout the day. In general, 25 to 50 milligrams of caffeine is sufficient for most people to report increased alertness and arousal as well as subjectively lower levels of fatigue.

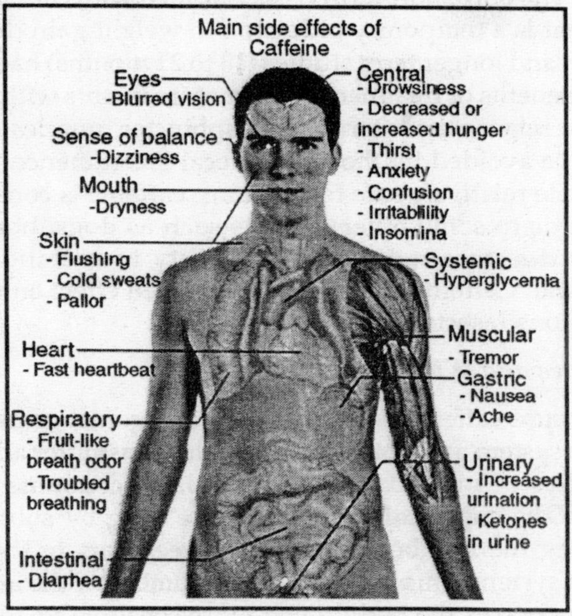


**Fig.** Overview of the More Common Side Effects of Caffeine, Possibly Appearing Even at Levels Below Overdose.

With these effects, caffeine is an ergogenic, increasing a person's capability for mental or physical labour. A study conducted in 1979 showed a 7% increase in distance cycled over a period of two hours in subjects who consumed caffeine compared to control subjects.

Other studies attained much more dramatic results; one particular study of trained runners showed a 44% increase in "race-pace" endurance, as well as a 51% increase in cycling endurance, after a dosage of 9 milligrams of caffeine per kilogram of body weight. Additional studies have reported similar effects. Another study found 5.5 milligrams of caffeine per kilogram of body mass resulted in subjects cycling 29% longer during high intensity circuits.

Caffeine citrate has proven to be of short and long term

benefit in treating the breathing disorders of apnea of prematurity and bronchopulmonary dysplasia in premature infants. The only short-term risk associated with caffeine citrate treatment is a temporary reduction in weight gain during the therapy, and longer term studies (18 to 21 months) have shown lasting benefits of treatment of premature infants with caffeine. Caffeine relaxes the internal anal sphincter muscles and thus should be avoided by those with fecal incontinence.

While relatively safe for humans, caffeine is considerably more toxic to some other animals such as dogs, horses, and parrots due to a much poorer ability to metabolize this compound. Caffeine has also a pronounced effect on mollusks and various insects as well as spiders.

### *Tolerance and Withdrawal*

Because caffeine is primarily an antagonist of the central nervous system's receptors for the neurotransmitter adenosine, the bodies of individuals who regularly consume caffeine adapt to the continual presence of the drug by substantially increasing the number of adenosine receptors in the central nervous system. This increase in the number of the adenosine receptors makes the body much more sensitive to adenosine, with two primary consequences.

First, the stimulatory effects of caffeine are substantially reduced, a phenomenon known as a tolerance adaptation. Second, because these adaptive responses to caffeine make individuals much more sensitive to adenosine, a reduction in caffeine intake will effectively increase the normal physiological effects of adenosine, resulting in unwelcome withdrawal symptoms in tolerant users.

Other research questions the idea that up-regulation of adenosine receptors is responsible for tolerance to the locomotor stimulant effects of caffeine, noting, among other things, that this tolerance is insurmountable by higher doses of caffeine (it should be surmountable if tolerance was due to an increase in receptors), and that the increase in adenosine receptor number is modest and does not explain the large tolerance which develops to caffeine.

Caffeine tolerance develops very quickly, especially among heavy coffee and energy drink consumers. Complete tolerance to sleep disruption effects of caffeine develops after consuming 400 mg of caffeine 3 times a day for 7 days. Complete tolerance to subjective effects of caffeine was observed to develop after consuming 300 mg 3 times per day for 18 days, and possibly even earlier. In another experiment, complete tolerance of caffeine was observed when the subject consumed 750–1200 mg per day while incomplete tolerance to caffeine has been observed in those that consume more average doses of caffeine.

Because adenosine, in part, serves to regulate blood pressure by causing vasodilation, the increased effects of adenosine due to caffeine withdrawal cause the blood vessels of the head to dilate, leading to an excess of blood in the head and causing a headache and nausea. Reduced catecholamine activity may cause feelings of fatigue and drowsiness. A reduction in serotonin levels when caffeine use is stopped can cause anxiety, irritability, inability to concentrate and diminished motivation to initiate or to complete daily tasks; in extreme cases it may cause mild depression. Together, these effects have come to be known as a "crash".

Withdrawal symptoms—possibly including headache, irritability, an inability to concentrate, drowsiness, insomnia and pain in the stomach, upper body, and joints —may appear within 12 to 24 hours after discontinuation of caffeine intake, peak at roughly 48 hours, and usually last from one to five days, representing the time required for the number of adenosine receptors in the brain to revert to "normal" levels, uninfluenced by caffeine consumption.

Analgesics, such as aspirin, can relieve the pain symptoms, as can a small dose of caffeine. Most effective is a combination of both an analgesic and a small amount of caffeine. This is not the only case where caffeine increases the effectiveness of a drug. Caffeine makes pain relievers 40% more effective in relieving headaches and helps the body absorb headache medications more quickly, bringing faster relief.

For this reason, many over-the-counter headache drugs include caffeine in their formula. It is also used with ergotamine in the treatment of migraine and cluster headaches as well as to overcome the drowsiness caused by antihistamines.

## OVERUSE

In large amounts, and especially over extended periods of time, caffeine can lead to a condition known as *caffeinism*. Caffeinism usually combines caffeine dependency with a wide range of unpleasant physical and mental conditions including nervousness, irritability, anxiety, tremulousness, muscle twitching (hyperreflexia), insomnia, headaches, respiratory alkalosis, and heart palpitations.

Furthermore, because caffeine increases the production of stomach acid, high usage over time can lead to peptic ulcers, erosive esophagitis, and gastroesophageal reflux disease. There are four caffeine-induced psychiatric disorders recognized by the Diagnostic and Statistical Manual of Mental Disorders, Fourth Edition: caffeine intoxication, caffeine-induced anxiety disorder, caffeine-induced sleep disorder, and caffeine-related disorder not otherwise specified (NOS).

### Caffeine Intoxication

An acute overdose of caffeine, usually in excess of about 300 milligrams, dependent on body weight and level of caffeine tolerance, can result in a state of central nervous system over-stimulation called *caffeine intoxication* (DSM-IV 305.90), or colloquially the "caffeine jitters". The symptoms of caffeine intoxication are not unlike overdoses of other stimulants.

It may include restlessness, nervousness, excitement, insomnia, flushing of the face, increased urination, gastrointestinal disturbance, muscle twitching, a rambling flow of thought and speech, irritability, irregular or rapid heart beat, and psychomotor agitation. In cases of much larger overdoses, mania, depression, lapses in judgment, disorientation, disinhibition, delusions, hallucinations, and psychosis may occur, and rhabdomyolysis (breakdown of skeletal muscle tissue) can be provoked.

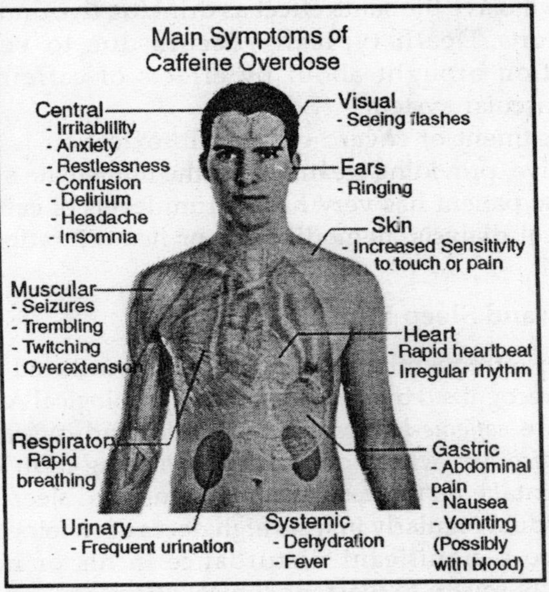


**Fig.** Main Symptoms of Caffeine Intoxication.

In cases of extreme overdose, death can result. The median lethal dose ($LD_{50}$) given orally, is 192 milligrams per kilogram in rats. The $LD_{50}$ of caffeine in humans is dependent on weight and individual sensitivity and estimated to be about 150 to 200 milligrams per kilogram of body mass, roughly 80 to 100 cups of coffee for an average adult taken within a limited time frame that is dependent on half-life.

Though achieving lethal dose with caffeine would be exceptionally difficult with regular coffee, there have been reported deaths from overdosing on caffeine pills, with serious symptoms of overdose requiring hospitalization occurring from as little as 2 grams of caffeine. An exception to this would be taking a drug such as fluvoxamine which blocks the liver enzyme responsible for the metabolism of caffeine, thus increasing the central effects and blood concentrations of caffeine dramatically at 5-fold.

It is not contraindicated, but highly advisable to minimize the intake of caffeinated beverages, as drinking one cup of coffee will have the same effect as drinking five under normal conditions. Death typically occurs due to ventricular fibrillation brought about by effects of caffeine on the cardiovascular system.

Treatment of severe caffeine intoxication is generally supportive, providing treatment of the immediate symptoms, but if the patient has very high serum levels of caffeine then peritoneal dialysis, hemodialysis, or hemofiltration may be required.

## Anxiety and Sleep Disorders

Two infrequently diagnosed caffeine-induced disorders that are recognized by the American Psychological Association (APA) are *caffeine-induced sleep disorder* and *caffeine-induced anxiety disorder*, which can result from long-term excessive caffeine intake. In the case of caffeine-induced sleep disorder, an individual regularly ingests high doses of caffeine sufficient to induce a significant disturbance in his or her sleep, sufficiently severe to warrant clinical attention.

In some individuals, the large amounts of caffeine can induce anxiety severe enough to necessitate clinical attention. This caffeine-induced anxiety disorder can take many forms, from generalized anxiety to panic attacks, obsessive-compulsive symptoms, or even phobic symptoms.

Because this condition can mimic organic mental disorders, such as panic disorder, generalized anxiety disorder, bipolar disorder, or even schizophrenia, a number of medical professionals believe caffeine-intoxicated people are routinely misdiagnosed and unnecessarily medicated when the treatment for caffeine-induced psychosis would simply be to stop further caffeine intake.

A study in the British Journal of Addiction concluded that caffeinism, although infrequently diagnosed, may afflict as many as one person in ten of the population. Co administration of theanine was shown to greatly reduce this caffeine-induced anxiety.

## Effects on Memory and Learning

An array of studies found that caffeine could have nootropic effects, inducing certain changes in memory and learning. Researchers have found that long-term consumption of low dose caffeine slowed hippocampus-dependent learning and impaired long-term memory in mice.

Caffeine consumption for 4 weeks also significantly reduced hippocampal neurogenesis compared to controls during the experiment. The conclusion was that long-term consumption of caffeine could inhibit hippocampus-dependent learning and memory partially through inhibition of hippocampal neurogenesis.

In another study, caffeine was added to rat neurons *in vitro*. The dendritic spines (a part of the brain cell used in forming connections between neurons) taken from the hippocampus (a part of the brain associated with memory) grew by 33% and new spines formed. After an hour or two, however, these cells returned to their original shape.

Another study showed that human subjects—after receiving 100 milligrams of caffeine—had increased activity in brain regions located in the frontal lobe, where a part of the working memory network is located, and the anterior cingulate cortex, a part of the brain that controls attention.

The caffeinated subjects also performed better on the memory tasks. However, a different study showed that caffeine could impair short-term memory and increase the likelihood of the tip of the tongue phenomenon.

The study allowed the researchers to suggest that caffeine could aid short-term memory when the information to be recalled is related to the current train of thought, but also to hypothesize that caffeine hinders short-term memory when the train of thought is unrelated. In essence, caffeine consumption increases mental performance related to focused thought while it may decrease broad-range thinking abilities.

## Effects on the Heart

Caffeine binds to receptors on the surface of heart muscle cells which leads to an increase in the level of cAMP inside the cells (by blocking the enzyme that degrades cAMP), mimicking the effects of epinephrine (which binds to receptors on the cell that activate cAMP production). cAMP acts as a "second messenger," and activates a large number of protein kinase A (PKA; cAMP-dependent protein kinase).

This has the overall effect of increasing the rate of glycolysis and increases the amount of ATP available for muscle contraction and relaxation. According to one study, caffeine in the form of coffee, significantly reduces the risk of heart disease in epidemiological studies.

However, the protective effect was found only in participants who were not severely hypertensive (i.e. patients that are not suffering from a very high blood pressure). Furthermore, no significant protective effect was found in participants aged less than 65 years or in cerebrovascular disease mortality for those aged equal or more than 65 years.

## Effects on Children

It is a common myth that excessive intake of caffeine results in stunted growth within children (particularly younger children) and teenagers. Recently, though, scientific studies have disproved the notion. Children are found to experience the same effects from caffeine as adults.

However, subsidiary beverages that contain caffeine, such as energy drinks, most of which contain high amounts of caffeine, have been banned in many schools throughout the world, due to negative effects having been observed in prolonged consummation of caffeine.

## Caffeine Intake During Pregnancy

Despite its widespread use and the conventional view that it is a safe substance, a 2008 study suggested that pregnant women who consume 200 milligrams or more of caffeine per day have about twice the miscarriage risk as women who consume none.

However, another 2008 study found no correlation between miscarriage and caffeine consumption. The UK Food Standards Agency has recommended that pregnant women should limit their caffeine intake to less than 200 mg of caffeine a day – the equivalent of two cups of instant coffee or a half to two cups of fresh coffee.

The FSA noted that the design of the studies made it impossible to be certain that the differences were due to caffeine per se, instead of other lifestyle differences possibly associated with high levels of caffeine consumption, but judged the advice to be prudent.

Dr De-Kun Li of Kaiser Permanente Division of Research, writing in the American Journal of Obstetrics and Gynecology, concluded that an intake of 200 milligrams or more per day, representing two or more cups, "significantly increases the risk of miscarriage".

However, Dr. David A. Savitz, a professor in community and preventive medicine at New York's Mount Sinai School of Medicine and lead author of the other new study on the subject published in the January issue of Epidemiology, found no link between miscarriage and caffeine consumption.

## Genetics and Caffeine Metabolism

A 2006 study by Dr. Ahmed El-Sohemy at the University of Toronto discovered a link between a gene affecting caffeine metabolism and the effects of coffee on health.

Some people metabolize caffeine more slowly than the general population due to variations in a specific cytochrome P450 gene and there is evidence people with this gene may be at a higher risk of myocardial infarction when consuming large amounts of coffee.

For rapid metabolizers, however, coffee seemed to have a preventative effect.

Slow and fast metabolizers are comparably common in the general population, and this has been blamed for the wide variation in studies of the health effects of caffeine.

## Intraocular Pressure and Caffeine

Recent data has suggested that caffeine consumption can raise intraocular pressure. This may be a significant consideration for those with open angle glaucoma.

## DECAFFEINATION

Decaffeination is the act of removing caffeine from coffee beans, mate, cocoa, tea leaves and other caffeine-containing materials. (While caffeine-free soft drinks are occasionally referred to as "decaffeinated," some are better termed "uncaffeinated": prepared via simply omitting caffeine from production.)

In the case of coffee, various methods can be used. The process is usually performed on unroasted (green) beans, and starts with steaming of the beans. They are then rinsed with a solvent that contains as much of the chemical composition of coffee as possible without also containing the caffeine in a soluble form.

The process is repeated anywhere from 8 to 12 times until it meets either the international standard of having removed 97% of the caffeine in the beans or the EU standard of having the beans 99.9% caffeine-free by mass.

Coffee contains over 400 chemicals important to the taste and aroma of the final drink; it is, therefore, challenging to remove only caffeine while leaving the other cnemicals at their original concentrations. Coffea arabica normally contains about half the caffeine of Coffea robusta. A *Coffea arabica* bean containing little caffeine was discovered in Ethiopia in 2004.

### Roselius Process

The first commercially successful decaffeination process was invented by Ludwig Roselius and Karl Wimmer in 1903. It involved steaming coffee beans with a brine (salt water) solution and then using benzene as a solvent to remove the caffeine.

Coffee decaffeinated this way was sold as Kaffee HAG after the company name *Kaffee Handels-Aktien-Gesellschaft* (Coffee Trading Company) in most of Europe, as *Cafe Sanka* in France and later as Sanka brand coffee in the U.S. Cafe HAG and Sanka are now worldwide brands of Kraft Foods. Due to health concerns regarding benzene, this process is no longer used commercially and Coffee Hag and Sanka are produced using a different process.

### Swiss Water Process

The Swiss Water Process is a method of decaffeinating coffee beans developed by the Swiss Water Decaffeinated Coffee Company. To decaffeinate the coffee bean by the Swiss Water method, a batch of green (unroasted) beans is soaked in hot water, releasing caffeine. When all the caffeine and coffee solids are released into the water, the beans are discarded.

The water then passes through a carbon filter that traps caffeine but lets the coffee solids pass through. The resulting solution, called "green coffee extract (GCE)" by the company, is now available for decaffeinating coffee. New green coffee beans are introduced to the GCE.

Since the GCE is coffee solids without caffeine only the caffeine diffuses from the new beans. The GCE passes through proprietary carbon which captures the caffeine. The process repeats, filtering out all the caffeine until the beans are 99.9% caffeine-free. These beans are removed and dried, and thus retain most if not all of their flavour. Although the process was pioneered in Switzerland in the 1930s, today the world's only Swiss Water Process decaffeination facility is based near Vancouver, British Columbia, Canada.

### Direct Method

In the direct method, the coffee beans are first steamed for 30 minutes and then repeatedly rinsed with either methylene chloride (Dichloromethane/DCM) or ethyl acetate for about 10 hours. The solvent is then drained away and the beans steamed for an additional 10 hours to remove any residual solvent.

Sometimes coffees that are decaffeinated using ethyl acetate are referred to as naturally processed because ethyl acetate can be derived from various fruits or vegetables; but, because of the impracticality of gathering natural ethyl acetate, the chemical used for decaffeination is synthetic.

### Indirect Method

In the indirect method, beans are first soaked in hot water for several hours, in essence, making a strong pot of coffee

Then the beans are removed and either methylene chloride or ethyl acetate is used to extract the caffeine from the water. As in other methods, the caffeine can then be separated from the organic solvent by simple evaporation.

The same water is recycled through this two-step process with new batches of beans. An equilibrium is reached after several cycles, where the water and the beans have a similar composition except for the caffeine. After this point, the caffeine is the only material removed from the beans, so no coffee strength or other flavourings are lost. Because water is used in the initial phase of this process, sometimes indirect method decaffeination is referred to as "water-processed" even though chemicals are used.

### $CO_2$ Process

This process is technically known as supercritical fluid extraction. Pre-steamed beans are soaked in a bath of supercritical carbon dioxide at a pressure of 73 to 300 atmospheres. After a thorough soaking for around ten hours, the pressure is reduced allowing the $CO_2$ to evaporate, or the pressurized $CO_2$ is run through either water or charcoal filters to remove the caffeine.

The carbon dioxide is then used on another batch of beans. This liquid works better than water because it is kept in supercritical state near the transition from liquid to gas, combining favourable diffusivity properties of the gas with increased density of a liquid. This process has the advantage that it avoids the use of potentially harmful solvents.

### Triglyceride Process

Green coffee beans are soaked in a hot water/coffee solution to draw the caffeine to the surface of the beans. Next, the beans are transferred to another container and immersed in coffee oils that were obtained from spent coffee grounds.

After several hours of high temperatures, the triglycerides in the oils remove the caffeine - but not the flavour elements - from the beans. The beans are separated from the oils and dried. The caffeine is removed from the oils, which are reused to decaffeinate another batch of beans. This is a direct contact method of decaffeination.

## Decaffeinated Tea

Tea may also be decaffeinated, usually by using processes analogous to the Direct Method or the $CO_2$ process as described above. Fermentation (i.e., the process of oxidizing tea leaves to create "black," "white," or "oolong" tea leaves from green leaves) does not affect the amount of caffeine in the tea, though tea plant species (i.e., Camellia sinensis sinensis vs. Camellia sinensis assamica) may differ in natural caffeine content. Younger leaves and buds contain more caffeine per weight than older leaves and stems.

Also, certain processes during production might lend a hand in either decreasing the caffeine content directly or simply lowering the rate at which it is released throughout each infusion. Several instances in China where this is evident is in many cooked pu'er teas, as well as more heavily fired Wuyi Mountain oolongs; commonly referred to as 'zhonghuo' (mid-fired) or 'zuhuo' (high-fired).

A generally accepted statistic is that a cup of tea contains 40–50 mg of caffeine, roughly half the content of a cup of coffee. Although a common technique of discarding a short (30– to 60-second) steep is believed to reduce caffeine content in a subsequent brew by 80–90%, research suggests that a five-minute steep yields up to 70% of the caffeine, and a second steep has one-third the caffeine of the first (about 23% of the total caffeine in the leaves).

## Caffeine Content of Decaffeinated Coffee

Almost all brands of decaffeinated coffee still contain some caffeine. Drinking five to ten cups of decaffeinated coffee could deliver as much caffeine as would one or two cups of regular coffee, according to research at the University of Florida Maples Centre for Forensic Medicine. In one independent research on 10 popular decaffeinated coffees, researchers found that all but one contained caffeine.

The 16-ounce (473-milliliter) cups of coffee samples

contained caffeine in the range of 8.6 milligrams to 13.9 milligrams. In another similar study of popular brands of decaf coffees, the caffeine content was anywhere from 3 milligrams up to 32 milligrams. The need to remove caffeine could vanish if coffee growers begin using a naturally caffeine-free bean first produced in June 2004.

# Index

**N**



**O**



**P**

## U



## V



## W